LABOUR'S GRASS ROOTS

LABOUR'S GRASS ROOTS

The Politics of Party Membership

PATRICK SEYD
AND
PAUL WHITELEY

CLARENDON PRESS · OXFORD
1992

Oxford University Press, Walton Street, Oxford OX2 6DP
Oxford New York Toronto
Delhi Bombay Calcutta Madras Karachi
Petaling Jaya Singapore Hong Kong Tokyo
Nairobi Dar es Salaam Cape Town
Melbourne Auckland
and associated companies in
Berlin Ibadan

Oxford is a trade mark of Oxford University Press

Published in the United States
by Oxford University Press, New York

British Library Cataloguing in Publication Data
Data available

Library of Congress Cataloging in Publication Data
Seyd, Patrick.
Labour's grass roots: the politics of party membership/Patrick Seyd
and Paul Whiteley.
p. cm.
Includes bibliographical references and index.
1. Labour Party (Great Britain) 2. Party affiliation—Great Britain.
I. Whiteley, Paul. II. Title.
JN1129.L32S439 1992 324.241—dc20 92-3016
ISBN 0-19-827357-6
ISBN 0-19-827358-4 (Pbk)

Typeset by BP Integraphics, Bath, Avon
Printed and bound in
Great Britain by Biddles Ltd.
Guildford & King's Lynn

ACKNOWLEDGEMENTS

The initial stimulus for this national survey of Labour party members came from Lewis Minkin and throughout he has provided assistance, encouragement, and advice for which we are grateful. The research would have been impossible without support from three sources. First, the Economic and Social Research Council provided the bulk of the money (Grant No: R000231522). The University of Sheffield Research Fund provided additional funds and we are grateful to the members of the Research Fund committee for their support.

Secondly, the project would have been impossible without the Labour party's support. It was a brave decision to open up the membership lists to academic inspection knowing that parts of the media were likely to interpret the initial results in as damaging a manner as possible. Larry Whitty and Joyce Gould have encouraged us in our endeavours. Among Labour party staff, Deborah Lincoln and John Braggins answered all our queries with unceasing goodwill. Roy Hill was responsible for producing the Labour party membership lists in the form we required. His enthusiasm for the project was such that his work went way beyond the normal calls of duty. Maggie Paun and Janice Mundy typed out these membership lists for us in a very short space of time. Individual Labour party members in Sheffield Central and Bristol East constituencies were very willing participants in the initial pilot surveys which ensured the effectiveness of the final questionnaire. Without the willingness of the individual party members to take the time and trouble to complete the questionnaires our initial efforts to establish the research project would have been in vain.

Thirdly, the administration of the survey depended upon the enthusiastic support of Sheffield University students Sue Kirk, Tom Donaldson, Steve Longden, Kevin Byrne, Susan Wright, Ingrid-Maria Sauer, Cathy Canman, Keith Mason, Daniel Ballard, Chris Wales, Lynn Sargeant, Shirley Howarth, Georgina Hirsch, and Emma Davey. We promised them that the survey would have practical relevance to their social science training and we hope their experiences confirmed this. Jane Blower was the main coder of the questionnaires, along with Daniel and Rachel Seyd; and Jean Orme inputted the data. All of them worked with unfailing good humour and co-operation. Don Callister and John Underwood in the University Finance Office, and Mrs McCullen in the Academic Secretary's Office, were of considerable help. We are also grateful to Martin Fenwick at Slater Printing for producing the questionnaires with such speed and accuracy.

David Broughton was the project Research Officer in day-to-day charge of the survey. His efficiency and commitment ensured its completion. Since leaving to take up a teaching post at the University of Cardiff he has continued to provide a great deal of help and advice. Andrew Gamble, as Chairman of the Department of Politics at the University of Sheffield, provided consistent support and assistance.

We would like also to thank the operators of the UK and US academic computer networks Janet and Bitnet. This project would have been very much more difficult to complete without the help of transatlantic electronic mail.

Finally, our transatlantic research co-operation has necessitated weeks away from home with the subsequent domestic upheaval and we are grateful to Ros and Sue for their continual support and for their patience in listening to our endless talk about party members.

P.S. and P.W.

Sheffield and Williamsburg, Virginia
September 1991

CONTENTS

FIGURES

TABLES

1

Introduction and Overview

Party members and party activists are the 'Cinderellas' of British politics. Few people, particularly journalists and academics, have much to say in their favour. Some see them as unrepresentative extremists, a vocal minority whose tiresome demands interfere with the 'true' processes of democracy. Others see them as 'film extras', whose task is basically to provide an appreciative audience for their respective party leaders during election rallies. Few think that they have any really important role to play in British politics.

One of the main reasons we have for writing this book is to try to change this widespread image of party members. In the book we try to understand the motives, aspirations, beliefs, political roles, and political actions of a representative cross-section of Labour party members. Our results show that, in general, they are a relatively active group of people, some of whom give up a great deal of their spare time in order to keep the Labour party in business. This in turn, as we argue below, helps to keep democratic politics alive in Britain.

This book is written with several audiences in mind. First, it is written for a Labour party audience; we hope that some party members will want to read it to find out more about the organization to which they belong. They may be put off at first sight by all the tables, figures, and diagrams. But we hope that they will persevere, since anyone who understands the meaning of a percentage will be able to follow most of the argument, and we hope that they will be pleasantly surprised by some of the findings and not unduly offended by others.

Secondly, it is written for journalists, politicians, full-time party workers, pollsters, and other professional communicators, who in the past have had access to little or no research on the social characteristics, attitudes, and opinions of a representative sample of Labour party members. This dearth of information about party members has often resulted in them being stereotyped. If the book convinces some of these professional communicators, particularly the journalists, to take the role of the party member in British

politics more seriously in the future, then we will have achieved one
of our objectives. We have included a percentage breakdown of
responses to our survey in Appendix II, which should provide a
source of reference for anyone wanting to know more about the
detailed responses to questions in the survey.[1]

Thirdly, it is written for an academic audience of political scientists, and also political sociologists and political economists who
might be interested in various aspects of the study of political participation. The study of political participation involves addressing
such questions as 'Why should people join voluntary organizations
like the Labour party?'; 'Are political activists more left-wing than
the politically inactive?'; and 'Do party members have any role in
increasing the vote for the Labour party in General Elections?'. Our
attempts to provide answers to these and other questions means that
this book is not simply a descriptive account of the social characteristics and attitudes of party members. We are trying, rather, to
provide a theoretical account of Labour party membership.

By theoretical account we mean a set of simple, general, and
coherent propositions which help to understand and explain the
political world. For example, one of our key theoretical arguments
is that individuals join the Labour party, and some of them subsequently become very active, in response to incentives of various
kinds. These incentives are such as to motivate only a relatively
small percentage of the population to become involved in party
politics, but nevertheless they explain why party membership exists
in the first place.

In some respects party members are very similar to voters, sharing
many of their opinions and beliefs. In other respects they are very
different from Labour voters, being considerably more middle class
and more male than the latter. It is hard to characterize an 'average'
or 'typical' party member, since they are a diverse group of people.
But they all have in common one thing; their contribution to British
politics goes further than occasionally turning out to vote, the only
significant contribution which most people in Britain make to democratic politics.

Party members contribute to British politics in a number of
different ways; first, they provide a lot of voluntary work without
which party politics could not function. There are few 'law-like'

---

[1] If anyone wants to go further and actually access the data for their own use, it is
deposited in the ESRC archive at the University of Essex.

generalizations in social science, but one of them is the proposition that democratic politics in advanced industrial societies cannot operate without political parties. Without parties the mass of interests in society cannot be properly aggregated, resulting in a politics dominated by a cacophony of special interests, most of them representing the rich and the powerful. In such a system what passes for government would consist of a shifting coalition of political 'entrepreneurs' none of whom has the authority to govern in the sense of making enforceable decisions. In this situation democratic politics would rapidly break down. Since political parties cannot operate without a significant group of party members, in a real sense party members make democratic politics possible.

A second contribution is in recruiting and socializing future political leaders. Political parties are the training grounds for the local councillors, Members of Parliament, and ultimately national political leaders. Within the party organizations these individuals acquire the skills of political argument, they develop policy preferences and learn to organize coalitions of interests and to bargain between opposing groups, all of which are indispensable skills required by a political leader in a democratic society.

A third contribution is in political communication or the complex interaction between political leaders and voters about the issues which emerge on the political scene. It is easy to fall into the trap of thinking that this is a one-way process, from the élites downwards as many Tory historians would argue, or from the mass upwards as public-choice theorists like Anthony Downs (1957) have assumed. The precise role of party members in transmitting political values and ideas at the face-to-face level in British politics is unknown, but it is a topic which fascinates many people researching the question of how political ideas are transmitted in our society. Our guess is that ordinary party members at the workplace and in the community play a very important role in political communication, even as we concede that this is a very difficult topic to research.

A fourth contribution is in policy-making. The existence of various think-tanks, government research organizations, and networks of government advisers and consultants, tends to obscure the point that much policy-making goes on within parties. Of course parties are not places where policies are implemented, but they are important 'breeding grounds' for new ideas. In the language of the policy analyst, they are often places where policies get on to the agenda of political debate. As has often been pointed out, 'Thatcherism' started out as a set of radical right ideas developed within think-tanks associated with the Conservative party. But it was the party connection which eventually made these ideas powerful.

The Labour party is unique among British political parties in adhering to a constitution which concedes the ultimate authority in determining policy to the party conference. As is well known, the actual political practice differs considerably from the official con-stitution, but that fact should not obscure the important role of the party conference and party meetings in legitimizing certain policy options. The importance of the party connection was seen in 1978 when the Labour government of Jim Callaghan lost touch with its party supporters on the issue of incomes policy. This produced the ill-fated 'winter of discontent' which led ultimately to the election defeat of 1979.

A fifth contribution, which is not much recognized, is in mobilizing the vote during a general-election campaign. There has been a dearth of research into this issue in the literature on electoral behaviour, but our findings in Chapter 8 show that Labour party members and activists play a very significant role in mobilizing electoral support for the party at the constituency level. Indeed we believe that one of the factors which explains the decline in the Labour party's share of the vote in general elections since the 1950s is the decline in the party membership.

Democracy in Britain is often taken for granted. Some people believe that democratic institutions are protected by abstractions like the 'rule of law', or by constitutional documents, or Acts of Parliament. Unfortunately there are numerous examples in the world of regimes with constitutions which guarantee a full range of human rights and the rule of law, but where in practice these things exist only on paper. In the final analysis democracy is possible only because enough citizens care sufficiently about politics to get in-volved and participate. If for any reason, citizens in general lose interest and become passive observers who choose not to participate, democracy will not survive in the long run.

One of our most important research findings is that ordinary Labour party members are more actively involved in politics than the conventional wisdom would suggest. Apart from anything else this helps to keep democracy alive in Britain, protecting it from the overbearing centralized state power which has threatened to undermine it in recent years.

In the remainder of this chapter we review the broad research findings of this book.

A SUMMARY OF THE RESEARCH

The analysis begins in Chapter 2 with a review of the literature on party members, together with information about the development of individual Labour party membership over the years. Changes in the party's rules of affiliation have made it very difficult to get an accurate picture of party membership over time since 1928, the first year that the Labour party published individual membership figures. However, the figures which are available suggest that the grass-roots party has declined significantly over the years.

There are different theories which try to explain this development, from the 'decline of working-class politics' thesis (Hindess, 1971) to the argument, which we feel has particular validity, that the party has neglected the grass-roots membership. The lack of a serious commitment to the recruitment and retention of members, can perhaps be partly explained by the party structure, particularly by the existence of a large indirect membership of trade-unionists. But it may also be as a result of a general perception common to most observers, that party members are not particularly important.

A second issue discussed in Chapter 2 is the change in the status of the individual party members which has been taking place in recent years. The party has moved away from a long tradition of delegatory democracy towards a system of individual participatory democracy. The expansion of the franchise for selecting the Party Leader was an example of this development, as was the decision by the 1990 Party Conference to move towards local party 'primary' elections for the selection of parliamentary candidates.

For reasons to do with the major internecine conflicts of the early 1980s the party leadership has increasingly sought to empower ordinary party members, at the expense of party activists. It is perhaps a vivid example of Schattschneider's thesis (1960) that the extension of the democratic franchise usually comes about as a result of élites seeking new allies in conflicts with other élites. In this case it was a conflict between the party leadership and some of the activists.

After discussing the history of individual membership and the political roles of members in Chapter 2, Chapter 3 provides a broad overview of the social characteristics and political views of the party members in our survey of Labour party members. This was a large survey with more than 5,000 respondents, carried out at the end of 1989 and the beginning of 1990 by means of a postal questionnaire. It was a representative random sample of Labour party members in Britain.

The analysis in Chapter 3 includes an examination of the socio-economic backgrounds of members, such as their age, class, gender, education, and income profiles. Some comparisons are made in this chapter with Labour voters, using data taken from the British Election Study of 1987 (see Heath *et al.*, 1991). In addition we look at members' attitudes to political issues and electoral strategy, their views on nationalization, unilateralism as well as other controversial political questions. Finally, we examine members' attitudes to the party leadership and to the modernization strategy instituted by Neil Kinnock. This chapter provides a quick overview of the topics which are discussed more fully in later chapters.

Chapter 4 introduces a major theoretical puzzle which has dominated discussions of political participation for some years. This is the influential thesis developed by the economist Mancur Olson (1965) which argues that in so far as individuals behave like rational actors, then they should not participate in politics. This argument might be regarded as something of a theoretical curiosity, were it not for the fact that in all types of democratic political systems, party membership and activism appear to involve relatively small minorities of individuals, even among parties which receive millions of votes in elections. Unlike more conventional theories of political participation, Olson has an explanation for this apparent paradox.

A theoretical model is developed in Chapter 4 which provides a general framework for understanding this paradox. It attempts to explain why some people join the Labour party in the first place, and why some of them go on to become very active once they have joined. The model takes into account the Olson thesis, but goes beyond the narrow conception of rational behaviour which it is based on, to consider a wider set of incentives for political action. It can be described as a 'general-incentives' theory of participation.[2]

---

[2] We are grateful to Professor Edward Muller of the University of Arizona, a former colleague of Paul Whiteley, who introduced the term 'general-incentive theory', and has applied it to the study of unorthodox political participation in a variety of political systems. Our framework is a development and extension of his approach.

The basic idea is that individuals are motivated to join the party, and to become active because of a variety of incentives which they face. Some of these incentives provide private returns of the type familiar to the economist operating in a world in which individuals base their decisions on calculations of the private costs and benefits of different courses of action. But other motives enter into the decision process, some of which are based on altruistic concerns, and some of which are based on social norms, or the pressures to conform to the opinions of other people. Neither of these types of motives figure in the classical rational choice analysis of decision-making.

The general-incentives framework makes it possible to classify members according to their dominant motives for joining the party, and to make predictions about the relationship between their socio-economic characteristics, particularly social class, and their motives for joining the party. It also predicts observable differences between Labour voters and Labour party members. In addition, Chapter 4 contains a discussion of the relationship between incentives for joining the party and political ideology.

In Chapter 5 the general-incentives framework is applied to the question as to why some individuals are very active in the party, whereas others are relatively inactive. A starting-point for this analysis is an examination of the meaning and measurement of party activism. Traditional discussions of this question have tended to divide party members into two groups: the activists and the members. Many commentators believe that the great mass of party members are very inactive, and that in addition a small minority of very left-wing activists control the local party organizations. Our results show that this is a very misleading picture of the Labour party.

It turns out that party activism is not a single homogeneous concept which can be accurately measured, for example, by the number of meetings which an individual attends. There are at least three distinct, though related dimensions to party activism. First, there is a 'contact' dimension, which measures the extent to which the individual party member has contact with other party members, often in party meetings, but also in other ways. Secondly, there is a 'campaigning' dimension which measures the extent to which individuals are involved in various political campaigns, both within the Labour party and outside in related political organizations. Thirdly, there is a 'representation' dimension which measures the extent to which individuals are elected or nominated into various offices both within the party and in the outside community.

We develop a scale which provides an overall measure of these different aspects of party activism, and the survey shows that there is a lot more political activity undertaken by ordinary party members than the conventional wisdom would suggest. There is in fact a continuum of activism, rather than a dichotomy of 'activists' and 'members'. The scale is used to examine the relationship between social backgrounds, political attitudes, and activism.

The results show that middle-class party members tend to be more active than working-class party members; men are more active than women; and educated members are more active than uneducated members. However, differences between these groups in levels of activism are not large, and it would be quite wrong to suppose that, for example, middle-class members are very much more active than the working-class members.

At the end of Chapter 5 the general-incentives model of political activism is tested. Some of the findings confirm conventional wisdom; for example, the very active are more left-wing than the inactive members, but again this effect is not all that strong when other factors are taken into account. Other findings are against the conventional wisdom. For example, one of the most interesting findings is that one of the strongest motives for activism is political ambition, or a desire to build a career in politics at the local or national levels. Party activists may be idealists, but many of them are also career-minded! One important implication of this finding is that very active members have a personal stake in the electoral success of the party.

Chapter 6 is about the relationship between ideology and party membership. The terms 'left' and 'right' are used in political analysis, often in very imprecise ways. The purpose of this chapter is to examine the ideological beliefs of Labour party members, to determine how these are structured in relation to all the major issues of British politics.

Attitude structuring is important, since it determines how easy it is to change existing political views. If attitudes to issues are all highly structured along a single left–right continuum, then attitudes are likely to be rigid, since changing one involves changing all the others. If, on the other hand, attitude structures are weak, then attitude change is more easily accomplished. These points are particularly relevant when considering the reaction of party members to the modernization strategy, or the series of reforms initiated by the leadership to change the policies, image, and organizational structure of the party, following the electoral defeats of the 1980s.

The findings indicate that the political attitudes of members are structured to a significant extent, but it would be wrong to conclude that all the important issues of British politics are classified in their minds along a single 'left–right' ideological dimension. The structure of beliefs is loose enough, for example, so that attitudes to nationalization, a long-running issue within the party, are largely independent of attitudes to nuclear disarmament. This means that a party member who is, say, strongly in favour of more nationalization is quite likely to be neutral or even against unilateral nuclear disarmament; a left-wing position on one issue does not translate into a left-wing position on the other.

Members have four distinct 'clusters' of attitudes to the major issues of British politics, and each of these is independent of the others. This means that a particular individual who is 'left-wing' on some issues, such as environmental pollution, can be 'right-wing' on other issues such as the role of trade unions in British politics.

At first sight interesting class differences emerge among members in their attitudes to these issue-clusters, the middle-class members being left-wing on some and right-wing on others. But further analysis suggests that education rather than class explains these differences, and this is accounted for by a model of the evolution of issues over time. Education makes individuals more responsive to changes in issue-saliency over time, and this can account for apparent class differences in attitudes.

Chapter 7 focuses on the attitudes of the members to the Labour party, its leaders, and some of the major institutions in British politics. The main aim of this chapter is to examine members' attitudes to the modernization strategy. The chapter begins by examining members' images of the party, or their beliefs about what it stands for and whom it seems to represent. This leads into the development of an 'attitudes to modernization' scale, which distinguishes between 'traditionalists' on the one hand, and 'modernizers' on the other.

Interestingly enough, there appears to be little difference between traditionalists and modernizers, with regard to their social backgrounds, but there is a very sharp difference between them with regard to political ideology. The 'hard left', who make up about 17 per cent of the sample are very much more hostile to modernization than anyone else. On the other hand, there appears to be little difference between the 'soft left', the 'centre', and the 'soft right' on this question, and so the 'hard left' stand out as a distinct group in this regard. This is because they have their own distinct views about the correct electoral strategy for the party, which motivates the modernization programme.

On the whole, the results show that members are very supportive of both the modernization strategy and the leadership of Neil Kinnock. Above all they are very attached to the Labour party, more so than to any individual or other institution in British politics.

Chapter 8 changes the focus of the discussion completely from examining the party members, to examining the effects of party membership on the all-important question of Labour's electoral support. The influence of party membership and local political activism on voting behaviour in Britain has not been properly researched before, although there is a good deal of indirect evidence to suggest that local campaigns might be quite important during general elections.

One of the main reasons for selecting an unusually large sample for this study was to facilitate an examination of the influence of local activism and party membership on the vote. The analysis in this chapter shows that local activism has a very important influence on the Labour vote at the constituency level; it is important for explaining why some constituencies experienced an above-average swing to the Labour party between 1983 and 1987. The key problem in this type of analysis is to separate out the effects of party activism on the vote from the effects of other factors, such as the geographical location or the size of the working class in a constituency.

This is done with the aid of a multiple-regression model which shows that activism is important even when a variety of other factors is taken into account. The importance of an active local campaign in a general election is underscored by a simulation of the 1987 general election using the multiple-regression model, building in a variety of assumptions about the size and level of activism of local Labour parties. These results show, for example, that if the Labour party had been about one-third larger than it was at the time of the election, it would have received nearly 5 per cent more of the total vote than it actually did receive. Thus the model suggests that local campaigns are extremely important.

The final chapter brings the threads of the argument together and looks at some of the dangers for the party inherent in present trends of declining party membership. In addition some people have suggested that in the late 1980s the party has become 'de-energized' and more passive. This is partly a result of the massive electoral defeats of the 1980s, but it may also be to some extent a by-product of the modernization strategy, which has heavily emphasized the importance of centralized communication and campaigning. The leadership is all too conscious of the electoral damage done by the internecine conflict of the early 1980s, and this has helped to produce, along with an increasing emphasis on the centralized media campaign, a 'nationalization' of party activity.

Our conclusions on this development are fairly unequivocal: the Labour party is unlikely to survive as the main alternative party of government, and a major electoral force in British politics, without a thriving grass-roots organization. The party needs to be 'energized' at the grass-roots level, and this points to the need for resources to be devoted to recruiting and retaining new party members.

The present survey cannot determine if this 'de-energizing' process has occurred, and it will require another type of research design to establish that.[3] But if it has, the party may be suffering from the tremendous increase in the centralization of state power which has occurred over the past ten years. The model developed in Chapter 4 suggests that if one removes incentives for grass-roots activism by taking away powers from the locality, then one result of this will be a decline in voluntary work of the type which sustains the local party organization and local government. This of course creates a problem for all political parties, not just the Labour party. But Labour may have added to this problem, by over-emphasizing national rather than local campaigning in the modernization strategy.

In conclusion, we think these findings have wider implications for British politics than just for the Labour party. Grass-roots activists require incentives, particularly in the face of the theoretical argument which suggests that activism looked at in narrow cost-benefit

---

[3] The authors of this study are currently working on a panel survey of Labour party members, which involves re-interviewing the participants in the original sample to isolate trends in party membership over time.

terms is 'irrational'. This means that local people require genuine control over their own lives if they are going to participate. Thus a revitalization of the Labour party requires action both within the party organization, and in the wider political system in Britain.

There is a severe 'democratic deficit', or a loss of control to the centre in British politics which is undermining democratic government, and which ultimately and ironically subverts efficiency, the usual justification for such centralization in the first place. We see revitalization of the Labour party as being part of a wider effort to rescue the principle of accountability in British politics, something which has been increasingly under threat in the 1980s. Thus our discussion of the future for the Labour party is intimately linked to a wider debate in Britain about constitutional change.

2

Party Members: A Review

The subject of our research is the party member, but how one defines such a person varies according to the particular party under consideration. What one party means by membership will not agree with the definition of another. In this chapter, firstly we consider what the Labour party means by an individual member and what the trends have been in recruiting such people. Then we consider the formal powers that individual members possess and the manner in which these powers have changed in the past ten years. Thirdly, we summarize some of the key findings of previous research on the social composition and political attitudes of Labour party members. And, finally, we examine the place of parties in the British system of government.

EVOLUTION OF LABOUR PARTY MEMBERSHIP

Maurice Duverger (1954) in his classic study *Political Parties* argues that the mass party with its clearly defined political programme, branch-based structure, and individual, dues-paying membership is the norm in advanced industrialized societies. In 1918 the Labour Party established the framework for such a mass party—a wide-ranging programme, an elaborate extra-parliamentary party structure and, for the first time in its history, an opportunity for individuals to join as members. Before 1918 individuals could only join indirectly through membership of an affiliated trade union or socialist organization. The party's new constitution stipulated the conditions for individual membership as being a willingness to 'subscribe to the Constitution and Programme of the Party'.[1]

McKibbin (1974: 141) notes that the Party did not give much priority in the early 1920s to the development of an individual membership. In these years little sustained effort was made to recruit individual members: the party's only initiative was directed towards

---

[1] *Labour Party Constitution*, 1918, Clause 2.

attracting newly enfranchised women. It was assumed that males would belong to a trade union and would therefore become members indirectly. When the first Labour Government lost office in 1924 the party launched a national drive to recruit members which included targeting trade-unionists already paying the political levy. This was the first occasion since the creation of an individual membership in 1918 that the party went out to recruit men (Cole, 1948: 174). The impetus to recruit individual members became more imperative from 1927, however, as a consequence of the Trade Union Act which replaced contracting out with contracting in for political levy-payers.[2] By the end of the 1920s the creation of a mass party with a nation-wide individual membership was well under way.

The party first published figures of individual membership in 1928 and from then until 1937 they record a fairly steady rise. Nevertheless the years immediately before World War II and the first years of the war were ones in which the party experienced a decline in membership to the point at which the figure was back to the 1928 level. Only after 1943 did membership grow and at such a rapid rate that by 1952 there were over one million individual party members. There is no reason to believe that the figures at that time were a gross distortion of reality. The fact that the records were devised from information provided by lay personnel in party wards and constituencies throughout Great Britain means that inaccuracies were inevitable. Nevertheless the fact that all constituency parties were deemed by the party's national office to have a minimum of 250 members—the figure upon which the minimum annual subscription fee paid by constituency parties to the national office was based—means that the distortion of national records was unlikely to have been too great. Only after 1957 when the minimum figure that constituency parties were required to register for affiliation to the national party was raised to 800, and then to 1,000 in 1963, did the membership figures become inaccurate and seriously overstate the true number. During the 1960s and 1970s the published membership figures, which range from one-half to three-quarters of a million, are of little value. Various attempts were

[2] Individual trade-unionists had to make a conscious decision to pay the political levy rather than their payment being automatic unless they had contracted out. Whereas political-levy payers totalled 3,388,000 in 1926, by 1928 the total had declined to 2,077,000.

made (Butler and Pinto-Duschinsky, 1971; Report of the Committee on Financial Aid to Political Parties, 1976; Pinto-Duschinsky, 1981; and Whiteley, 1983) to estimate the true individual membership figure and their conclusions suggest a figure around one-half of that published. Only in the early 1980s, when the party reduced the minimum affiliation for local parties, do the figures again become reasonably accurate.

These published membership figures are for Great Britain as a single entity. What is unclear is the pattern of membership within Great Britain. Has the tradition of party membership been stronger in some parts of the country than others? Has membership been higher in safe Labour or safe Conservative constituencies? Or has it been in marginal constituencies that party membership has been best developed? Have there been differences in the membership of inner-city and suburban constituencies? What impact has trade-union sponsorship of Labour MPs had upon individual membership in the constituencies where this has occurred? Where a city-wide organization, such as a Trades and Labour Council, has existed have constituency politics and thus membership been of little importance?

We know very little about the nature of party membership at the micro level. Labour party membership records provide little evidence which can assist these queries. The party has published some limited figures on the size of local parties in the National Executive Committee (hereafter the NEC) reports to the annual conference. For example, it reported 45 parties with an individual membership larger than 3,000 in 1955. These reports reveal that local constituency parties in Woolwich West, Lewisham South, Salford West, Faversham, Southampton Test, and Eastleigh had a tradition of high membership in the 1950s. The reasons for this high membership are unclear. Whether it was due to the existence of a full-time local party agent, to an attractive local social club, or to a local tote-scheme (i.e. a cheap, weekly form of gambling in which party membership is a legally necessary part of the stake) is unknown.

It is clear that party membership peaked in the early 1950s. The decline commenced in the 1950s and continued over the ensuing thirty years. Goss (1988: 135) records an individual membership in the four inner London constituencies of Bermondsey, Peckham, Dulwich, and Southwark of 12,500 in 1952 but by the late 1960s these parties 'could not have mustered 2,000 members between them'. Research by Seyd and Minkin (1979) into the records of local

Party Members: A Review

TABLE 2.1. *Total Individual Party Membership*

Year	No. of members	Year	No. of members
1928	214,970	1960	790,192
1929	227,897 (250*)	1961	750,565
1930	277,211	1962	767,459
1931	297,003	1963	830,346 (1,000*)
1932	371,607	1964	830,116
1933	366,013	1965	816,765
1934	381,259	1966	775,693
1935	419,311	1967	733,932
1936	430,094	1968	700,856
1937	447,150	1969	680,656
1938	428,826	1970	690,191
1939	408,844	1971	699,522
1940	304,124	1972	703,030
1941	226,622	1973	665,379
1942	218,783	1974	691,889
1943	235,501	1975	674,905
1944	265,763	1976	659,058
1945	487,047	1977	659,737
1946	645,345	1978	675,946
1947	608,487	1979	666,091
1948	629,025	1980	348,156 (256*)
1949	729,624	1981	276,692 (128*)
1950	908,161	1982	273,803 (167*)
1951	876,275	1983	295,344
1952	1,014,524	1984	323,292
1953	1,004,685	1985	313,099
1954	933,657	1986	297,364
1955	843,356	1987	288,829
1956	845,129	1988	265,927
1957	912,987 (800*)	1989	293,723
1958	888,955	1990	311,152
1959	847,526		

* minimum affiliation

Source: NEC Reports

Note: Prior to 1928 the Labour party did not publish a record of individual membership.

constituency parties confirms this decline in Salford, Bermondsey, Battersea, Lewisham, and Brixton. Whether the decline varied from region to region is impossible to judge from the records.

Explanations for this collapse vary. One has to do with the changing social composition of the party. Barry Hindess (1971) was one of the first to argue the decline of working-class politics and, in particular, the party's loss of its traditional working-class support. His evidence was drawn from a study of Liverpool and its politics but other authors also referred to the decline of traditional working-class communities. Labour was the victim of social change. Modern society was becoming more diversified and the sociological ties between party and member were weakening. Labour's decline was not exceptional: throughout Western Europe a new politics was emerging and all social democratic parties were suffering a loss of members (Von Beyme, 1985: 167–87).

Furthermore, the nature of inner-city parties was changing. Goss's (1988) study of the inner area of South London makes it clear that the local Labour party had been an established part of the local community. From the 1930s onwards it was 'a centre of social and political life' (pp. 20–1). Nevertheless, by the late 1960s it had become nothing more than 'a rusty and seldom activated election machine' (p. 79). Generational and demographic changes meant the local party was no longer a part of this local community.

At national level the increasingly middle-class composition of the parliamentary party, and Labour government policies in the mid-1960s of curbing the living standards and bargaining power of working-class members of society were additional reasons for the exit of the party's traditional adherents. Whiteley (1983) argues that the party's policies alienated its more instrumental working-class supporters.

Membership decline was not unique to the Labour party. Both major parties were experiencing similar trends in the 1950s and 1960s. One explanation for this phenomenon was that they had been replaced by pressure groups as the major channel for citizen opinion. McKenzie (1974) argued that pressure groups had become 'a far more important channel of communication than parties for the transmission of political ideas from the mass of the citizenry to their rulers'. Moran (1985: 120) also argued that 'pressure groups now seriously rival parties in the system of representation'. An academic explanation for party membership decline was, therefore, that as

British society was becoming more affluent, citizens' interests were becoming more diverse and pressure groups were better able to represent these diverse demands than parties. In addition, people's greater concern with individual life-style was reducing the numbers willing to become involved in such time-consuming public activities as party membership. Individuals were either opting out of political activity altogether or identifying with specific, one-issue groups. The foundation and rise of the 'good cause' groups in the 1960s (for example, Shelter, the Child Poverty Action Group, and the Disablement Income Group) was felt to be particularly damaging to the Labour party as many individuals who previously might have been recruited to the party would now channel their commitments into these new bodies. Furthermore, many of these 'good causes' would attract young people who, a generation previously, might have been engaged in radical political activity through the Labour party.

Another explanation of the decline in membership was the political disillusion many experienced at the direction the Labour party was taking particularly in government during the late 1960s and late 1970s. Over a thirty-year period the party's ideologists on both the left and right became so disappointed by the prevailing party programme as to exit. Whether more from the left or right of the party departed is impossible to calculate with any accuracy.

What was the party's attitude towards this haemorrhage of its most committed supporters? With the exception of a very few senior party figures little concern was expressed. A subcommittee of the NEC, established after the party's 1955 election defeat to examine the state of party organization, defined the membership purely in electoral terms and made no recommendations for expanding numbers. In fact in the late 1950s the party leadership displayed little concern with the declining membership. The prevailing wisdom of the Gaitskellite leadership (Crosland, 1960) and some academic commentators (Butler and Rose, 1960; Epstein, 1967) appeared to be that television and political advertising had replaced the need for campaigning foot-soldiers. The local candidate, local party organization and party membership had little impact on the uniform national swing of voters which was determined by national campaigning. So long as the trade unions provided the funds to pay for party campaigning then there was little need for the individual, dues-paying members. And so for almost twenty years the party

gave only perfunctory attention to the question of declining individual membership. Another committee of inquiry into party
organization in the mid-1960s was very much concerned with
administrative issues and made only passing reference to individual
membership. The National Agent's office periodically initiated a
membership recruiting drive but by the end of the 1970s membership
was down to an estimated 275,000, a return to the figures of the
1920s. Only in 1980 did another party enquiry take some note of the
parlous state of the party membership and it recommended that an
increasing membership 'must be of a prime importance to the future
work of the party'.[3] But, in fact, only two pages of its report were
devoted to this question and its proposals were devoid of any in-
spiration. No wonder then that one academic commentator (Ware,
1987: 146) has written that 'of all the mass membership parties, the
British Labour Party is perhaps the one where membership recruitment has been taken least seriously'.

By the 1980s, therefore, as a consequence of inertia, inefficiency,
and political design, the grass roots of this old established mass
party had withered.

THE POLITICAL AND CONSTITUTIONAL ROLE OF
THE PARTY MEMBER

The Labour party, as a modern mass party, had its origins in the 1918
party constitution which remained almost untouched and the organizational basis for its activities until the late 1970s. This constitution
legitimized the individual member's right to play a prominent part
in the party's affairs through the local branch and constituency
party, the NEC, and the annual party conference. These constitutional powers have been repeatedly reinforced by leadership statements confirming the individual member's rights in policy-making.
An example is provided by the opening words of *Labour's Programme 1973*, written by the party's General Secretary, in which he
states: 'In the Labour Party policy is made by the members.'

In practice, for much of the party's history, power has been a
subtle and complex process in which the parliamentary leadership
has been sustained by the block vote of a small number of trade
unions. Thus the party leadership has been able to use the rhetoric of

---

[3] *Report of the Labour Party Commission of Enquiry*, 1980: 10.

member sovereignty knowing full well that its point of view would prevail within the deliberative process. Nevertheless, the fact that the constitution legitimizes the authority of the membership means that the party leadership has been forced to argue and defend its position, and to mobilize majorities, in the day-to-day running of the party. Perhaps the classic case of the Party Leader arguing his point of view within the party, losing the vote at the party conference and then, after losing, promising to continue to argue within the party and to return to the conference and win his argument, was Hugh Gaitskell in 1959 on the issue of unilateral nuclear disarmament.

Both Robert McKenzie (1964) and Lewis Minkin (1978) have examined Labour's intra-party democracy. McKenzie's conclusions are that the Labour party at work was no different from the Conservative party. The parliamentary leadership, irrespective of the party constitution, dominates the policy-making process and, furthermore, parliamentary democracy requires that this should be the case. It would be unconstitutional for party activists to determine party policy. Cabinet government requires that parliamentarians make policy and are accountable solely to their electors. McKenzie therefore concludes that the Labour party has been forced to adapt its procedures and practices, if not its constitution, accordingly.

Minkin argues that intra-party democracy is a subtle process in which the party leadership is required to proceed by bargaining and conciliation with the extra-parliamentary party, and leadership concessions are sometimes necessary in order to maintain its overall authority. His detailed and intricate study of the annual party conference reveals a party leadership which uses many procedural devices but necessarily is also involved in bargains and concessions in order to maintain its authority. Minkin disagrees with McKenzie concerning the norms of parliamentary democracy; for him parliamentary and party democracy can coexist.

Minkin suggests that the party leadership's attitude towards the extra-parliamentary party has shifted over time: in early years the deliberations of the party conference were treated with respect and authority, but by the late 1960s the party leadership treated its decisions with a calculated disregard. The consequence was a concerted move to restore the party members' rights to play an active role in the party's affairs. A campaign for greater intra-party democracy developed in the late 1970s which concentrated upon the right of the individual party member to select and reselect the Labour

MP, the right to take part in the election of the Party Leader and Deputy Leader, and the right to have a greater influence in the party's election manifesto (Kogan and Kogan, 1983; Seyd, 1987). At this time, however, this was a campaign to give powers only to those active in their local branches and constituency parties rather than to the individual member at large. Why was this the case?

First, the organization leading the campaign for increased party activist powers—the Campaign for Labour Party Democracy— argued that only the activists had the political knowledge and sophistication to resist the pe ressures of outside media campaigns to determine the internal politics of the party. Experience of media intervention in the 1970s on behalf of two Labour MPs, Dick Taverne and Reg Prentice, in their long-drawn-out and bitter dis- putes with their local constituency parties, influenced the attitudes of many of those campaigning for membership rights. Second, many members must have felt that participation in party decision-making should be a prize for those working hard on behalf of the party. Third, if individual members were to participate directly in matters previously reserved for the party's delegates this would undermine the principle of delegatory democracy which had been a funda- mental feature of the party since its foundation: clearly eighty years' practice was a powerful factor in resisting any proposal to give more direct powers to individuals. And, finally, the Left was in the politi- cal ascendancy within the party by the late 1970s and regarded the party activists as its power-base and believed that an extension of decision-making powers to the individual membership would weaken its newly found position of strength. After a long period of right-wing dominance of the party machine it was unlikely that the Left would willingly concede its chances to direct party affairs for a change.

The campaign for activist democracy was triumphant in the late 1970s to early 1980s. A regular reselection procedure of all incum- bent Labour MPs by constituency parties was introduced, and the election of the Party Leader and Deputy Leader was removed from the sole authority of the parliamentary party and given to an electoral college in which the constituency parties cast 30 per cent of the total vote.

The price paid for activist democracy was Labour's damaging electoral defeat in 1983 when Labour came very close to becoming the third party in terms of electoral support. Many factors explain the Conservative's electoral victory and Labour's disastrous loss of support, but two are directly associated with activist democracy. First, intra-party factionalism was so intense, as Left and Right fought for command of the party, that outsiders believed the Labour party was so divided as to be unfit to govern. Second, as activist democracy triumphed the party adopted policies which alienated Labour's traditional supporters. In particular, the commitments to unilateral nuclear disarmament, to the expansion of public ownership, and to oppose the sale of council houses were not popular with Labour voters (Crewe, 1983).

A new party leadership emerged from this crushing electoral defeat committed to a reduction in the powers of party activists. Either party democracy had to be reduced or, assuming individual party members were more representative than activists of the Labour voter, all individual party members had to be given extensive powers. At this time there was little likelihood that party democracy could have been reduced and therefore the leadership's strategy was to involve more party members in the selection and reselection of MPs and in the election of the party leadership.

In 1981 the principle of 'one person, one vote' had received only derisory support among annual conference delegates in the deliberations over any new procedure to be adopted for electing the party leadership. It was only the party Right who argued this point of view.[4] The party leadership's attempt at the 1984 Party Conference to enable all individual members to participate in the parliamentary candidate reselections failed to win a majority.[5] It was still regarded with suspicion by very many in the party as a right-wing tactic to reassert the supremacy of the parliamentarians. However, at the following year's conference a resolution calling for all candidate selections to be on the basis of 'one person, one vote' was remitted to the NEC.[6] As a consequence, a NEC Working Party was established to examine ways of extending the franchise in candidate selections. It recommended two options if the principle of extending the franchise was accepted; either 'one person, one vote' or the creation of local electoral colleges. The 1988 Conference opted for the second of these options, the local electoral college, in order to

---

[4] 6.2 million votes were cast in favour of some form of electoral college to elect the party leadership. Only 400,000 votes were cast in favour of the party leadership being elected by a ballot of individual members.

[5] *Report of the Annual Conference of the Labour Party*, 1984: 66.

[6] *Report of the Annual Conference of the Labour Party*, 1985: 194.

protect the affiliated trade-unions' institutional role at the local party level, but for the first time the principle that all individual party members had the right to participate in candidate selections was accepted. In addition, the party leadership encouraged all local parties to consult their individual members before casting their votes in the 1988 leadership elections and it is estimated that just under 350 constituencies carried out this participative exercise. The party leadership's long-term objective since 1983 has remained, however, an individual membership party at the local level and the 1990 Party Conference agreed that parliamentary selections and reselections should be based upon this principle after the next general election.

In a short period of seven years the party had abandoned the principle of delegatory democracy enshrined in its constitution for over sixty years and had begun the process which leads to individual member democracy. At the time of writing the party combines an uneasy mix of delegatory, activist, and individual member democracy. The party structure maintains indirect membership through trade-union affiliation. Only with the abolition of this indirect membership and the creation of a party composed entirely of individual members can this tension be resolved.

THE SOCIAL AND POLITICAL COMPOSITION OF THE MEMBERSHIP

Since the creation of an individual membership in 1918 almost nothing has been known about its social composition or its political views. Between 1933 and 1970 the party distinguished the male and female membership; but even this simple information is no longer available. Up to the time of the present survey scholars have been reliant therefore for information on hunch or limited surveys. The hunch tends towards the view that party members are an unrepresentative body of people. Symptomatic of this point of view was Sydney Webb's assertion that constituency parties were frequently made up of 'unrepresentative groups of nonentities dominated by fanatics and cranks, and extremists ...' (McKenzie, 1964: 505).

Specific studies suggest, however, that this hunch should be treated with some caution. Rose (1976) studied annual party conference resolutions submitted by constituency parties between 1955 and 1960 and discovered a wide span of opinions. Rose slightly underestimates the extent of 'extremism' among constituency parties because he takes no account of the process of resolution exclusion which operated prior to the publication of the conference agenda upon which he based his analysis (see Minkin, 1978: 77–80). Nevertheless he challenges the conventional wisdom that party members participating in the process of submitting conference resolutions are situated at the extreme of the political spectrum. Minkin (1978) argues that a wide span of opinions are expressed by constituency parties in their conference resolutions, nevertheless he draws attention to the fact that during the period 1956–70 the overwhelming body of constituency views were of a left-wing nature on many of the major issues such as nuclear disarmament, the EC, Vietnam, and prices and incomes legislation. Other commentators have noted that the constituency parties' representatives on the NEC, first elected by constituency delegates in 1937, have been consistently and overwhelmingly on the party's left. From 1952 onwards the Left has secured almost uninterrupted dominance of this section of the party's ruling body. Again, however, the extent of left opinions in the local constituency parties should not be exaggerated since other factors also prevail in securing election to the NEC, such as incumbency and personality.

Numerous studies of local constituency parties (Bealey, Blondel and McCann, 1965; Forrester, 1976; Barker *et al.*, 1978; Turner, 1978; Bochel and Denver, 1983; Whiteley, 1983; Seyd, 1987; and Goss, 1988) suggest a wide spectrum of political opinions among party members. No common factor, such as the social composition of the membership or the political opinions of the incumbent Labour MP (assuming the constituency returns a Labour MP), appear to have any significance in determining the political opinions of local party members. The commonly held assumption of their politically extreme views should be treated with caution. These assumptions, as we argued earlier, have been based upon hunch or upon limited surveys of particular localities or groups of members. We now have the benefit of a national survey which has extracted basic information concerning the political and social characteristics of the membership, and in the following chapters we will outline and elaborate on our findings. But before commencing the analysis we need to consider, finally, the position of party members in the wider political system.

THE PARTY MEMBER IN BRITISH POLITICS

Political parties are the life-blood of liberal democracy. They institutionalize political conflict and they help ensure political accountability of leaders. They are an essential part of the British state. A government committee set up to examine the funding of political parties stated that 'the existence of political parties is an essential feature of our system of parliamentary democracy' (Report of the Committee on Financial Aid to Political Parties, 1976: 19). This viewpoint was repeated by the Hansard Society in its report on the financing of parties in which it stated that 'parties play a vital role in the working of democratic government' (Hansard Society, 1981: 9). Nevertheless parties play a shadowy role within the British state because they are only partially recognized. Parties have a recognized legitimacy in Parliament but not, until recently, within the electoral process. For example, until 1970 no party label was included on the ballot paper, even though the overwhelming majority of candidates at general elections were party nominees. Parties, outside of parliament, are essentially private organizations. Keith Ewing (1987: 7) states that they are 'truly autonomous in the sense that there is no direct statutory regulation of their affairs'. Therefore who joins and what are the rules by which they conduct their affairs are matters left to the parties themselves. Parties are dependent for most of their funds and labour upon private subscription and voluntary involvement. The state provides only limited subsidies for electioneering and parliamentary activities. Members are therefore of value in British parties. They provide their party leadership with important resources. For example, they contribute money and labour and they may act as a channel for political communication. Sporadic attempts have been made recently to increase state funding of parties. Both the Houghton and the Hansard committees proposed forms of state funding but both foundered on the opposition of the Conservative governments. For the time being therefore parties remain autonomous agencies with limited state support and reliant on the contributions, both of money and time, of a reserve army of voluntary labour. They are organizations which are an essential part of civil society.

It is somewhat surprising when parties are so dependent upon volunteers that academic studies of the amateur grass roots have been so limited. Who are they? What opinions do they hold? Why do they join? What do they perceive as the costs and the benefits? We hope to remedy this absence of study of the voluntary partisans in the following chapters.

3

Who Are The Members?

> ... the broader the base of the party's membership the deeper
> will go the roots and the more in tune the party's policies will
> be with the hopes, experiences and aspirations of the British
> people.[1]

We pointed out in the previous chapter that, until now, no comprehensive study of the members of one of Britain's major political
parties has ever been conducted and therefore no profile of the party
membership has been available. In this chapter we will fill this gap
and provide an overview of our research findings. We will consider
Labour members' socio-economic background, and then their attitudes and, in particular, their views on the reorganization of the
Labour party. We will compare their background and attitudes with
those of Labour voters, in order that we might draw conclusions
about the representativeness of the party membership.

In 1989 exactly 293,723 individuals, according to the Labour
party's records, signified their support for the declared objectives of
the party by paying either a full or a reduced subscription of £10 or
£3 and by becoming an individual member.[2] Who are these people
and what are their opinions?

We know from the Labour party's published figures that they are
more likely to be located in the party's London region than elsewhere. In the early 1980s when the Left was in the ascendancy within
the Labour party there were many, both on the left and right of the

[1] Tom Burlison, delegate from the General and Municipal Workers' Union,
speaking at the Labour Party Conference in 1988. (*Report of the Eighty-seventh Annual
Conference of the Labour Party*, 1988: 32.)

[2] To become an individual member a person has to 'subscribe to the conditions of
membership' and not be a member of a political party or organization 'declared by
the Annual Conference of the Labour Party ... or by the National Executive Committee ... to be ineligible for affiliation to the Party'. In addition, the individual has
to 'Accept and conform to the Constitution, Programme, Principles and Policy of the
Party', and 'If eligible, be a member of a Trade Union affiliated to the Trades Union
Congress'. Clauses II(4) and III(3), *The Constitution and Standing Orders of the
Labour Party*.

party, who believed that London members were playing too prominent a role in party affairs. This was a time when parts of the media were concentrating on certain so-called 'loony-left councils' in London and some members felt this was giving the party bad publicity. There is no doubt that this media attention had more to do with the concentration of the media in London rather than any distinct regional distribution of opinions among party members. Nevertheless the view was expressed in Labour party circles that provincial members needed to wrest the political initiative from London members in order to reassert a more traditional party image. Whether the London members are as distinctive in their political attitudes as this view supposes we will leave to an examination in Chapter 6, but for the moment we should note the strength of party membership in the London region relative to the rest of Great Britain. Fig. 3.1 displays the regional breakdown of the party membership.[3] Then in Fig. 3.2 we show the regional distribution of Labour's vote in the 1987 General Election. We can then see in Fig. 3.3 that, in relation to the overall distribution of the Labour vote, as measured at the 1987 General Election, the distribution of the individual membership is skewed. The London, Southern, Eastern, and South-Western regions have a higher proportion of members than voters whereas in the Scottish, Yorkshire, West Midlands, North-Western, Northern, and Welsh regions the reverse is the case. Labour's total membership is skewed, in other words, towards the more Conservatively inclined regions of the country.

This is the extent of the details in the party's published records. We can now supplement this by, first, revealing the social make-up of this membership.

A SOCIO-ECONOMIC PROFILE

In Table 3.1 we examine some of the socio-economic characteristics of party members. This shows that the typical party member is a middle-aged, middle-class man. Almost two-thirds of the party membership is male. If the party was intent on achieving a gender profile which reflects the distribution of the adult population then it

[3] We are grateful to Professor Ron Johnston for his advice and to Graham Allsopp for the drawing of the maps.

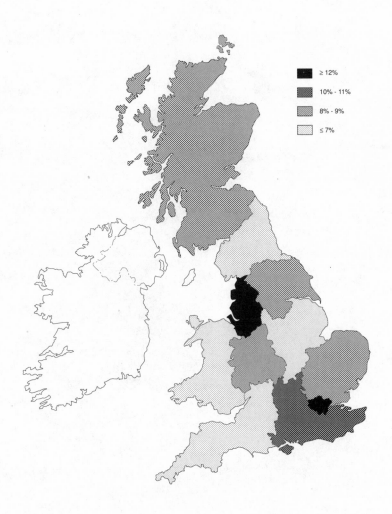

FIG. 3.1 Percentage of total individual Labour party membership by region

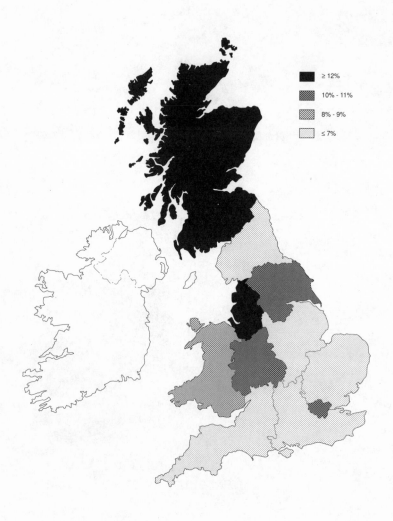

FIG. 3.2 Percentage of total 1987 Labour vote by region

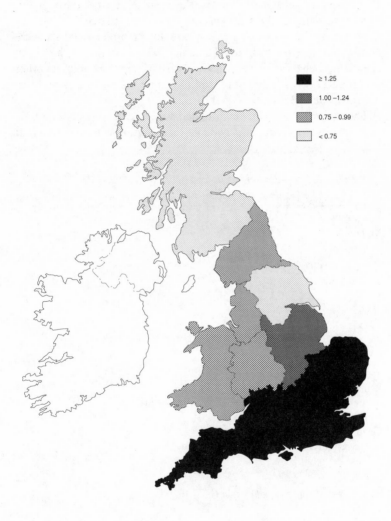

Fɪɢ. 3.3 Individual Labour party membership as a proportion of 1987 Labour vote by region

would have to redouble the attempts it has made in recent years to recruit more women into its ranks. It would also need to recruit more young people since the average age of the membership is 48. There are very few members under the age of 25. Part of the explanation for this may be the problems the party has experienced in organizing young people. For many years the Young Socialists were dominated by the Militant Tendency whose policies, the party leadership believes, alienate the majority of young people. Another explanation is that the young tend not to be joiners of any political organizations (Bynner and Ashford, 1990).

The majority of members attended state secondary schools. Less than one in ten attended private or direct grant schools. Over half

TABLE 3.1. *Socio-economic Characteristics of the Party Membership: Gender, Age, and Schooling* (percentages)

Gender (N = 5032)	
Male	61
Female	39
Age (N = 5007)	
25 and under	5
26–35	17
36–45	26
46–55	17
56–65	16
66 and over	19
Type of school last attended (N = 4872)	
Primary/Elementary	16
Secondary Modern/Technical/Scottish Secondary	31
Comprehensive	12
Grammar/Scottish Senior Secondary	28
Direct grant/Grant-aided	4
Private fee-paying	5
Other	3
Age at end of full-time education (N = 4893)	
16 and under	58
17–18	12
19 and over	30

Note: Figures in this table, and all subsequent tables, have been rounded and therefore may not total 100.

(58 per cent) left full-time education at 16 or under and 29 per cent have no educational qualification of any kind; in contrast, over one-quarter (30 per cent) remained in full-time education until the age of 19 or over, and 29 per cent have either a University or CNAA/ Polytechnic degree. There is a very sharp divide therefore in the party between those members who have succeeded educationally and are well qualified and those who left school at the earliest possible opportunity and lack any educational qualifications.

Table 3.2 shows that party members are very likely to be working

TABLE 3.2. *Socio-economic Characteristics of the Party Membership: Work Sector, Class, Accommodation, and Income* (percentages)

Type of work organization (N = 4633)	
Private firm	37
Local authority/Local education authority	27
Nationalized industry/Public corporation	10
Health authority/Hospital	5
Central government/Civil Service	5
Other (e.g. University/Polytechnic)	16
Socio-economic occupational classification (N = 4621)	
Salariat	49
Routine non-manual	16
Petty bourgeoisie	4
Foreman and Technician	5
Working-class	26
Type of accommodation (N = 5029)	
Own property	71
Rented from council	17
Rented privately	4
Rented from housing association	2
Live with family/friends	5
Household income (£ p.a.) (N = 4960)	
Under 5,000	17
5–10,000	21
10–15,000	18
15–20,000	15
20–25,000	10
25–30,000	8
30,000 and over	12

in the public sector. Almost two-thirds have a public sector job in either local government, a public corporation, a local health authority, a polytechnic, or a university. Whether they work in the public sector because their political values are anti-capitalist and anti-business, or whether as public sector workers they are more likely to gravitate towards the Labour party because its programme is likely to enhance their employment and career prospects, is unknown.

If we use the classification of occupations employed in the British Election Study (Heath, Jowell, and Curtice, 1985), one-half of the members are salariat (for example, lecturers, teachers, social workers, solicitors, dentists, and doctors). In fact, there are more schoolteachers in the party than any other occupational grouping. There is a common misconception that the majority of schoolteachers are Labour voters, but it is certainly the case that a large proportion of Labour members are schoolteachers.[4] Only one-quarter of the members are manual workers. The party's electoral appeal has always been to 'workers by hand or by brain', nevertheless it has always relied on the organized working class for the bulk of its electoral support. Now the contemporary Labour party, however, recruits only a very small part of its individual membership from this traditional constituency. If the current party leadership maintains its commitment to reduce the role of the affiliated membership within the party (see later in this chapter) then one of the means by which working-class opinions can be expressed within the party will have been reduced. The party needs to consider alternative ways in which this voice can be heard. We will return to this question in a later chapter.

Finally, on the pattern of work among members, just over one-half (52 per cent) are in full-time work and another one-tenth (8 per cent) work part-time. Almost one-fifth (19 per cent) are retired.

The sense of class politics among this overwhelmingly non-manual membership is high. Almost three-quarters (73 per cent) regard themselves as belonging to a class, and for this class-conscious group 70 per cent see themselves as working class. Members were even more aware of their parents' class identity: 90 per cent of respondents believed that when they were teenagers their

---

[4] In surveys on teachers' voting behaviour it was revealed that only 26 per cent in 1983, and 28 per cent in 1987, voted Labour. *Times Educational Supplement*, 27 May 1983, and 29 May 1987.

families belonged to a social class and, among these class-conscious members, over three-quarters (77 per cent) identified themselves as working class. Class-awareness and identity is therefore very strong among members. Upward mobility presumably explains the slippage (17 per cent) in class-awareness from teenager to adult, but members clearly identify subjectively with a different class from that which their occupation would suggest is their objective position.

Two-thirds (64 per cent) of members are trade-unionists and, not surprisingly in the light of the occupational profile, it is a white-collar union (NALGO), not affiliated to the Labour party, to which more party members belong than any other union. Table 3.3 shows the eight trade unions recruiting upwards of 5 per cent of the party membership.

Four trade unions with the largest affiliated membership to the Labour party have a significant number of their members who also belong to the party as individuals, but some other major affiliated trade unions, such as the Union of Shop, Distributive and Allied Workers, or the National Union of Mineworkers, are underrepresented among the individual membership. The existence of an affiliated, indirect category of party membership perhaps leads to an underestimate of the party commitment amongst members of the traditional manual trade unions. A politically committed member of a non-affiliated trade union, such as NALGO or the NUT, who wishes to identify with the Labour party has more incentive to join than a member of an affiliated union who, by paying the political levy, is already contributing in an indirect manner to it. This will be one factor explaining why, for example, there are more members of

TABLE 3.3. *Trade-union Affiliations of Party Members (unions recruiting 5 per cent or more of the membership)* (percentages)

National Association of Local Government Officers	12
Transport and General Workers' Union	11
National Union of Teachers	9
Amalgamated Engineering Union	7
Manufacturing, Science, Finance Union	7
General and Municipal Workers' Union	6
National Union of Public Employees	5
National Association of Teachers in Further/Higher Education	5

the Association of University Teachers than members of the National Union of Mineworkers in the Labour party.

Party members are home owners. Only 17 per cent live in council housing. Among the home owners almost one-fifth (17 per cent) have taken advantage of the Conservative government's 'right to buy' legislation and have purchased their council house.

There is a clear disparity in the financial resources of party members. One measure of disposable income is car ownership. One-half of members own a car, and a further one-quarter own two; one-quarter possess no car. Overall household income is another measure of the financial resources available to party members. The average household income is £18,000, but there are wide income disparities. Almost one in five (17 per cent) have a household income below £5,000 per year, whereas another one in five (20 per cent) take home £25,000 or more per year. Taken together these two sets of figures reveal that between one-fifth and one-quarter of members are poor, and one-tenth are very well-off.

Finally, party members are overwhelmingly white-skinned; there are very few who are of African or Asian origin. Two-fifths (41 per cent) declare themselves to be religious non-believers, but those who do have a religious commitment are more likely to be attached to the established Protestant or Roman Catholic churches. Nonconformism was a significant influence during the party's formative years (Pelling, 1965), but it has little presence in the contemporary Labour party. Neither is the Jewish presence of any significance in today's Labour party.

What is clear from these findings is that there is a division among the members between the relatively poor and under qualified and the relatively well-off and well qualified. There are two distinct universes that party members inhabit which is exemplified by their newspaper-reading habits. Among those purchasing a morning newspaper there is a clear divide between the readers of the *Guardian* and the *Daily Mirror*.

This profile confirms a common journalistic assumption that middle-class, public-sector professionals predominate among Labour party members. What has been missed, however, in the conventional wisdom is the existence of a significant group of members with very limited resources, either financial or educational. There is a class of member who has missed out on the expansion of educational opportunities, on the rise of living standards, and the growth

TABLE 3.4. *Socio-economic Characteristics of the Party Membership: Colour, Religion, and Newspaper Readership* (percentages)

Ethnic origin (N = 4810)	
White/European	96
Afro-Asian	3
Other	1
Religion (N = 4983)	
Non-believer	41
Protestant (Churches of England, Scotland, Wales)	28
Nonconformist (Methodist, Baptist, United Reform)	8
Roman Catholic	11
Christian, but no denomination	6
Jew	1
Moslem	1
Other	3
Newspaper readership (N = 4772)	
No daily	13
Guardian	35
Daily Mirror/Record	29
Independent	7
Other (*Daily Express, Daily Mail, Star, Today, Sun, Daily Telegraph, Financial Times, The Times*)	15

of home-ownership. The 'new model' Labour party of the 1990s may perhaps be in danger of becoming too responsive to the demands of the affluent radical rather than of the poor proletarian. If the middle-class membership is growing as a proportion of the total then the party leadership needs to ensure that the diminishing working-class membership does not feel excluded from party affairs. Otherwise the working-class membership will either create internal trouble or exit.

The party leadership also needs to ensure that the party membership is not too unrepresentative of the party's potential voters, either socially or politically. If the members are socially unrepresentative they will be less able to fulfil their role as 'ambassadors to the community' (Scarrow, 1990) in such a way as to generate electoral support and, in fact, they may alienate potential voters. If they are politically unrepresentative they will demand policies which may

not attract widespread support from the voters. We will examine
members' political representativeness later in this chapter: here we
consider their social representativeness.

In Table 3.5 we compare some of the social characteristics of
party members and Labour voters, where the information for the
latter is taken from the British Election Study of 1987. The Labour
party attracts more women as voters than it does as members. The
party has made efforts to encourage women to take a more active
part in the party's affairs. For example, women are now guaranteed
three places in the Shadow Cabinet and parliamentary selection
short lists must include at least one woman, if women have been
nominated. Nevertheless the party needs to concentrate on recruiting more women members if it wishes its membership to be more
representative of its electoral support.

There is, however, a closer age approximation between the party
members and voters, apart from an underrepresentation among
members of the very young (18–25 years) and an overrepresentation
of the middle aged (36–45 years).

There is an almost perfect reversal of occupational groups among
party members and voters. Whereas one-half and one-fifth of
Labour voters belong to the manual working class and salariat
respectively, the opposite is the case among Labour members. If the
gender composition of the party membership is out of line with the
party's voters, then this is even more so with its class composition.
Britain's social structure is changing, nevertheless the Labour party
still relies on the manual working class for a substantial part of its
electoral support. In order to ensure that the party is both sensitive
to the needs of this constituency and a credible ambassador in this
community it needs to recruit more manual workers as members.
Establishing workplace party branches in the 1980s was one attempt
to make more working-class members but this has had little
success.[5] The Labour party is confronted with the fact that by tradition the working class is less likely to join political organizations
than the middle class, nevertheless it has to consider new ways of
ensuring that the voice of this significant constituency is heard within
its councils. This is especially the case when the party leadership is
considering a reduction in the trade-unions' influence in the party as
affiliated members.

Home-ownership is the norm among both party voters and

[5] In the survey only 1% of members belong to a workplace branch.

TABLE 3.5. *Social Characteristics of Labour Party Members and Voters* (percentages)

	Members	Voters
Gender		
Male	61	48
Female	39	52
Age		
18–21	2	8
22–25	3	10
26–35	17	20
36–45	26	18
46–55	17	14
56–65	16	16
Over 66	19	15
Social class		
Salariat	49	14
Routine non-manual	16	19
Petty bourgeoisie	4	4
Foreman and Technician	5	6
Working-class	26	57
House tenure		
Owner	75	53
Rented from local authority	18	39
Private renting	4	6
Housing association renting	2	3
Household income (£ p.a.)		
Under 5,000	17	36
5,000–10,000	21	31
10,000–15,000	18	18
15,000–20,000	15	9
20,000–25,000	10	4
25,000–30,000	8	1
30,000 and over	12	1

members, although there is a greater preponderance of home owners among members than voters. Finally, party members are richer than their voting counterparts. There is again, as with occupational grouping, almost a complete reversal of economic fortunes between member and voter. Two-thirds of Labour voters had a household annual income of *under* £10,000 whereas two-thirds of Labour members had a household annual income of *over* £10,000.

The party membership is clearly socially unrepresentative of Labour voters in some significant ways. Whereas a large part of Labour's electoral support is drawn from manual workers and from people with average or below-average levels of household income, a large part of Labour's membership support is drawn from middle-class professionals and from people with above-average levels of household income. Does this matter? It might in two ways. First, the general image conveyed through behaviour, language, and concerns by the party, via its membership, might be alienating to potential supporters. Second, specific policy commitments might be entered into by the members which run counter to the views of its supporters and will therefore antagonize and drive them away. It is difficult to assess whether the first of these prevails. There are Labour parties in working-class areas of cities which seem no longer to be the natural inhabitants of the local community culture in the way in which Goss (1988) describes for the inter-war and immediate post-war years. One reason why Labour lost the traditional inner-city constituency of Bermondsey in the 1980s was because the local party, and its parliamentary candidate at the time of the by-election in 1982, were socially and politically unrepresentative of the community. On the other hand, there are examples of inner-city parties, increasingly represented by middle-class members, which continue to attract electoral support from among Labour's traditional working-class supporters. Regarding the second of the problems that might arise from having a socially distinctive party membership, we can draw some conclusions by comparing Labour voters' and members' political opinions to see whether there are significant differences between the two.

THE POLITICAL ATTITUDES OF PARTY MEMBERS[6]

Since Labour's calamitous electoral performance in 1983 the party leadership has been steadily engaged in a simultaneous twin-track strategy of policy reformulation and party reorganization in order to win back political office. The party leadership's belief has been

---

[6] The questionnaire contains a wide range of 'agree/disagree' questions dealing with policy attitudes mainly assessed using Likert-scales.

that for the party to be electable some of the party's policy commitments had to be abandoned and the party activists' powers within the
party had to be reduced.

Policy reformulation was implemented by means of a wide-
ranging policy review initiated in 1987 and completed in 1989 with
the publication of *Meet the Challenge, Make the Change.* It is not our
intention to examine either the progress of that policy review or the
fine details of the end-result, since this has been well documented
elsewhere (Hughes and Wintour, 1990). Suffice to note that the bulk
of the document caused little intra-party controversy. Only in the
areas of the economy and defence did disagreements emerge. There is
a very clear commitment in the policy-review document to an efficient market economy in which a good working partnership between
capital and labour is established. Public ownership is regarded as a
fall-back option to be used only in certain limited circumstances.
Similarly, on the question of defence, first, the party's unilateralist
stance on nuclear disarmament has been abandoned and, secondly,
the document argues the need for adequate and efficient conventional defence forces which might involve maintaining high defence
expenditure. Both of these issues were debated at the 1989 Party
Conference and clear majorities secured for the new policies.[7]

Policy reformulation was generated primarily by electoral
pressures. The need to win voters' support has necessitated the aban-
donment of commitments unpopular with the party's traditional
supporters, such as unilateral nuclear disarmament, extensive
nationalization, withdrawal from the European Community, and
an unwillingness to sell council houses to sitting tenants. This process of policy modification was further stimulated by external and
internal institutional pressures. Labour's alternative economic
strategy of the early 1980s was predicated upon a domestic state
controlling the commanding heights of the economy, but by the end
of the decade the party had shifted its position to a recognition that
economic policies needed developing in a European context and
should include membership of the European Exchange Rate
Mechanism, the development of a politically accountable European central bank, and a well-developed European regional policy.
The Labour party had abandoned its national, Labourist solutions
to Britain's economic problems.

The Labour party has been always very traditional in its approach

[7] *Report of the Eighty-eighth Annual Conference of the Labour Party*, 1989: 152–6.

to the institutions of the British state. Apart from reducing the House of Lords' delaying powers in 1949 it has been reticent about introducing any basic reforms of the political system. Only when the institutions of the British centralized state attracted increasing criticism, and there were demands from a section of the population for constitutional reforms in the late 1980s, did the Labour party respond in part to some of these criticisms by promising devolved powers to an elected Scottish assembly, elected regional authorities in England and Wales, and an enquiry into the electoral system.

Party members were asked questions in the survey on a wide range of issues and enough of their responses will be examined here to obtain an overall picture of their political attitudes. At first glance these middle-class radicals are, perhaps surprisingly, attached to the politics of traditional, industrial Britain in the sense that two-thirds (66 per cent) of them believe that the class struggle between labour and capital is the central issue in British politics. The party membership seems wedded to a very traditional class-politics at a time when the party leadership is attempting to adapt to the new formations and attitudes emerging in the post-industrial state. However, if on the basis of this response on class-politics, it might be thought that members believe the party should adopt policies of specific benefit to the working class, then they are revealed as more equivocal. They are equally divided over whether the party should have a strategy of adopting policies only approved of by the working class. Furthermore, a majority believe that the party should adjust its policies 'to capture the middle ground of politics'. It would appear therefore that the members share the party leadership's desire to position the party in the political spectrum in such a manner as to maximize its electoral support. Furthermore, this suggests that the class struggle is important as a symbolic totem for members[8] but the stark realities of winning power demand a less class-specific party strategy. Members would appear to distinguish, however, between adjusting party *policies* to win electoral support and shifting party *principles*. A majority want the party to maintain its principles, even if this does result in the loss of an election.

But what are these party principles? Between 1985 and 1988 the party leadership made various attempts to reformulate Labour's

---

[8] Asked whether they were aware of belonging to any one class as they were growing up, 77% placed themselves in the working class. Their sense of class-awareness is high which would contribute to this prevailing commitment to the idea of class struggle.

TABLE 3.6. *Members' Attitudes on Class Politics and Electoral Strategy*
(percentages)

	(a)	(b)	(c)	(d)
Agree	66	41	57	60
Disagree	20	42	33	28
Neither	14	18	10	12

Notes: Party members were asked to respond on a five-point scale ('strongly agree'; 'agree'; 'neither'; 'disagree'; 'strongly disagree') to the following statements:

(a) 'The central question of British politics is the class struggle between labour and capital.'

(b) 'The Labour Party should only adopt policies supported by a majority of working-class people.'

(c) 'The Labour Party should adjust its policies to capture the middle ground of politics.'

(d) 'The Labour Party should always stand by its principles even if this should lose an election.'

In all cases the 'strongly agree' and 'agree'; and the 'disagree' and 'strongly disagree' have been summated.

basic beliefs but the end result, *A Statement of Democratic Socialist Aims and Values* never became the ideological foundation of the party's activities (Hughes and Wintour, 1990: ch. 5). The party therefore remains unclear about its underlying beliefs, but the membership does have principled commitments. On examination of the survey data they appear committed to four socialist 'touchstones'.

First, they believe in public ownership and they are very critical of market forces. Asked whether they are committed to more nationalization of companies, more privatization, or to leaving things as they are, over two-thirds (71 per cent) opt for more nationalization. Furthermore, over three-quarters of the membership believe that the public enterprises privatized by the Government should be returned to the public sector. The majority of party members do not believe that the production of goods and services should be left to the free market.

This positive enthusiasm party members feel for nationalization is not reflected in the updated policy-review document, *Looking to the Future*, (Labour Party, 1990) in which only the water industry is itemized for public ownership. A word of caution should be expressed, however, concerning the survey response on nationaliz-ation. The survey was conducted at the time that water privatization was prominent in the news; even Conservative voters expressed some apprehensions about this policy and public support for water remaining a state-owned undertaking was high. The survey did not ask respondents to itemize the industries which should be publicly owned: perhaps enthusiasm for public ownership is high for the basic utilities (e.g. water, gas, and electricity) but wanes for other industries.[9] It should also be noted that one-quarter of all members believe the production of goods and services should be left to the free market—which challenges the notion of ideological uniformity among members. There is no way of discovering whether this figure is larger than in the past but one might deduce that 'Thatcherism' has had an impact on a significant number of members as far as their views on the running of the economy are concerned.

Second, party members remain strong defenders of the legitimacy of trade unions in the economy. They do not believe that Britain benefits from trade-union powers being weaker. Nor do they believe that stricter laws should be introduced to regulate the trade unions. Furthermore, they approve of sympathy strikes by workers, even when not in the same workplace, in order to reinforce worker soli-darity.

The 'new model' Labour party has tried to distance itself from too close a general association with the trade unions and, in particular, from any return to the legal position and bargaining rights they enjoyed in the late 1970s. How far the Labour leadership can go in this disengagement strategy before seriously antagonizing the party members is unclear. We have discovered a general pro-trade-union sentiment among members, more so than the party leadership might care to identify with, but we are unable to highlight specific trade-union legal measures introduced by Conservative governments since 1979 that members would wish to repeal against the wishes of the party leadership.[10]

Third, party members are sceptical about the benefits of defence expenditure. Asked whether more or less should be spent on

---

[9] A follow-up national survey of party members will include a question on the public ownership of specific industries.

[10] Whether party members would wish to restore the legally based closed shop, and remove the legal restraints imposed upon unions before taking industrial action, are issues to be followed up in our later survey.

defence, over three-quarters of the sample (86 per cent) believe in lower expenditure. Asked also for their views on nuclear weapons, two-thirds believe Britain should have nothing to do with nuclear weapons.

The party leadership's fears that it will lose a general election if it can be portrayed by its opponents as leaving Britain defenceless are very strong. For this reason unilateral nuclear disarmament was abandoned and the party leadership has been at pains to stress its commitment to maintain Britain's defence forces: for example, it opposed a resolution at the party's 1990 Conference which would have committed a future Labour government to a reduction in defence expenditure to the Western European average.[11]

The fourth socialist touchstone is public expenditure. Party members almost unanimously believe in high public expenditure even if it means raising taxation.

On this issue there is less division between the party leadership and the membership. The leadership is at pains, however, to ensure there are no grounds for the accusation that a future Labour government would expand public expenditure and pay for it by raising taxes. Leaders stress that no rise in public expenditure is possible without sustained economic growth and that not all the public projects deemed worthy of support will be funded in the lifetime of a single parliament. The leadership is nervous of the electoral consequences of higher tax commitments and therefore emphasizes the need for a fair and progressive income tax without being too specific. In the initial policy-review document there was a commitment to secure the effective taxation of wealth but this was not referred to in the later, updated version.

Our first conclusion therefore regarding party members' attitudes and opinions is that they believe in a principled approach to politics and any attempts by the party leadership to reduce this principled approach would be unpopular. Furthermore, they have distinct opinions on four areas of policy which are not always in accord with the party leadership's renewal strategy. Nevertheless, they also want to win a general election and are conscious of the need to pursue an electoral strategy which will maximize their electoral support. It is not possible to ascertain here what the exact 'trade-off' is between these four socialist touchstones and electoral office but it

[11] See, the *Independent*, 4 Oct. 1990.

TABLE 3.7. *The Core Beliefs of Members regarding Trade Unions, Nationalization, Defence, and Public Expenditure* (percentages)

	(a)	(b)	(c)
Should	12	86	21
Should not	78	11	73
Doesn't matter	10	3	6

Notes: Party members were asked to respond on a five-point scale ('definitely should'; 'probably should'; 'doesn't matter'; 'probably should not'; 'definitely should not') to the following statements that the government should/should not:

(a) 'Introduce stricter laws to regulate trade unions.'
(b) 'Spend less on defence.'
(c) 'Reduce government spending generally.'

In all cases the 'definitely should' and 'probably should'; and the 'probably should not' and 'definitely should not' have been summated.

Trade unions

	(a)	(b)	(c)	(d)
Agree	13	72	82	25
Disagree	73	17	8	58
Neither	14	11	10	17

Notes:

(a) 'It is better for Britain when trade unions have little power.'
(b) 'Workers should be prepared to strike in support of other workers, even if they don't work in the same place.'
(c) 'The public enterprises privatized by the Tory government should be returned to the public sector.'
(d) 'The production of goods and services is best left to a free market.'

Nationalization/privatization

Are you generally in favour of:	
More nationalization	71
More privatization	2
Leave as now	28

Defence

Britain should maintain independent nuclear weapons	5
Britain should maintain nuclear weapons in Western defence system	21
Britain should have no nuclear weapons	68
No opinion	6

Public expenditure

Reduce taxes/spend less on services	2
Tax and spend the same as now	6
Increase taxes/spend more on services	92

is the essence of political leadership to calculate that point and act accordingly.[12]

Mention was made earlier in this section that Labour has made some significant changes in its approach to both economic policy and state institutions; it has moved away from its isolationist stance towards the European Community and has begun to critically re-examine the working of some British institutions. We explore here whether members share the view that a reappraisal of two traditional aspects of Labour policy is now necessary.

Members were asked whether Britain should remain a member of the European Community or withdraw: overwhelmingly (89 per cent) they opt for remaining a member. Their commitment goes further: fewer than one in five (16 per cent) would resist moves to further integrate Britain into the European Community.

Asked also whether Labour should create a directly elected Scottish assembly with its own taxing powers, a majority (59 per cent) approve. A majority (58 per cent) believe Britain's electoral system should be replaced by one based upon proportional representation. When asked, however, for their views on coalition government, which it is reasonable to assume would be the consequence of such an electoral system, fewer than one in ten (7 per cent) express their approval. Party members appear to be critical of the present electoral system yet are also hostile to the practical consequences of a proportional system. Finally, even though the party leadership has expressed its opposition to a Bill of Rights because it would

[12] One of the issues we will be pursuing in the follow-up survey of party members is the nature of the 'trade-off' between principles and power.

TABLE 3.8. *Members' Attitudes on the European Community and Institutional Reforms* (percentages)

Attitudes to EC

Continue	89
Withdraw	11

Attitudes to Institutional Reforms

	(a)	(b)	(c)	(d)	(e)
Agree	16	59	58	7	12
Disagree	72	20	31	81	78
Neither	12	22	11	13	11

Notes: Party members were asked to respond on a five-point scale ('strongly agree', 'agree', 'neither', 'disagree', 'strongly disagree') to the following statements:

(a) 'Labour should resist further moves to integrate the European Common Market.'

(b) 'A future Labour government should introduce a directly elected Scottish Assembly with taxing powers.'

(c) 'Britain's present electoral system should be replaced by a system of proportional representation.'

(d) 'Coalition governments are the best form of government for Britain.'

(e) 'There is no need for a Bill of Rights in this country.'

place powers in the hands of unelected judges, three-quarters (78 per cent) of the membership believes such a constitutional reform is required.

Our findings are that members are in advance of the party leadership in wanting to make changes in these two areas. They are more integrationist than the party leadership might care to be on the European Community and, on the question of electoral reform and constitutional safeguards for the citizen's civil liberties, they are supporters of fundamental reforms. While the membership is resistant to the party leadership's wishes to abandon a commitment to public ownership, it is a stronger advocate of change than the party leadership regarding constitutional reforms.

Neil Kinnock's party-renewal strategy has been two-pronged. First, it has been an endeavour to make the party's policies electorally more attractive. Secondly, it has been concerned to reorganize the party structure primarily because, in his view, the organization and distribution of power within the party as prevailed in the early 1980s would leave it with policies unpopular with the voters. We will now examine the party members' views on this second aspect of party renewal, namely party reorganization.

MEMBERS' VIEWS ON INTERNAL PARTY REFORM

Since his election as party leader in 1983 Neil Kinnock has been very closely identified with moves to reform the party's internal procedures. For example, he was closely involved in reducing the NEC's overall powers to determine the general direction of the party in opposition, he took a prominent part in forcing Militant sympathizers out of the party, and he was instrumental in securing powers to ensure that parliamentary by-election candidates were more representative of his 'new model' Labour party. There have been two underlying purposes to his drive for internal party reform. First, to increase the powers of the individual party members relative to the party activists by giving them the right to choose their Party Leader, their parliamentary representative, and their NEC representatives. Secondly, to reduce the relative strength of the affiliated trade-union vote at the party's annual conference and within the local constituency parties. Recently, a third objective in party reform has emerged, namely to improve the party's policy-making procedures by reorganizing the structure and operation of the annual conference.

Kinnock's commitment to these internal party reforms has prompted his critics to complain of his autocratic and arrogant leadership. For example, Ken Livingstone commented that 'the methods used inside the Labour Party to achieve the present position have been completely Stalinist'.[13] Our survey enables us to examine whether members share this type of criticism. When asked to express their feelings towards various senior party personnel on a thermometer scale ranging from zero to one hundred, one in three (34 per cent) ranked Kinnock at eighty or above. More members ranked him at this high point than any of his other colleagues. So in terms of a general estimation of Kinnock the man, there is more personal support for him than the criticisms might suggest. It is worth noting, however, that John Smith attracts equal high support and less dislike (namely, a ranking below 50) than his leader. This is perhaps

[13] The *Guardian*, 24 Mar. 1990.

TABLE 3.9. *Party Members' Ratings of Labour Leaders out of 100*
(percentages)

	0–10	11–50	51–80	80+	Mean
Neil Kinnock	2	14	51	34	73
Roy Hattersley	4	29	56	10	60
John Smith	2	10	59	29	73
Gordon Brown	3	14	58	24	70
Robin Cook	2	15	65	18	69
John Prescott	1	20	64	14	66
Joan Ruddock	3	22	63	13	64
David Blunkett	2	12	66	21	71
Harriet Harman	2	18	65	15	67
Bryan Gould	3	23	63	11	63
Tony Benn	6	31	46	17	60
Dennis Skinner	5	26	52	18	63
Ken Livingstone	9	35	44	12	55

unsurprising, however, because as leader Kinnock is inevitably going to attract more criticism than a Shadow Chancellor of the Exchequer who, because he is not a member of Labour's NEC, is less identified with the internal party reorganization.

Members do not agree with the point of view that Kinnock is too authoritarian in his behaviour. Almost three-quarters (71 per cent) reject the view that a problem with the party is that the leader is too powerful. Nevertheless, members are sceptical of Kinnock's principled commitments. Asked whether he would stick to his principles, even if this meant loss of an election, almost one-half (46 per cent) believe he would abandon them.

It is clear that members are overwhelmingly in favour of Kinnock's desire for a party structure in which individual members play a prominent part. Eight in ten (81 per cent) believe the party leader should be elected by individual members on a 'one member, one vote' basis. There is less agreement, however, on the role of trade unions within the party. Members are equally divided over whether or not the trade-union movement has too much power over the party, which suggests that any proposal to eliminate the role of the affiliated membership will generate significant hostility. There is very strong support, however, for the view that the trade-union

TABLE 3.10. *Members' Attitudes towards the Party Leadership and Block Vote* (percentages)

	(a)	(b)	(c)	(d)	(e)	(f)
Agree	15	37	81	72	43	63
Disagree	71	46	12	16	42	26
Neither	15	17	7	12	15	11

Notes:

(a) 'A problem with the Labour party today is that the leader is too powerful'.

(b) 'Neil Kinnock will stick to his principles even if this means losing a general election.'

(c) 'The Labour party leader should be elected by a system of one party member, one vote.'

(d) 'The trade-union block vote at conference brings the party into disrepute.'

(e) 'The trade-union movement has too much power over the Labour party.'

(f) 'Constituency Labour parties should have the exclusive right to select their own parliamentary candidates.'

block vote at party conferences brings the party into disrepute, suggesting that the internal balance of trade-union and individual-membership powers, and the manner in which trade unions operate within the party, are unpopular with members but they retain a belief in the legitimacy of the trade-union position in the party. Finally, members are committed to their local constituency parties maintaining some of their key powers relative to the party leadership: for example, almost two-thirds (63 per cent) believe constituency parties should have the exclusive right to select their parliamentary candidates. The NEC now possesses extensive powers to determine the choice of the party's candidates in parliamentary by-elections. Any extension of these powers to cover general elections would clearly be resisted by the members.

Our conclusion, therefore, is that the attempts to give the individual member a more direct part in electing the party's political élite are very popular among the membership. However, any attempt to restructure the party and abandon the role of the party's affiliated membership, a principle enshrined in the party's constitution since its origins, would not find universal favour. Furthermore, if the party leadership is intent on establishing a party in which the individual member might be more easily managed from the top, it will find strong resistance from the majority who believe local members' rights are paramount.

Finally, we need to consider the attitudes of the party members and the party voters. We referred earlier to the dangers for the party if its membership is unrepresentative of its voters. If they are socially unrepresentative their role as 'ambassadors to the community' is less effective and if politically unrepresentative their chances of damaging the party's electoral prospects are considerable. We will concentrate on the four areas referred to earlier as the members' socialist 'touchstones', namely public ownership, trade-union bargaining rights, defence, and public expenditure.

THE POLITICAL ATTITUDES OF PARTY MEMBERS AND VOTERS: A COMPARISON[14]

We have already noted that almost three-quarters (71 per cent) of members would prefer more nationalization. In contrast, only just over one-third (38 per cent) of Labour voters share this view; their preference is to leave the public–private mix as it stands. While, therefore, very few Labour voters share the Conservative party's liking for privatization, neither do the majority of them share Labour members' desire for renationalization of the privatized industries.

Labour members and voters are in closer accord over the question of trade-union powers in the economy than they are over public ownership. Both a majority of members and voters are supportive of the trade unions possessing collective-bargaining powers. They are opposed to the government introducing stricter laws to regulate the trade unions and they believe strongly that workers should have more say in the workplace.

Similarly, both Labour member and voter share the view that the government should spend less on defence, and that Britain should remain a member of NATO. Where they differ is on the question of nuclear weapons; a majority of Labour voters want Britain to maintain a nuclear defence force, either independently or

[14] Political attitudes change over time and therefore we are conscious that our conclusions, based upon a two-year time gap between the British Election Study of 1987 and our research, can only be tentative.

as a contribution to the Western defence system, but almost three quarters (72 per cent) of members prefer a non-nuclear defence policy.

Finally, Labour voters and members share an almost similar approach to the question of welfare and taxation. Both are strongly in favour of increasing taxes in order to increase public expenditure on health, education, and social benefits, both approve of the redistribution of wealth to working people, but they do disagree on the impact of taxation on the incentives to work. No doubt this disagreement is, in part, a reflection of the income differences between voters and members which we examined earlier. Fewer members than voters experience a high marginal rate of taxation.

We conclude therefore that Labour voters and members have more political attitudes in common than might have been expected considering their social differences. They seem to share a value system which results in similar opinions on trade unions, defence, and public expenditure. On just two specific issues—nationalization and nuclear weapons—are the members out of step with Labour voters. Whether this will have embarrassing electoral consequences is too early to say. We mentioned earlier, however, that the Labour leadership is committed in its latest policy document to the re-nationalization of only one privatized industry—water. The Labour leadership has calculated the 'trade-off' value of nationalization and concluded that party members will accept this concession to electoral opinion. The 'trade-off' on nuclear weapons may be more costly for the leadership if unilateralists are more committed to their belief than nationalizers. Perhaps, however, the cost of this policy change may be eased by developments in international politics which reduce the tensions in Europe. The state of international politics, especially relations between the USA and the USSR, are of considerable importance to the Labour party leadership's attempts to undermine future Conservative attacks on its defence policy whilst, at the same time, not alienating those who regard nuclear weapons as obnoxious.

One note of caution is necessary, however, in making these observations since the Labour vote of 1987 had been reduced to a hard core of support. There were many voters, previously attracted to the Labour party, who had been alienated by its policies and had drifted away. While we argue, therefore, that there is more consistency between voters and members than might have been expected, we

TABLE 3.11. *A Comparison of Members' and Labour Voters' Attitudes on Public Ownership, Trade Unions, Defence, and Taxation* (percentages)

Public ownership

	Members	Voters
More nationalization of companies	71	38
More privatization of companies	2	6
Things left as they are	27	56

Trade Unions

	(a) Members	Voters	(b) Members	Voters
Should	12	26	94	85
Doesn't matter	10	14	3	5
Should not	78	61	3	8

Notes:

(a) 'The government should/should not introduce stricter laws to regulate trade unions.'

(b) 'The government should/should not give workers more say in the place where they work.'

Defence

	Members	Voters
Britain should keep her own nuclear weapons, independent of other countries	5	26
Britain should have nuclear weapons as part of a Western defence system	23	38
Britain should have nothing to do with nuclear weapons	72	36
Britain should continue in NATO	72	86
Britain should withdraw from NATO	29	14
The government should/should not spend less on defence:		
Should	86	62
Doesn't matter	3	8
Should not	12	31

Table 3.11. *Continued*

Taxation

	(a) Taxes		(b) Redistribution	
	Members	Voters	Members	Voters
Agree	35	47	88	77
Not sure	11	13	8	16
Disagree	54	30	5	8

Which of the following options should the government choose?	Members	Voters
1. Reduce taxes and spend less on health, education, and social benefits	2	5
2. Keep taxes and spending on these services at the same level as now	6	26
3. Increase taxes and spend more on health, education and social benefits	92	69

Notes:

(a) 'High income tax makes people less willing to work hard.'

(b) 'Income and wealth should be redistributed towards ordinary working people.'

should also stress the need for the party to ensure a greater proximity of opinions between its members and *potential* voters if it is again to become a permanent contender for political office.

We now move from a general discussion of party membership to a more specific examination of particular features of this political activity and we start by examining the reasons why a person should decide to join the Labour party.

4

Why Join the Labour Party?

Joining a political party is very much a minority activity in Britain. Recent survey evidence from a comprehensive study of political participation concluded that only 7.4 per cent of the electorate are party members, and only 2.2 per cent party activists (Parry and Moyser, 1990). In the 1987 British Election Study individuals in the sample of the UK electorate were asked if they were members of a political party, and just under 1.5 per cent stated that they were members of the Labour party, which constituted about 5 per cent of Labour voters.

These figures suggest something of a paradox. If millions of people are willing to vote for the Labour party—enough to put it in power for some sixteen years since World War II, why are so few willing to join the party? Moreover this paradox is not confined to the Labour party, since the same election study showed that only just under 4 per cent of the respondents were members of the Conservative party, and only about 0.5 per cent were members of the Liberal party. Thus millions of people are willing to support political parties with their votes during an election, but cannot be persuaded to join those parties.

If we pose the broad question 'Why should anyone want to join a political party?', a plausible common-sense answer would seem to be 'Because they want to help to promote the goals of the party—to help get it elected so that it can implement the policies which they favour'. However, in an influential book *The Logic of Collective Action*, Mancur Olson (1965) persuasively argued that this common-sense answer is quite wrong. He demonstrated that if voters are rational individuals, they would not try to promote the goals of their preferred political party by joining it, even when they are enthusiastically in favour of party policies. His analysis suggests that the problem of understanding political participation lies not in explaining why so few people are party members, but why anyone is a party member at all!

To understand this theoretical account it is important to note that

Olson is writing in the tradition of the economist who assumes that individuals are rational actors, who seek to maximize returns and minimize costs in any course of action they undertake. This means if individuals can avoid incurring costs when they obtain benefits of some kind, then they will invariably choose a course of action which allows them to do this.

Olson's theory depends on the notion of a 'collective good', which has certain unique properties distinguishing it from private goods like houses and cars, etc. Collective goods have two important characteristics which make them different from private goods: jointness of supply and impossibility of exclusion. Jointness of supply means that one person's consumption of the good does not reduce the amount available to anyone else; and impossibility of exclusion means that individuals cannot be prevented from consuming it once it is provided, even if they did not contribute to its provision in the first place.

The economic textbook example of a collective good is national defence (Samuelson, 1954). Once a society has provided defence in the form of armed forces and weapons, etc. then a newly arrived member of that society immediately starts to consume that good, benefiting from the security it provides, even though he or she has not contributed towards its provision. It is not possible to exclude that individual from the consumption of that good, since it cannot be distributed only to those individuals who have paid for it. This is the impossibility of exclusion characteristic of a collective good.

Another feature of defence is that one person's consumption does not reduce the consumption of anyone else—once it is provided then it is just as effective if it is 'consumed' by 55 million people or by 55 million and one. This is the jointness of supply property. Because collective goods have these characteristics, individuals have an incentive not to contribute to their provision. Economists have long recognized that individuals may have to be coerced into contributing to collective goods of this type by taxation, if such goods are to be adequately provided.

Olson's key insight was to recognize that most of the 'products' of political parties or interest groups are collective goods, particularly the public policies advocated by these organizations; thus if individuals favour the policies advocated by a political party they will receive the benefits of those policies if it is elected to office, whether or not they worked to bring about that election win.

Moreover, the incentive not to contribute goes beyond that since their own contribution to any election victory is likely to be extremely small even when they are very active. It is not rational for them to get involved since their work will make no effective difference to the outcome. The logic of the choices they face is as follows: when they contribute to the party by working for it during an election, they as individuals, are not likely to increase the chances of the party winning the election. In addition they can avoid the costs and get the benefits by not participating if the party is elected, and avoid the costs while not receiving the benefits if it fails to be elected. Only in the unlikely situation where their participation is likely to be decisive in determining the outcome of the election is it rational for them to participate.

This theoretical argument suggests that rational individuals will not participate in politics, and so the problem lies in explaining why some people do actually join political parties, and why some of those who join become active. Clearly some people do join parties and become active in them, so how does the theory deal with this fact? Olson explains this by pointing out that politically active individuals receive 'selective incentives', or inducements to become active which are unrelated to the collective goods the organization is set up to provide. These selective incentives are private goods in the sense that anyone who does not contribute will not receive them.

In his book he illustrates such incentives in the case of trade unions (Olson, 1965: 73). The main 'outputs' of trade-union action are improvements in wages and conditions of service in the workplace, and these are collective goods, since they are available to non-union members of the work-force once the trade union has achieved them. This produces an incentive among potential members to free-ride on the efforts of others and refuse to join, something which trade-unionists have long recognized as being a potential problem.

Trade unions typically deal with this problem in one of two ways. First, they provide selective incentives like legal advice and insurance which are only available to members, and which provide an inducement to join. Alternatively they try to negotiate a closed shop, which prevents free-riding altogether. This means that potential trade-unionists join primarily because of selective incentives, or as part of a workplace closed-shop agreement, not because of the collective goods provided by the union.

As we have noted already, the interesting thing about party membership is that so few people out of the voting population do actually join parties. Moreover, cross-national research into political participation suggests that this is generally true in a wide variety of different political systems—relatively few people get involved in any forms of political participation which involve significant costs (Verba and Nie, 1972; Verba, Nie, and Kim, 1978; and Barnes and Kaase, 1979).

Unlike other theories of political participation, Olson has an explanation for this apparent paradox: political parties are primarily collective goods producing organizations which can in general provide only limited selective incentives for people to join. As a consequence few people join such parties, and the ones that do are not principally involved because they want to promote the collective goals of the party.

It would be tempting to dismiss the Olson theory as being unrealistic, since individuals in the real world are not rational in the sense defined by economists. But the theory makes the remarkable prediction that party membership in democratic systems is likely to be very limited, and this appears to be generally true. Moreover, it is certainly true of the Labour party when one compares the individual membership with the size of the Labour vote.

For this reason any theory of party membership has to deal with the 'paradox of participation' as it is known. In the next section we set out a 'general-incentives' theory of political participation which addresses this issue, and at the same time explains the fact that many people who join the Labour party claim to do so in order to promote the policy goals of the party, something which is inconsistent with the Olson model.

GENERAL INCENTIVES AND PARTY MEMBERSHIP

The essence of our theory is that the Olson model, while plausible and insightful is too narrowly focused to give an adequate account of why people should join a political party. To explain political participation in general and party membership in particular we need to consider a wider array of incentives than narrowly defined individual incentives. However, this does not ignore the central insight of Olson's theory, which is the idea that individuals respond to incentives in politics as in many other spheres of life. Thus perceptions of costs and benefits, play a key role in understanding political action.

We have already mentioned selective incentives, and these are relevant for explaining the motives of some people who join the Labour party. Selective incentives in politics are of two types: process and outcome incentives. Process incentives refer to motives for participating which are not linked to outcomes, but which derive from the process of participation itself. Different writers have referred to a number of different motives for participation which might be counted under this heading. Tullock (1971) has written of the 'entertainment' value of being involved in revolution; Opp (1990) writes about the 'catharsis' value of involvement in political protest. In essence the political process can be interesting and stimulating in itself, without regard to the outcomes or goals of the process. Party membership is a way of meeting like-minded and interesting people, and for some this is motive enough for getting involved.

In fact, as we argue in Chapter 5, this is more likely to be a motive for activism in the party, rather than a motive for joining the party. This is because many people join the party but remain inactive, which means that they do not receive these process benefits. However, such incentives are relevant for those who join with the intention of becoming active.

Selective-outcome incentives refer to motives concerned with achieving certain goals in the political process, but goals which are private rather than collective. A potential member might harbour ambitions to become a local councillor, for example, or the local mayor, or even to be elected to the House of Commons. Others may want the endorsement of the Labour party to be nominated as a school governor, or to further their careers in the trade-union movement. Yet others may be interested in business connections that party membership might bring in areas where the party is strong in local government.

There are many motives which fall under this heading, but all have the common characteristic of providing private rather than collective incentives for involvement, since they are not available to non-members. Again though, these are motives for the activist rather than the inactive member, since generally these benefits only accrue to those individuals who actively work for the party, and are judged as being worthy for nomination to these positions by the other party members.

It is also possible to explain why some individuals might join the party and remain inactive, and thus not receive these selective incentives, within the terms of the narrow cost–benefit framework of the Olson model. What matters in this model is the individual's perceptions of those costs and benefits. Thus the rational individual may perceive that their own contribution to the collective good is negligible, but collective action will still be rational for them if they also see the costs as being negligible. In other words it is the perceived difference between costs and benefits which matters, not some 'objectively' defined measure of the benefits alone.

This has a further implication, namely that when perceptions of both benefits and costs are small, it is not rational to precisely calculate them. The exercise of assessing costs and benefits is itself costly, and does not warrant the return when those costs are trivial. Thus it is rational to operate with a threshold below which one does not assess the precise costs and benefits of collective action in making a decision to participate (see Barry, 1970; and Niemi, 1976). In this situation becoming a member without receiving selective incentives is rational, providing that one believes that one is making a non-zero, if tiny, contribution to the collective good.

However, we do not accept the narrowly cast Olson model, even though it can explain why some individuals would want to become party members. This is because it does not allow individuals to think in solidaristic terms, to want to promote the interests of the group as a whole. Any adequate theoretical account of collective action needs to consider situations where the individual 'thinks' collectively rather than individually.

This is an important point, and might seem obvious, but in the narrow world of the economist such notions as 'collective rationality' are quite alien. The key to understanding this idea is the recognition of the fact that individuals can put themselves in the place of the group, and think about the group welfare rather than just their own individual welfare. The most obvious example of this is in the family, where the members often think collectively. For mothers and fathers, for example, the relevant question is very often not 'What is best for me?', but rather 'What is best for all of us?'.

If this idea is applied to the question of Labour party membership, then it implies that one reason why some individuals join is because they believe that the Labour party members collectively make a difference to outcomes. They still undertake a calculus of costs and benefits, but it is focused at the level of the Labour party as a whole and not just at the level of the individual. If they reach the conclusion that the party as a whole can make a difference both to their own lives, and to the lives of people with which they identify then they will join the party. The corollary of this is, of course, that if they conclude that the party cannot make a difference, then they will not join.

Collective incentives are motivated by collective goods, which in the present discussion represent the policy-goals of the Labour party. Individuals who think in these terms are motivated by a desire to improve health care, reduce poverty, and increase equality in society, and so on. Whether they join the party or not depends on whether they see it collectively as a vehicle for achieving those goals.

Clearly, such motives are subject to the 'free-rider' problem, in that individuals might be tempted to let other people do the work to advance such policy goals. In a purely individualistic world in which people do not think in collective terms at all, virtually nobody would participate for this reason. But our conjecture is that because people think collectively rather than individually, in terms of 'What can the party do?' rather than 'What can I do?', many will participate. Obviously, the party as a whole is much more likely to be able to implement public policies than any one individual.

The main objection to this idea is that the individual cannot make decisions for the group as a whole and so it appears irrational to try to work out the costs and benefits of different courses of action at the group level. This is a problem, but significantly it is also a problem for individual decision-making in the rational choice framework. Once it is accepted that decision-making is characterized by uncertainty, such that the probabilities of certain courses of action leading to given outcomes are often unknown, then individuals cannot know the costs and benefits of different choices in advance, and so they often cannot make informed choices about what to do. They may not be able to speak for the group, but they often cannot speak with any certainty for themselves either![1]

---

[1] The problem is even more complex than that, since the game-theory literature suggests that inconsistency in decision-making over time can be rewarding. Thus precommitment to a given course of action is irrational, in a situation where the individual faces strategic uncertainty. Another way of putting this is to say that it can be profitable to surprise other people, but that the actor does not necessarily know this in advance. For a discussion of some of the fascinating paradoxes and problems of individual rational action see Elster (1983).

These 'collective' incentives for joining the party can be of two kinds: positive and negative incentives. Individuals will participate not only because they want to achieve collective goals, but because they want to change current government policy goals. They may be motivated to get involved by a great sense of injustice associated with the actions of the Conservative government, or by some significant political event such as the miners' strike of 1984. Getting rid of collective 'bads' is the mirror image of seeking collective 'goods', and these should be incorporated into any analysis.

Muller and his associates, in a series of important papers on political participation, have developed the idea of the 'unity principle', that is a norm that all members of the group should contribute if the good is to be provided (Muller and Opp, 1986, 1987; and Finkel, Muller, and Opp, 1989). They describe this norm as 'calculating Kantianism'. When faced with the possibility of free-riding on the efforts of others, group members ask themselves the question 'What if everyone did that?'; and since the answer is that the collective good would not be provided if everyone tried to free-ride, they choose to participate.

The essence of this approach is the idea that individuals are motivated by altruism when making decisions. Potential members may realize that their individual contributions to the collective goals of the party are negligible, or even that party as a whole is not very important, but they contribute anyway out of a sense of loyalty or affection for the party. They have an emotional attachment to the party which has little to do with the policy positions which it espouses, and they contribute without considering the costs and benefits of their actions.

Very often altruistic concerns will be expressed in terms of idealistic goals, such as the desire to 'build Socialism', or create a 'more compassionate society', which have obvious policy implications. But the moral imperative is the driving-force behind the decision to participate, not the specific policy goal.

It is always possible to interpret altruism within the cost-benefit framework, arguing that individuals count the costs and benefits of altruistic goals in the same terms as they do policy goals. However, we take the view that while altruistic concerns may be influenced by such calculations, they are operated within a fundamentally different type of discourse than cost-benefit analysis.

Thus if the individual recognizes that idealistic goals are

unattainable in practice, that would not deter him or her from seeking them, much as the religious person does not require proof of the existence of God in order to go to church. They constitute a separate category of motives for participation which is different from individual or collective rationality of the types discussed earlier. The former are rooted in a calculus of costs and benefits, whereas the latter are rooted in emotional attachments.

Another type of motive for involvement also lies outside the traditional cost-benefit analysis, but differs from altruistic motives. These are motives which derive from a social norm favouring participation. The key characteristic of social norms, as Elster points out (1989: 97–9), is that they are not outcome-orientated, they do not rely on individual calculations of the consequences of political action. In this respect social norms are similar to altruistic motives for participation. However, social norms differ from altruistic motives because they are primarily determined by a desire to win the respect or approval of other people. In Riesman's phrase they are 'other-directed' rather than 'inner-directed': that is motivated by a desire to conform to the values of others, whose approval the individual seeks (Riesman, 1961). This means other people are important in enforcing such norms. More formally Hollander (1990) has developed a model in which actors contribute to the collective good even when they know that their own efforts have a negligible influence on outcomes because of a desire for social approval within the group.

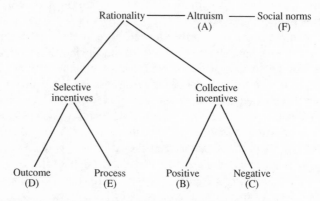

FIG. 4.1 A classification of incentives for political action

Applying this to membership of the Labour party, if an individual is raised in a family which has an active tradition of involvement in the party or the trade-union movement, then those norms of participation will very likely be passed on and influence their behaviour. Just as there is evidence to suggest that partisan attachments are handed down from generation to generation, albeit in an attenuated form (Butler and Stokes, 1974), then it seems likely that the same will be true of party membership and party activism.

The various components of the general-incentive theory are summarized in Fig. 4.1. In the light of this analysis we can go on to examine various predictions which can be derived from this analytical framework, which in turn can be tested with survey data.

THE IMPLICATIONS OF GENERAL-INCENTIVE THEORY

General-incentive theory can be tested in part by examining differences between Labour party members and Labour voters from the 1987 British Election Study. However, the data provided by the election study is limited, since it was not collected for the purpose of analysing party members, but it provides illustrative insights into the role of incentives in promoting membership.

A first and obvious difference between Labour party members and Labour voters is that the former should be more strongly attached to the Labour party than the latter. The attachment should derive principally from social norms and altruism, rather than instrumental concerns about selective or collective incentives. Indeed selective incentives should have no influence on the strength of party attachment at all, since the incentives to free-ride on the efforts of other people are the same for strongly attached individuals as they are for weakly attached individuals. However collective incentives should influence the individual's degree of support for Labour party policies, so that we would expect to see party members more supportive of Labour policies than Labour voters.

Another, rather less obvious prediction derives from the cost–benefit model of participation. We have argued that individuals will take into account their own influence on outcomes when assessing the benefits of collective action. This implies that members should have a greater sense of political efficacy than voters—they should feel more able to influence the political system than Labour voters, since low efficacy is a deterrent to political participation.

A third interesting hypothesis concerns social-background differences between Labour members and Labour voters, which in turn influence individuals' reactions to the incentives which they face. This is the proposition that members are much more likely to be high-status individuals than voters. This inference derives from an argument developed by Inglehart (1977) in his study of post-materialist values in advanced industrial democracies.

Inglehart's thesis derives from Maslow's (1962) 'hierarchy of needs' explanation of human motivations. Maslow argues that people act to fulfil a number of different needs, which are pursued in order, according to their relative importance for survival. Relatively deprived individuals on a low standard of living will therefore strongly value basic needs such as the need for physical and economic security.

By contrast, high-status individuals will have satisfied these basic needs, and will be more concerned with higher-level post-materialist values to do with the need for self-esteem, self-expression, and intellectual satisfaction. Inglehart (1977: 21–71) interprets post-material values as being manifested by a desire for greater political expression and political participation, as well as by a desire to seek collective goals like 'caring for the environment', and 'working with like-minded people'.

The obvious inference from this is that post-materialist values are much more likely to motivate party members than voters, and in addition because of the relationship between political values and socio-economic status they are more likely to be middle class than voters. This provides a theoretical account of 'middle-class radicalism' which has been much discussed in the literature (Parkin, 1968; and Forrester, 1976).

A fourth implication of the theory relates to a key open-ended question in the survey of party members, which asked 'What was your MOST important reason for joining the Labour party? (feel free to explain in detail)'. This provided a rich array of unprompted answers, which as we see below, classify fairly closely into the categories of general-incentive theory. The above discussion implies that collective incentives, whether positive or negative, should be less important than other types of incentives for joining the party because of the free-rider problem to which they are subject. Individuals motivated by selective incentives or by altruistic concerns, do not face this free-rider problem and as a consequence these motives for involvement should be stronger than collective motives.

A fifth implication arising from the open-ended question concerns the saliency of motives for membership as guides to political action. This concerns the status of altruistic as opposed to self-regarding or collective-regarding motives. Elster (1989) argues that altruistic motives are second-order motives for action, which are ultimately dependent on satisfying more basic self-regarding motives. He writes, for example, that 'the second-order pleasure from giving presupposes an expected first-order pleasure of the recipient' (Elster, 1989: 36). This suggests that there may be a hierarchy of motives for action analagous to the Maslovian hierarchy of needs. If altruistic motives are second-order motives for involvement, that implies that they are likely to be weaker than self-regarding motives.

The hierarchy of incentives for action would start with the most salient (i.e. selective incentives which provide the strongest motives) since they bring direct benefits to the participant. Collective incentives come next, since they also bring direct material or psychological benefits to the participant, but are subject to the free-rider problem. Altruistic motives come third, for the reasons described above, and social norms are weakest because they are motivated less by a desire to participate, as much as by a desire to please other people.

One way to examine whether or not there is such a hierarchy of motives is to use one of the survey questions, which asked respondents if they experienced difficulties contacting the party when they first decided to join. This question was asked of those respondents who set out to join the party on their own initiative. If selective incentives provide the strongest motives for joining, we would expect that individuals who experienced difficulty in joining would be more likely to have selective incentives, since they are the ones most likely to persist in their attempts to join in the face of adversity.

By contrast, if the weakest motives for joining are social norms, then very few individuals who experienced difficulty in joining should be motivated by social norms, since they would be most likely to abandon the effort in the face of difficulties. The other types of motives would be intermediate cases.

Perhaps one of the most important points in the earlier discussion of the costs and benefits of membership is that for the passive members who do not get involved in party activity, the costs of membership are small and possibly trivial. As we argued above, in this situation the free-rider question is not a major problem, since individuals will essentially discount costs as being a relevant factor in their decision to join. This hypothesis can be examined by means of questions in the survey concerning annual subscriptions. Respondents were asked first the size of the subscription they paid, and secondly the subscription which they felt they ought to pay. If the earlier analysis is correct few individuals should feel that their subscriptions are excessive.

A final point is that the motives for joining the party change over time, and so we should observe patterns in the recruitment of members over the years. When a Labour government is in power there is a greater likelihood that positive collective incentives can be provided, and so we should expect more individuals to join with those kinds of motives with a Labour government in office, in comparison with periods when Labour was in opposition. Similarly, when the Conservatives are in office there is a greater likelihood of members joining with negative collective incentives, particularly a desire to get rid of the Tory government. Such considerations may also influence selective incentives as well, although they are unlikely to be an issue in the case of altruistic motives or social norms.

In the remainder of this chapter we examine the evidence for this general-incentive theory of the motives for joining the Labour party. We begin with some suggestive evidence from the 1987 British Election Study, which as we pointed out earlier contains questions about the possible party membership of respondents.

EVIDENCE RELATING TO GENERAL INCENTIVES

The 1987 British Election Study[2] contained questions about party membership and just under 1 per cent of respondents (N = 54) stated that they were Labour party members. This makes it possible to compare Labour party members and Labour voters in the election study with the respondents in our membership survey. It should of course be noted that a direct comparison of these two studies is complicated by the fact that they were conducted at different times, but such comparisons are illuminating.

[2] The data for the election study was made available through the ESRC archive at the University of Essex.

TABLE 4.1. *The Relationship between Party Membership and the Strength of Partisan Support for the Labour Party* (percentages)

Partisan support	Election study		Membership Survey
	Voters (N = 880)	Members (N = 49)	Members (N = 5071)
Very strong	27	65	55
Fairly strong	48	35	38
Not very strong	25	0	6

We have argued that general-incentive theory makes several predictions about differences between members and voters which can be investigated using the election study data. First, there is the obvious, but important point that members should be more strongly attached to the party than voters. This is confirmed by the evidence in Table 4.1.

It can be seen that some 27 per cent of the voters were very strong Labour identifiers, compared with 65 per cent of party members in the election study and 55 per cent in the membership survey. The latter may be regarded as providing more reliable measures than the election study, because of the larger sample size. It can also be seen that 25 per cent of voters describe themselves as not very strongly attached, in comparison with zero per cent for the election study members and 6 per cent for the membership survey. Clearly, party members are more strongly attached than Labour voters.

In Table 4.2 we examine the support for various policy goals of members and voters in the election study and the membership survey. It will be recalled that incentive theory suggests that members should express greater support for these collective policy goals than voters, and this is confirmed by the results.

The policy goals in Table 4.2 are not of course precisely the same as Labour party policy aims, but the broad position taken by the party on these goals can be identified. Thus the party seeks to discourage, though not abolish private education and members are more in favour of such a goal than voters. On the goal of supporting private medicine, which obviously runs counter to party policy, members are much less supportive than voters. A similar pattern exists for all other policy areas; either there is a broad consensus on

TABLE 4.2. *The Relationship between Labour Voters, Members, and Support for Policy Goals* (percentages)

Policy goal	Labour voters (Election Study) (N = 940)			Labour members (Election Study) (N = 52)			(Membership Survey) (N = 4940)		
	Should	Doesn't matter	Should not	Should	Doesn't matter	Should not	Should	Doesn't matter	Should not
Get rid of private education	35	31	34	54	17	29	64	18	18
Spend more on poverty	96	2	2	98	0	2	99	0	1
Encourage private medicine	21	13	66	8	4	88	4	5	91
Spend more on the NHS	98	1	1	100	0	0	99	0	1
Reduce spending generally	44	13	43	27	4	69	21	6	73
Introduce stricter trade-union laws	27	14	59	11	4	85	9	10	81
Give workers more say in places where they work	87	5	8	88	2	10	94	3	3
Spend less on defence	61	8	31	73	4	23	86	3	11

items, like supporting the NHS, or members are more strongly in favour of Labour policy goals than voters, particularly on opposing stricter laws on trade unions and reducing government spending in general.

Thus Labour members are more in favour of broadly defined party-policy goals than are voters. The implication of this is that they have a greater incentive to be involved in politics, because they feel more strongly about the implementation of such goals, and this partly explains why they are members in the first place.

Another comparison which can be made between voters and members concerns feelings of personal influence over politics of political efficacy. Again, incentive theory would suggest that members should have a greater sense of political efficacy than voters, and this is one of the reasons why they are members. Once again this is confirmed in the data.[3]

It can be seen in Table 4.3 that members are more likely to disagree than voters with statements suggesting that the individual has little influence over government and politics. Perhaps the clearest example of this is the statement that, 'Politics is so complicated that it is difficult for a person like me to understand.' Some 65 per cent of voters agreed with this compared with only 48 per cent of members in the election study and 35 per cent in the membership survey. Thus members clearly feel themselves to be more influential in understanding and influencing politics than voters, another reason why they joined the party.

We have already discussed some of the social-background characteristics of party members in the membership survey in Chapter 3; in Table 4.4 we compare these characteristics with Labour voters and members in the election study, for four variables: occupational status, university education, self-assigned social class, and housing tenure.

It can be seen from this table that members are very much more likely to be middle class than voters, as measured by the Hope–Goldthorpe occupational scale. Equally, they are much more likely to have a degree or a diploma from a university, and to be owner-occupiers than the voters. Even in the case of self-assigned social class, more members claim middle-class status than do the voters.

---

[3] Note that two of the indicators used in the election study were omitted from the membership survey.

TABLE 4.3. *The Relationship between Party Membership and Feelings of Political Efficacy* (percentages)

Indicator	Labour voters (Election Study) (N = 935)			Labour members (Election Study) (N = 52)			(Membership Survey) (N = 5025)		
	Agree	Neutral	Disagree	Agree	Neutral	Disagree	Agree	Neutral	Disagree
'Politics is so complicated it is difficult for a person like me to understand.'	65	10	25	48	7	45	35	9	56
'Parties are only interested in people's votes, not in their opinions.'	62	15	23	39	16	45	41	12	47
'People like me have no say in what government does.'	63	13	24	50	7	43	—	—	—
'It doesn't matter which party is in power.'	41	10	49	23	2	75	—	—	—

TABLE 4.4. *Social-background Characteristics of Labour Voters and Members*

| | Voters | Members | |
	(Election Study) (N = 943)	(Election Study) (N = 54)	(Membership Survey) (N = 4621)
Hope–Goldthorpe occupational status			
Salariat	14	37	49
Routine non-manual	19	10	16
Petty bourgeoisie	4	6	4
Foreman and Technician	6	13	5
Working class	57	34	26
University degree or diploma			
Yes	6	33	29
No	94	67	71
Self-assigned social class			
Middle class	10	17	20
Working class	49	55	51
Other	2	0	2
None	37	28	27
Housing Tenure			
Owner-occupier	53	68	75
Rented accommodation	47	32	24

Responses to the self-assigned social-class question are interesting. Although members concede that they are more middle class than voters, they are also more likely to claim to be working class. Voters are more inclined to think they are not members of any class. For party members their own class-status is really an ideological question; they identify with the working class, even when they are not working class in the sociological sense of the term. This replicates earlier findings in research on Labour party candidates (see Whiteley, 1978).

Turning next to the responses to the open-ended question on motives for joining the party in the membership survey, the

TABLE 4.5. *The Most Important Reason for Joining the Labour Party (Membership Survey)* (percentages: N = 4700)

A. *Altruistic concerns*		
To create a more equal or compassionate society		9.6
Through a belief in Socialism or left-wing politics		14.2
Through a desire for social justice		3.9
To help the working class		10.5
To help the Labour party financially		1.2
To get the Labour party into power		2.9
	TOTAL A	42.3
B. *Collective positive incentives*		
Unemployment		0.4
The Health Service		0.7
Social policy/Social services		0.5
Unilateral nuclear disarmament		1.8
Education		0.6
Public ownership		0.7
The redistribution of wealth		1.2
Economic policy		0.2
To help minorities and women		0.4
A concern with local issues		1.0
	TOTAL B	7.5
C. *Collective negative incentives*		
To get rid of Thatcher and the Conservatives		16.9
To oppose the Social Democrats		0.2
To oppose extremists in the Labour party		0.3
	TOTAL C	17.4
D. *Selective outcome incentives*		
As a job requirement (e.g. MP's assistant)		0.1
To be selected as a local candidate		0.2
	TOTAL D	0.3
E. *Selective process incentives*		
To work with like-minded people		2.1
To be politically active		11.5
As a continuation of trade-union work		5.5
As a result of involvement in elections		3.4
As a result of specific political events (e.g. Suez)		1.4
	TOTAL E	23.9
F. *Social norms*		
Through the influence of parents		5.6
Through the influence of a spouse or children		1.4
Through the influence of friends and workmates		0.2
	TOTAL F	7.2
Unclassified		1.4

responses to this question were coded according to the categories of incentive theory displayed in Fig. 4.1. In the event only a relatively small percentage of the responses could not be coded into this scheme.

In the case of category A answers, which refer to altruistic concerns, a typical response from a 34-year-old male Polytechnic lecturer was: 'I wanted to show my commitment to Socialism.' A similar category A answer came from a 36-year-old male computer programmer: 'At the age of 17, when I joined, I already considered myself a socialist and wanted to put my beliefs into action.'

In the case of category B answers, relating to collective positive incentives, a 41-year-old deputy-headmistress wrote: 'The Labour Party in Scotland organised a march against unemployment, which was well attended with excellent speakers. I picked up one of the pamphlets and joined, so unemployment was the main reason I joined the Labour party.' In the same vein, another category B answer came from a 21-year-old female bank-clerk who wrote: 'I joined because of my views on nuclear disarmament'.

A typical category C answer, concerned with collective negative incentives, was given by a 40-year-old female voluntary worker: 'I could not sit at home any longer with the cruelty of the Thatcher Dictatorship; I felt I had to do something.'

A 48-year-old male electrician gave this category E answer, which relates to selective process incentives, when he wrote: 'Being a member of the EEPTU and active, I felt there was more to politics than trade unions.' A 34-year-old female probation officer was also coded into category E with the following answer: 'Originally it was to gain membership of the Labour club, and to mix with people who shared my views'.

Finally, a representative category F answer, concerned with social norms, was given by a 43-year-old female school-supervisor, who wrote: 'I come from a very political family, who are all Labour party members, so it seemed the natural thing to do'. Along the same lines, a retired male security-officer wrote: 'My family always voted Labour, so you could say that I was brought up Labour'.

In analysing Table 4.5, the first point to make is about the frequency of the responses in the various categories. We have suggested that collective motives for membership are likely to be less important than other types of motives. It is noteworthy that the largest category consists of altruistic responses with just over 42 per cent of the total; the second largest is the selective process-incentives category, which describes motives for participation in terms of enjoying the political process for its own sake. Thirdly, come the negative collective incentives, and fourthly the positive collective incentives. Thus the collective-incentives categories combined constitute only 25 per cent of the motives cited in the table.

The finding that negative collective incentives appear to be much more important than positive collective incentives is intriguing. Members were much more likely to cite a dislike of Mrs Thatcher and the Conservative government as a reason for becoming involved than the desire to promote a specific policy goal such as unilateral nuclear disarmament or the redistribution of wealth. As we show below, this is partly because the bulk of the anti-Conservative members joined during the period of the Thatcher era, when British politics was uniquely polarized in comparison with earlier years. This may be partly due to the fact that Labour was on the defensive during these years in trying to articulate a clear alternative set of values and principles to Thatcherism. In other words when the party can set out a positive alternative 'philosophy' to the Conservatives, then it is likely to do better in recruiting members for positive reasons.

Of course due recognition must be given to the fact that respondents were constrained to answer in terms of their most important reason for joining; no doubt many would also have cited policy goals as additional motives for becoming members if they had been able. But nevertheless this data supports the proposition that most people's first priority when they are considering joining the party are altruistic concerns or selective incentives, and not the achievement of specific policy goals.

One notable feature of Table 4.5 is that few cited selective outcome incentives as reasons for joining the party. In fact, part of the reason for this may be that such motives are not very socially acceptable in the party. Part of the ethos of the Labour party is to distrust the leadership to some extent and thus the personal ambitions of those who desire to become leaders. Thus it seems plausible that individuals will be reluctant to admit that they joined the party in order to build a political career. Consequently these responses may understate the true importance of political ambitions when it comes to motivating membership. We will return to this issue later in the chapter on activism.

TABLE 4.6. *Percentages of Different Categories Motives for Joining the Party by Experience of Joining*

Question: If you approached the local party when you first joined how easy or difficult was it to make contact with them?

	Easy	Difficult
Selective Incentives	80	20
Collective Incentives	82	18
Altruistic Motives	83	17
Social Norms	95	5
All respondents	83	17

Note: Chi-square = 32.6, sig. at $p < .01$, N = 3474.

We can address the question of whether or not there is a hierarchy of motives for participation by examining the relationship between types of incentives and the ease or difficulty that individuals experienced in joining the party in the first place. This is done in Table 4.6, which tabulates the relationship between motives for joining and the experience of joining.

The relationships in this table are not very strong, but they are interesting and support the inference that a weak hierarchy of motives for joining may exist. The prediction is that selective incentives are the strongest type of motives for involvement. If so, more of the respondents who cite selective incentives for involvement should also say they had difficulty in joining the party. This is because when motives for joining are strong, then individuals should persist with their efforts to join the party in the face of adversity; when they are weak, they should give up easily. This would account for the pattern of responses in Table 4.6.

Some 20 per cent of the respondents who cited selective incentives stated that they experienced difficulty in joining; thus these individuals were the least likely to be discouraged by difficulties experienced when they first joined the party. The respondents who cited collective motives for joining came next, followed by those with altruistic motives, and finally those citing social norms. Though the differences between the first three categories are relatively small, the social-norms category is significantly different from the others; it appears that individuals who join because of social norms are easily discouraged in the face of adversity, since only 5 per cent of them reported experiencing difficulties.

This suggests that a hierarchy of motives for membership may exist, but it seems clear that differences between motives in this hierarchy are not uniform. The Chi-square test written below the table indicates that there is a statistically significant relationship between motives for joining and the ease or difficulty of joining. Thus these differences, though small, are not trivial.

In the earlier discussion it was suggested that one of the key factors explaining why the free-rider problem does not influence the decision to join for many people, even in a narrowly cast model of collective action, is because the costs of membership are seen as relatively trivial. Moreover, individuals had no incentive to calculate such costs when they were below a certain threshold of importance. To test this we can compare two variables in the membership survey which concern the costs of subscription to the party. Respondents were asked the value of the subscription they paid to the party each year, and this was followed up by a question asking what annual subscription they felt they ought to pay.

If the costs of membership are regarded as being relatively trivial, then we would expect very few people to say that they ought to pay less than the subscription which they actually did pay. This inference is strongly supported by the evidence; some 43 per cent of respondents said they ought to pay a higher subscription than they actually did pay; 51 per cent said they ought to pay the same and only 6 per cent thought that they should pay less. Thus the only significant cost of party membership for the relatively inactive individual, the annual subscription, is seen as being no great burden by the vast majority of members.

Thus the costs of participation as measured by the annual subscription are essentially below the threshold of saliency for practically everyone. Thus even if members did operate in a narrowly defined world of costs and benefits, many of them would still join the party. The same reasoning, however, would not apply in the case of party activists, where the costs of membership are considerably higher than the annual subscription. This issue is taken up in Chapter 5.

A final test of the theory relies on the fact that incentives change over time. In particular when there is a Labour government in office the party can deliver policies, the positive collective incentives

TABLE 4.7. *Percentages of Respondents who joined under different Post-War Governments by Motives for Joining*

Government	Motives for joining				
	Selective incentives	Collective incentives		Altruistic motives	Social norms
		Positive	Negative		
1945–51 Labour	12	5	4	59	20
1951–64 Conservative	17	7	5	57	14
1964–70 Labour	26	7	5	55	7
1970–74 Conservative	25	6	5	59	5
1974–79 Labour	29	8	13	46	4
1979+ Conservative	26	8	27	36	4

Note: N = 4246.

referred to earlier, which is likely to make these motives for joining more salient. Alternatively, when the Conservatives are in power negative collective incentives are likely to be important. This can be tested by examining the relationship between motives for joining and the year in which each of the respondents joined. This is done in Table 4.7.

Table 4.7 has some interesting findings in it, but it has to be interpreted with some care. When one examines the motives of individuals who joined at the time of the 1945–51 Labour governments, for example, one is asking respondents to comment on events which took place nearly half a century ago. So the responses relating to the earlier periods have to be interpreted with that caveat in mind.

There is no clear evidence in this table that positive collective motives for joining are more salient during periods of Labour governments, but there is clear evidence that negative collective incentives have played a more important role during the Thatcher years than earlier. Mrs Thatcher has been an excellent recruiting-sergeant for the Labour party! This undoubtedly reflects the breakdown in consensus politics during the 1970s and 1980s. So there is qualified support for the proposition that collective incentives are influenced by the political context of the time.

The most interesting finding in Table 4.7 relates to trends in the types of motives cited for joining the party over time. There has been a clear decline in altruistic motives and social norms, and a clear rise in selective and collective motives for membership. These trends are not easy to interpret, however, because they are a mixture of life-cycle and cohort effects.

Life-cycle effects refer to changes in opinions and attitudes which can occur over the lifetime of an individual; for example, an individual may view their reasons for joining the party differently from the perspective of a 50-year-old, than they did when they were 30 years old. In contrast, cohort effects refer to the fact that the different age cohorts bring political experiences acquired in very different circumstances to the task of making political judgements, so that the post-war generation may differ from the 1960s generation in their reasons for joining, because the post-war years differed so much from the 1960s. Cohort effects are caused by new cohorts of members joining the party and replacing older cohorts over time; this could produce changes of the type observed in Table 4.7 even if there were no life-cycle effects at all.

In the absence of time-series panel data we cannot separate life-cycle from cohort effects, but there are good reasons for thinking that the latter may be more important than the former. First, respondents are not being asked for their views on contemporary issues, but rather for the reasons they joined the party in the first place; thus the only source of life-cycle effects in such a question is the decay of memory, and not potential changes in their political opinions over time.

A second and perhaps stronger reason for believing that cohort effects predominate is Inglehart's (1977, 1982) findings to that effect, in his longitudinal study of value-changes in Western democracies. In his research generational replacement was primarily responsible for attitude change over time, rather than any life-cycle effects. Accordingly we will interpret these results with that point in mind.

One of the main reasons why we observe these trends in motives for joining the party may be changes in the class composition of the Labour party membership over time. If middle-class members are motivated to a greater extent by policy goals in comparison with the working class, this would produce a rise in collective motives if the party was becoming more middle class over time. Equally if the working class are more motivated by social norms, often in the past associated with tightly knit working-class communities in inner-city areas like the East End of London, then again these motives for joining the party would decline over time if the party is becoming more middle class.

A number of researchers have suggested from survey evidence of different types, that Labour has become more middle class over time and this may have led to a change in reasons for joining the party (see Hindess, 1971; Brand, 1973; and Gordon and Whiteley, 1979). A rise in middle-class membership, and a decline in working-class membership would produce the patterns observed in Table 4.7. Policy goals would become more important, and social norms less important as motives for involvement over time.

We can throw some light on this issue by examining the motives for joining of the members in the survey broken down by social class. Some 29 per cent of the salariat cited collective incentives for joining the party, and only 5 per cent of them cited social norms. By contrast, 21 per cent of the working class cited collective incentives and 7 per cent social norms. Thus, while relationships are not strong, the results indicate that the middle class are more motivated by policy goals than the working class, who are marginally more likely to be motivated by social norms. Of course this cross-sectional evidence cannot be used to definitively measure the mix of motives which individuals had for joining the party over many years, but they are instructive.

Another and related trend which throws light on these changes is if middle-class party members tend to be more left-wing than working-class members. This issue is discussed more fully in Chapter 6, where we show that the middle class are more left-wing than the working class on some issues. This implies that an influx of middle-class members in the party would change the ideological centre of gravity of the party with respect to these issues, and might well change the motives that individuals have for joining the party, because motives for joining are related to ideology.

In Table 4.8 we tabulate the relationship between motives for joining the party and respondent scores on a left–right ideology scale. The ideology scale was constructed by asking respondents to code themselves along a 9-point left–right scale.[4] This was recoded into three categories, which appear in Table 4.8.

---

[4] Two left–right scales were constructed; the first was in response to the question: 'In Labour party politics people often talk about 'the Left' and 'the Right'. Compared with other Labour party members, where would you place your views on this

TABLE 4.8. *The Relationship between Motives for Joining the Party and the 'Left–Right' Scale*

	Percentages in each category of the Ideology Scale		
	Left	Centre	Right
Selective Incentives	63	27	10
Collective Incentives	74	20	6
Altruistic Motives	69	22	9
Social Norms	52	33	15
All respondents	67	24	9

Notes: Chi-square = 75.5; sig. at $p < 0.01$; N = 4560.

It can be seen in this table that respondents citing selective, collective or altruistic motives for involvement were significantly more likely to be left-wing than respondents citing social norms. The fact that working-class members are more likely to cite social norms as motives for joining the party suggests that a decline in working-class recruitment into the party would shift the ideological centre of gravity to the left on a number of important issues.

To summarize the discussion so far, party members joined for a variety of reasons. Collective incentives were important in explaining why some members joined, but only for a minority of members, since such motives are subject to the 'paradox of participation'. However the paradox did not eliminate collective incentives as a motive for joining altogether, partly because members think collectively as well as individually, but also because the costs of membership are regarded as being trivial for the vast majority of individuals.

The motives for joining have changed over time and one of the key reasons for this may be a change in the class composition of the party over time which has had ideological effects as well. We return to the discussion of ideology and membership more fully in Chapter 6.

---

scale?'; and the second, which we use in Table 4.8 asked 'And where would you place your views in relation to British politics as a whole (not just the Labour party)?'. The nine-point scale was recoded into three categories: 1–3 as Left, 4–6 as Centre, and 7–9 as Right.

The discussion up to this point has focused exclusively on the question of why people should join the party, but a related and equally interesting question is how they joined. This refers to the 'pathways' to membership, or the routes by which people become involved. Over the last few years the national party has promoted a membership drive, using party-political broadcasts which ask people to write to party headquarters for information, and which allows them to join by mail. The survey throws light on the success of this campaign, and we discuss this next.

THE PATHWAYS TO MEMBERSHIP

In designing this study we hypothesized that members would join the party via a variety of routes. Some would seek out party membership, either at the local or national level and we might describe these people as self-starters; others would be recruited, usually as a result of being canvassed by party activists either during an election or in the course of a membership drive. In Table 4.9 we describe the various routes by which members joined.

The table shows that the vast majority of party members were self-starters, since only 21 per cent joined as a result of being approached by the local party. Moreover, a significant group of these self-starters experienced difficulty in joining the party. The most plausible explanation for this is that their local party was inactive. The evidence suggests that the national membership drive of recent years has had only a limited effect, since only 6 per cent of members joined by approaching the national party. However, it is possible that some people approached their local parties after seeing a party-political broadcast targeted at potential members.

Further light can be thrown on the effects of the national membership drive, by examining the proportion of those who approached the national party since the 1987 election, the start of the national membership drive. However, none of the members who approached the national party joined within the period 1987 to 1989, which suggests that the national membership drive has had limited success!

The only evidence to suggest that the national membership drive might be having some effect is that the percentage of respondents who joined as a result of being approached by the local party increased from 21 per cent before 1987 to 23 per cent after. So it is

TABLE 4.9. *Routes to Membership of the Party* (percentages)

Question: Thinking back to the time you first joined the Labour party, did you approach the party to apply for membership or did they approach you?

Approached the local Party	71
Approached the Regional Party	2
Approached the National Party	6
The local party approached me	21
	(N = 4900)

Question: If you approached the local party did you find it easy or difficult to make contact with them?

Very Easy	40
Easy	43
Difficult	13
Very Difficult	4
	(N = 3777)

possible that the national membership drive has had an influence on the local activists, encouraging them to seek out new members.

Once new members have been recruited there is the question of whether or not the party retains them. Respondents were asked whether or not they had kept up continuous membership since they first joined. Altogether 86 per cent said they had kept up continuous membership. Again, this is not surprising if one recalls the earlier discussion which suggested that respondents did not really worry about the costs of membership. This is however encouraging for the party as it plans future membership drives, since it appears that the great majority of new members will remain in the party once they have joined.

Part of the reason why there is a high retention rate of members is that they appear to have fairly regular contact with the party activists. Members were asked 'Thinking over the last year, how often have you had contact with people active in your local branch or Constituency Labour Party?' The responses to this question were 'Not at All' (10 per cent); 'Rarely' (17 per cent); 'Occasionally' (29 per cent); and 'Frequently' (44 per cent). This question indicates that a large majority of members had some sort of contact with the party in the previous year, and a large number had quite a lot of contact. This is a fairly good record by the standards of any large voluntary organization.

To return to the question of pathways into membership, we hypothesized that some members would be drawn into the party by becoming active in single-issue pressure groups, or alternatively within the trade-union movement.[5] Some 14 per cent of members joined as a result of voluntary work in their trade unions, and 9 per cent joined as a result of campaigning in a pressure group at the local or national levels. Thus activism outside the party is a source of recruitment for a significant minority of members.

In conclusion there are a variety of pathways into the party; some are recruited because of their involvement in outside voluntary organizations or trade unions; others are recruited in the course of canvassing at election time or during local membership drives. However, most appear to recruit themselves, and a significant minority appear to have experienced difficulty in doing this. Clearly, if the party wishes to widen its membership base, any reforms which facilitate recruitment, such as the national membership scheme are a good thing. There is no way of knowing how many potential recruits have been lost to the party because of the difficulties they experienced in trying to join.

This concludes our discussion of why and how the members come to join the party. In the next chapter we consider an issue which is very much related to the present discussion. This is the question of why members become active in the Labour party.

---

[5] The questions were 'Did you become a party member as a result of voluntary work in your trade union or staff association?'; and 'Did you become a Labour party member as a result of campaign activity in an interest group? (e.g. such as CND, or a local campaign to prevent hospital closures in your area)'.

5

Why be Active in the Labour Party?

We have developed the theoretical framework for the analysis of political participation in the Labour party in Chapter 4, and we will apply the same framework to the analysis of activism in this chapter. It will be recalled that even within the terms of a narrowly focused model of rationality of the type discussed by Olson, membership of the party could be explained by the fact that individuals did not perceive the costs of membership as being at all salient.

However, the costs of membership for the party activists can be considerable, as the evidence below suggests. Accordingly, the same explanation cannot be used to understand party activism. Some of the other factors discussed in general incentives theory come to the fore in this situation, and so much of the time in this chapter is spent discussing how these factors might be measured and analysed.

The discussion is divided into three sections; first, there is an analysis of the problems of measuring political activism. This shows that the conventional dichotomy between activists and members which is often referred to in journalistic accounts, is rather misleading. Political activism appears to be distributed along a continuum from low-level sporadic activism at one end of the scale, to high-level activism amounting virtually to full-time employment at the other.

The second section in this chapter discusses some of the important correlates of activism, particularly the social-background profiles of the activists. This generally reinforces the findings in Chapter 4; it may be recalled that the analysis in that chapter showed that Labour party members are generally higher-status individuals than Labour voters. These findings apply again here, since party activists are higher-status individuals than passive party members. This conclusion is of course qualified by the point that passive and active membership of the party are not precisely defined categories.

In the third section we discuss the determinants of activism, in order to answer the general question of why some people are active in the party and others not. As incentives theory suggests, the findings show that selective incentives are particularly important in explaining activism, although other types of incentives play a role as well.

MEASURING PARTY ACTIVISM

There are a number of different dimensions to party activism. Most obviously, there are the activities of keeping the party in existence at the local level on a day-to-day basis, which means arranging and attending meetings, fund-raising, organizing membership drives, and campaigning on local and national issues. Another and related aspect of activism concerns preparations for elections; this involves recruiting candidates for local or general elections, and promoting those candidates during the run-up to elections. For general elections the 'long campaign', or the eighteen months or so leading up to the election is particularly important (Miller *et al.*, 1990). Then there is the work involved in running the election campaign itself, such as preparing and delivering leaflets and election literature, canvassing, holding meetings, and seeking local publicity. Election-day activity is the culmination of a lot of pre-election work.

For a few individuals party activism involves holding elective office either inside the party organization, or on the local council, or a quasi-official body of some kind such as a local health authority. The regular rounds of party and local council meetings each month can take up a great deal of time, particularly when the Labour party is in control of the local authority. This is also true for members who represent the party on outside bodies such as school or college governing-boards, police authorities, or trades councils.

Clearly an individual member may be involved in some of these activities on an occasional basis, and another involved in most of the activities on a regular basis. Thus the first step in the analysis is to map out these different dimensions of activism, in order to get a clearer idea of the numbers involved in each type of activity.

We can begin with a question in the survey which simply asked respondents to indicate how much time they devoted to party activities in the average month. This provides a baseline measure of the amount of work done by the members as a whole.

Some 50 per cent of the party members devote no time at all to

TABLE 5.1. *The Amount of Time devoted to Party Activities by Members in the Average Month* (percentages)

Question: How much time do you devote to party activities in the average month?

None	50
Up to five hours	30
Five to ten hours	10
Ten to fifteen hours	4
Fifteen to twenty hours	2
More than twenty hours	4

party activities in the typical month, although as we shall see below this does not mean that they are inactive all of the time, particularly during the period of an election. The remaining 50 per cent of members devote at least some of their time in the average month, which implies that the average member is more active than the conventional wisdom would suggest. At the lower end of the 'activism' scale some 30 per cent of the members spent up to five hours, and at the other end of the scale around 10 per cent spent more than ten hours on party matters in the average month.

This table indicates, not surprisingly that the higher the costs of political participation, in terms of hours spent working for the party, the fewer the numbers of people who get involved. Nevertheless if these figures are translated into national terms, using the national membership figures for 1989 cited in Chapter 2, they indicate that approximately 147,000 people devote at least some time to party matters in the average month, and nearly 30,000 devote more than ten hours. Clearly, there is a lot more work done by party members than many observers of Labour party politics suspected.

It is useful to classify party activism into the three dimensions or characteristics discussed above. First, there is the dimension of contact with the party, which is measured by the extent to which respondents attend meetings or have regular contact with other activists. A second dimension is that of campaigning which examines the extent to which respondents are associated with various campaign activities, both within the party organization and outside in related political campaigns of various kinds. A third dimension is that of representation which measures the extent to which

TABLE 5.2. *The 'Contact' Dimension of Party Activism* (percentages)

Question: Thinking back over the last year, how often have you had contact with people active in your local branch or constituency Labour party?

Not at All	10
Rarely	17
Occasionally	29
Frequently	44
	(N = 5042)

Question: Thinking back over the last year, how often have you attended a Labour party meeting?

Not at All	36
Rarely	14
Occasionally	20
Frequently	30
	(N = 5043)

Question: Have you responded to any of the national appeals for money by the Labour party in the last year?

Yes	35
65	
	(N = 5009)

Question: Are you more active or less active within the party than you were five years ago, or about the same?

More active	20
Less active	43
About the same	37
	(N = 4913)

respondents represent the party both by holding office within the party organization, or on external bodies as a party nominee.

Table 5.2 contains various indicators of the contact dimension. These show that the majority of party members have fairly regular contact with the party over the period of a year. Some 73 per cent had occasional or frequent contact with activists; the 44 per cent of respondents in the category who had frequent contact will obviously include those who regularly attend meetings, although not all of the people in this category will necessarily be activists in that sense.

Another interesting finding in Table 5.2 is that 30 per cent of respondents claimed to have frequently attended party meetings within the last year. Again, this is a higher figure than conventional wisdom would suggest, which often sees the party as being dominated by a handful of regular attenders who represent only a tiny fraction of the membership. Translated into national terms that means that approximately 88,000 members frequently attend party meetings. In interpreting this figure it is also important to remember that the period referred to in the question was not a general election year. Arguably, a number of inactive party members might be persuaded to attend a party rally during a general election campaign. But in the absence of such a campaign it is interesting to see that about half the members occasionally or frequently attended some type of party meeting in the average year.

A similar point could be made about the fact that 35 per cent of the members said that they had responded to one of the national appeals for money by the party during the previous year. Obviously the party could do more to attract money from the other 65 per cent, but again translating this figure into a national context means that more than 100,000 members donated money to the party during the period of one year.

One of the most intriguing findings in Table 5.2 is the responses to the question concerning activism over time. Interestingly enough, more than 40 per cent of respondents felt they were less active than five years before, and these outnumber the respondents who felt they were more active by more than two to one. In the absence of longitudinal data it is difficult to say precisely why this is the case. Part of the explanation may simply be age, since some 52 per cent of respondents over the age of 65 stated that they were less active than five years previously, in comparison with 38 per cent of respondents under the age of 26 who gave this answer.

If there is a trend decline in activism in the party, and this data only hints at it, there are a number of factors in the recent history of the party which might explain such a development. First, there is the growing dominance of centralized media campaigns, particularly during general elections; when the party leaders reach out to the electorate directly this is likely to weaken the role of the activists. A second factor arises from the perception of the damage which can be

inflicted on the party by dissent; this has turned the party conference, for example, into an increasingly sedate affair in comparison with the early 1980s. This is not simply a matter of the
leadership controlling the agenda and debate, although this may
very well be part of it, but a self-denying ordinance may have
emerged in the party not to damage its electoral chances by the
kind of internecine strife which contributed to the electoral disaster
of 1983. However, in the absence of time-series data it is difficult to
be sure about the precise reasons for this development. We return
to this question later.

The second dimension of activism is the campaigning dimension
which is analysed in Table 5.3. The first question in this table shows
that a remarkably high percentage of members claim to have
actively supported one or more of the political campaigns run by the
party in the previous year. Many of these will have been local
campaigns, since the national party has not been particularly active
in running campaigns in the past. The meaning of 'actively supported' is slightly vague in this question, and for some members this
might mean nothing more than trying to persuade their friends or
workmates of the validity of the campaign. But it does show that
most of the party members see themselves as active in one way or
another in supporting party campaigns. It also underscores the point
that there is much more to party activism than attending meetings, so
that an analysis of activism which focuses exclusively on that aspect
of party activity will considerably underestimate rates of participation.

Another approach to the measurement of campaign activity is to
find out how many respondents are members of campaigning groups
both within and outside the party. The evidence suggests that only a
relatively modest percentage of respondents are members of party-
based groups like the Fabian Society or the Labour Co-ordinating
Committee. However, many more are members of outside campaigning organizations like Greenpeace, the Campaign for Nuclear
Disarmament, or Friends of the Earth. In addition many members
were also involved in local groups of various kinds such as com-
munity-action organizations or tenants groups.

We have listed only the major groups cited by members in reply to
questions about campaigning. In an additional open-ended question
which asked members to write in the names of various groups they
were involved in, members cited a total of eleven party groups, and

TABLE 5.3. *The 'Campaigning' Dimension of Party Activism* (percentages)

Question: Within the last year have you actively supported (for example by signing a petition or attending a meeting) any political campaigns promoted by the Labour party? (e.g. the Poll Tax campaign, or the NHS campaign).

Yes	82
No	18
	(N = 5020)

Question: Are you currently a member of any of the following groups within the party?

Young Socialists	0.7
Tribune Group	0.5
Co-operative Party	5.5
Black Section	0.4
Fabian Society	2.7
Campaign Group	2.4
Women's Section	4.7
Workplace Branch	1.2
Campaign for Labour Party Democracy	1.1
Labour Co-ordinating Committee	0.9
	(N = 5071)

Question: Are you a member of any of the following interest groups?

Anti-Apartheid Movement	11.8
SHELTER	2.5
Amnesty International	6.8
OXFAM	7.0
Friends of the Earth	8.2
MIND	1.7
Campaign for Nuclear Disarmament	18.9
Child Poverty Action Group	2.4
National Council for Civil Liberties	3.1
Greenpeace	16.0
A local community action group	18.8
A local anti-Poll Tax group	4.0
A local tenants' or housing group	16.5
A local charity	7.9
A local women's group	5.3
	(N = 5071)

TABLE 5.4. *The 'Representation' Dimension of Party Activism*
(percentages)

Question: Do you at present hold any office(s) within the Labour party
(e.g. branch secretary, constituency treasurer, branch membership
secretary)?

Yes	14
No	86
	(N = 5015)

Question: Are you currently a Labour councillor?

Yes	6
No	94
	(N = 5032)

Question: Do you currently represent the Labour party on any official
bodies (e.g. as a school governor, or member of an Area Health
Authority)?

Yes	15
No	85
	(N = 5038)

no less than sixty-five non-party groups other than those listed in
Table 5.2; examples of the former included the Christian Socialist
Movement, the Socialist Educational Association, and the
Socialist Health Association; examples of the latter included War-
on-Want, the World Wildlife Fund, Save the Children, and
Charter 88.

Many of the respondents were members of several groups at the
same time; for example 27 per cent of the members of the Fabian
Society were also members of the Co-operative party, and no less
than 50 per cent of members of Amnesty International were also
members of the Campaign for Nuclear Disarmament. Some people
appear to be involved both in a number of party and outside interest
groups, suggesting that there is a 'network' of highly active people
within the party who are clearly involved in many kinds of political
campaigns as well as in the party organization.

In Table 5.4 we examine the 'representation' aspects of activism.
Not surprisingly only a relatively small percentage of respondents

are office holders within the party or elected representatives on the local council. These individuals might be described as the élite party activists, who are likely to have disproportionate influence over the local party organization.

The information in these tables is very interesting but does not allow us to get an overall measure of activism in the party, since we cannot tell easily the interrelationships between these types of activities. For example, it is not clear how many individuals are active campaigners but not interested in being elected representatives, or how many have quite a lot of contact with the party, but do not get involved in many meetings. Clearly, there is a need for some overall index of party activism, so that the very active can be distinguished from the semi-active, who in turn can be distinguished from the inactive party members.

Table 5.5 contains responses to a set of questions in the survey designed to measure the overall levels of activism within the party. Respondents were asked about their involvement in eight specific political activities within the party, over the previous five years. The activities were arranged in an ascending order of 'costliness' in the sense of taking up the individual's time and effort. Thus 'displaying an election poster' is a relatively low-cost activity, which we might expect most party members to have done frequently over this period. By contrast 'delivering party leaflets during an election' is a higher-cost activity, which should therefore involve fewer participants. The highest-cost activity on the scale is 'standing for elected office'. This type of 'increasing cost' scale of participation has been used successfully to measure political participation in a variety of political systems in different countries, including Britain (Marsh, 1977; and Barnes and Kaase, 1979).

It can be seen that the activities in Table 5.5 cover the three dimensions of contact, campaigning, and representation fairly well. Moreover the higher-cost activities such as canvassing involved significantly fewer party members than lower-cost activities like delivering leaflets. There is a relatively sharp discontinuity in the table when it comes to the indicators of representation; significantly fewer party members have stood for office within the party or in the outside community, than have canvassed or attended meetings. Despite this, a statistical analysis of the items, using a technique known as factor analysis which is designed to estimate how well these measures group together in a single active–passive dimension,

TABLE 5.5. *The Components of the Activism Scale* (percentages)

Question: How often have you taken part in political activities during the last five years?

Activity	How often have you done this? (%)			
	Not at all	Rarely	Occasionally	Frequently
Displayed an election poster in a window	10	4	21	65
Signed a petition supported by the Labour party	6	5	30	59
Donated money to Labour party funds	18	15	34	33
Delivered party leaflets during an election	17	5	21	57
Attended a party meeting	18	14	26	42
Canvassed voters on behalf of the party	34	9	21	36
Stood for office within the party organization	71	5	10	14
Stood for elected office in a local or national election	85	2	4	9

Note: N = 4825

demonstrated that the items could indeed be aggregated into an overall activism scale fairly well.[1]

The activism scale was constructed by adding together the responses for each individual (not at all = 1; rarely = 2; occasionally

---

[1] This involved a principal-components analysis of the eight items with pairwise deletion of missing observations and a varimax rotation of the components. The analysis produced a two-factor solution with an eigenvalue for factor one of 3.71, and for factor two of 1.1. Factor one explained 46 per cent of the variance, and factor two 14 per cent of the variance. All the loadings on the first factor of the principal-components analysis exceeded 0.55, and this together with the fact that the eigenvalue for factor two barely achieved significance using Kaiser's criterion, suggests that the items can be represented adequately by a single overall scale. For a full discussion of factor analysis see Harman (1967).

= 3; frequently = 4;), so that a very inactive respondent would score 8 (i.e. a score of one for each of the eight items), and a very active respondent would score 32 (i.e. a score of four for each of the eight items).[2] The distribution of scores over this 24 point scale for all the respondents appears in Fig. 5.1.

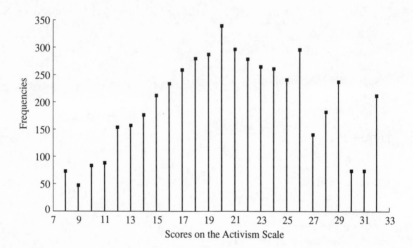

FIG. 5.1 The activism distribution

The distribution of scores in the histogram of Fig. 5.1 is surprisingly symmetrical, so that there is no obvious tendency for respondents to cluster, for example, at the inactive end of the scale. Only 1 per cent of respondents scored the minimum which indicates that they are totally inactive, whereas 4 per cent scored the maximum, which indicates that they are extremely active. Thus the superactivists outnumber the totally inactive party members.

The mean score on the scale was 21, which was also the mid-point or median score. Of course this mean score can be achieved in a wide variety of different ways; a respondent could have done all the items up to, and including delivering leaflets frequently, but none of the

[2] Some respondents omitted to answer some of the higher-cost items in the scale, perhaps because they felt that these were not relevant to themselves, and so the aggregate scores for a few individuals were less than 8. These are omitted in Fig. 5.1, but are incorporated into the analysis of Tables 5.12–5.14.

items beyond that at all, and still get just below the mean score (i.e. 20). Alternatively they could have done the first two items frequently, the second two occasionally, the third two rarely, and the last two not at all, and get the same score (20).

With that caveat in mind the last example provides an illustrative profile of how active the average or 'typical' member of the party is; he or she is very likely to have displayed a poster at election times and signed a petition sponsored by the party; quite likely to have delivered leaflets at election times; likely to have given money occasionally to Labour party funds, attended a party meeting or canvassed; and unlikely to have stood for office in the party or in a local election.

In the light of this discussion the next question is to examine the relationships between political activism and the social and demographic backgrounds of party members.

THE CORRELATES OF PARTY ACTIVISM

One of the most interesting questions about the Labour party members is the relationship between their demographic characteristics such as class, gender, and age, and their levels of activism within the party. To facilitate the analysis of this question the activism scale will be divided into four categories; scores up to 13 will be described as 'inactive'; 14 to 19 'occasionally active'; 20 to 25 'fairly active'; and 26 to 32 'very active'.

The relationship between various social-background characteristics and activism appears in Table 5.6. This table should be interpreted by comparing rates of activism for all members which appear first, with rates of activism for various subgroups which appear lower down.

The first sub-table examines the relationship between activism and age. Overall, middle-aged members, particularly those in the age-group 46–65 are more active than the young members, or the retired members. It is possible that the amount of spare time individuals have available to devote to party matters could be one of the factors which influences their levels of activism within the party. If this is true then younger party members, who on the whole do not have large family commitments, and retired members who have a lot of spare time, should be more active than middle-aged members in full-time jobs and with families to raise.

However the evidence clearly does not support this reasoning. It is noticeable that the retired members are much more likely to be inactive than middle-aged members, or even the young. Similarly, the young are rather less active than the middle-aged. Thus having spare time available does not appear to influence rates of political participation.

Another approach to the same question involved examining whether or not unemployed party members, who constitute about 4 per cent of the sample, were more active than the others. Again, since the unemployed have more spare time than members in full-time occupations, it is possible that they are more active. However, the evidence does not support this conclusion, since unemployed members did not differ from members as a whole in their rates of activism.

It may be recalled from the discussion in Chapter 4 that party members were more likely to be middle class than Labour voters. The same applies to the very active members in comparison with inactive members, as can be seen in the second sub-table in Table 5.6; members of the salariat are overrepresented in the very active group in comparison with members of the working class. Similarly, the middle class are underrepresented in the inactive group in comparison with the working class.

The relationship between gender and party activism can be observed in the third sub-table of Table 5.6. It is clear that women are less likely to be active than men in the party; we saw earlier that women are underrepresented in the party anyway, in relation to their numbers in the voting population, and it appears that this under-representation extends further into the highly active group of party members.

The fourth sub-table in Table 5.6 examines the relationship between activism and income. Once again there is evidence of a class relationship, with members of the high-income group more likely to be active than members of the low-income group.

Finally, another important social characteristic which might have an influence on activism is education. We saw in Chapter 4 that graduates were very much overrepresented among party members than they were among Labour voters. Obviously the same kind of factors which explained that should also serve to make graduates more active than non-graduates in the party. In addition to possessing more post-materialist values, graduates should have a greater

TABLE 5.6. *The Relationship between Activism and Social Characteristics* (percentages)

	Inactive	Occasionally active	Fairly active	Very active
All respondents	14	29	34	24
Age				
17–25	16	37	32	15
26–45	9	30	36	26
46–65	13	27	33	27
66+	24	27	30	19
Class				
Salariat	10	29	34	27
Routine non-manual	13	30	34	23
Petty bourgeoisie	12	31	31	26
Foreman and technician	14	31	27	28
Working class	16	27	34	23
Gender				
Female	15	30	36	19
Male	13	28	32	28
Income				
Under £10,000	19	27	33	22
£10,000–£25,000	10	30	35	26
£25,000+	12	30	32	26
Graduate				
Yes	9	30	34	27
No	14	29	34	23

sense of personal efficacy—they should feel more able to influence politics than non-graduates. This hypothesis is confirmed in the fifth sub-table of Table 5.6 where graduates are overrepresented in the 'very active' category and underrepresented in the 'inactive' category.

However, differences between graduates and non-graduates in this table are not nearly so marked as the differences between voters and members in Table 4.4. Thus education has a much stronger influence on the decision to join the party than it has on the decision to be active once the individual has joined.

One final relationship we shall consider is between activism and ideology. This has been much discussed in journalistic accounts of the Labour party which tend to assume that activists are significantly more left-wing than the inactive members. This argument has also been developed in the academic literature (see McKenzie, 1964, 1982) and is formalized in the so-called 'law of curvilinear disparity' (May, 1973; and Kitschelt, 1989). This is the proposition that middle-level élites or rank-and-file activists in a political party are more radical than the party leadership on the one hand, and the party voters on the other.

This produces a curvilinear relationship between ideological radicalism and the position of the individual within the organizational hierarchy of the party. It implies that Labour activists are to the left of both the inactive members and the party leadership. The assumption is that because they are more left-wing than the voters, they are more likely to want to become active in the party.

This idea has mainly been discussed in relation to party strategies; it implies for example that parties can pursue electoralist strategies only in so far as the leadership can control the activists. However, within the general-incentive model it can be used to provide an interesting theoretical explanation of activism. Ideological radicalism should motivate activists to become more involved than the inactive members, because the reward for their involvement is the ability to give expression to deeply held beliefs. Their involvement is prompted by similar motives to those of the active church-goer—church attendance allows them to give expression to religious convictions. Thus ideological radicalism provides an additional selective process incentive for involvement.

Of course the same argument could be used about right-wingers in the party, namely that involvement allows them to interact with others and thus express their beliefs. However, left-wingers and right-wingers are not in the same political position. Parkin (1968) points out that a dominant set of ideological values exist in British society concerned with support for inequality, deference to authority, and a belief in the private market. He distinguishes between these values and what he terms 'deviant' left-wing values, which emphasize egalitarianism, public intervention in the market place, and an absence of deference towards authority. Clearly, right-wing values within the Labour party conform more closely to

TABLE 5.7. *The Relationship between Ideology and Activism* (percentages)

	Inactive	Occasionally active	Fairly active	Very active
All respondents	14	29	34	24
Left–Right scale in Britain				
Left	10	26	35	30
Centre-left	12	33	34	22
Centre	21	28	30	20
Centre-right	17	28	31	24
Right	27	24	34	15
Left–Right scale in the party				
Hard left	10	24	34	32
Soft left	10	29	35	27
Centre	15	32	32	21
Soft right	14	33	35	18
Hard right	29	27	28	16

the dominant ideology, and individuals with those values do not need to seek out others to give expression to their beliefs, since society is pervaded by such values. This asymmetry in the position of left-wingers in comparison with right-wingers is likely to make the former more active than the latter.

This 'law of curvilinear disparity' assumes that radicalism motivates participation, but obviously the process can work in the opposite direction; as individuals become drawn into the party for a variety of reasons they become radicalized by contact with other activists. In so far as this happens then activism sustains itself, as individuals become socialized into the norms and ethos (Drucker, 1979) of the party, and are rewarded for this by interacting with other like-minded people.

The two left–right ideological scales referred to in Chapter 4 have been recoded into five categories for purposes of comparison in Table 5.7. It will be recalled that one scale asks respondents to code themselves along a nine-point scale in relation to British politics as a whole, and the other asks them to code themselves along a similar scale relating to Labour party politics.

The evidence in Table 5.7 suggests that activists are more left-wing than inactive members, since for both scales the left-wing members are markedly overrepresented in the 'very active' category, and significantly underrepresented in the 'inactive' category. Equally, the right-wing respondents are significantly overrepresented in the 'inactive' category and underrepresented in the 'very active' category. Centrist respondents appear to be slightly overrepresented in the 'occasionally active' category. We discuss ideology more fully in Chapter 6, but for the moment these results lend support to the 'curvilinear disparity' hypothesis.

The relationships between social-background characteristics and activism are interesting, but they are not very strong, certainly not strong enough to explain the observed variations in activism within the party. To explain this we need a clear theoretical framework, of the type provided by general incentives theory. In the remainder of this chapter we apply this theoretical framework to the issue of explaining variations in activism within the party.

THE DETERMINANTS OF PARTY ACTIVISM

It will be recalled that incentives theory is based on the idea that individuals calculate the costs and benefits of any course of action before they undertake to do it. This can be set out in the form of a 'calculus' of participation as follows (Barry, 1970; and Olson, 1965):

$$R_i = (p_i)\,(B) - C_i \tag{1}$$

where

R_i measures the returns from participating in politics for a given individual i;

p_i measures the probability that i's participation will bring about the policy outcomes desired (or collective goods);

B measures the benefits to society of implementing the policy proposals of the party (collective benefits);

C_i measures the costs of participation for individual i.

The benefits of collective action B, are collective goods as defined in Chapter 4. When they are provided, by the party winning office and implementing new policies, they cannot be restricted to those individuals whose efforts made it possible to win the election in the first place. Since they are collective goods and available to all, a rational actor would work out his or her own individual contribution, p_i, the provision of the policies, and use this to weight B when calculating whether or not to participate. Only if he or she can make a difference to the outcome, i.e. when p_i is non-zero, is it rational to get involved, since only then will his or her own actions increase the chances of the good being provided, and the benefits of action outweigh the costs.

The paradox of participation arises because in most situations p_i is vanishingly small. Thus the individual has very little influence over the policy programme of a political party, or over the outcome of an election acting as a single person, so even if they perceive the benefits of collective action to be large in relation to costs, it will not be rational to participate once p_i is incorporated into the analysis.

However, as we pointed out in Chapter 4 a number of other factors need to be taken into account in order to explain political participation, namely, selective incentives, altruistic concerns, and social norms. To incorporate these into the analysis it is necessary to measure them with suitable indicators.

We can begin the exercise of deriving suitable indicators of the various measures with equation (1). The dependent variable in this equation is the return from political participation; if we assume that activism is a direct function of R_i, i.e. the higher the return, the greater the rate of activism, then the activism scale discussed above can be incorporated directly into the model in the place of R_i. It will be labelled A_i.

The individual influence variable p_i is measured by means of three Likert-scaled items:[3] 'people like me can have a real influence on politics if they are prepared to get involved'; 'sometimes politics seems so complicated it is difficult for a person like me to understand what is going on'; and 'parties in general are only interested in people's votes, not in their opinions'. High scores went to those respondents who perceived themselves to have most influence,[4] and

[3] A Likert scale is constructed by asking respondents to indicate if they agree or disagree with a set of statements, using a five point scale (1 'strongly agree'; 2 'agree'; 3 'neither'; 4 'disagree'; 5 'strongly disagree'). Statements are designed to be controversial, taking a clear position in favour or against some issue, so that responses will elicit the emotional reaction of the individual to the issue in question.

[4] The individual scores associated with each statement are aggregated into an overall score. Thus a respondent who strongly agreed with the first of these statements and strongly disagreed with the second and third would score 5 points in each case, to give an overall total of 15 points. Obviously, this person would feel very influential in politics. An individual who strongly disagreed with the first and strongly agreed with the second and third would score one point each, giving an overall total of 3 points.

the measure was transformed into a probability scale ranging from 0 to 1 in order to use it as a weighting measure with the B index.

Thus if an individual scores highly on the B scale, but low on the personal influence scale, they are unlikely to become very active in the party despite strongly agreeing with its policy goals, because they do not feel able to influence policy outcomes.

Turning to the measurement of the collective-benefits scale B, in the earlier discussion collective incentives for participation were of two types, positive and negative. Thus members become active in order to support some policies or parties, or alternatively to oppose some policies or parties. Both of these types of incentives can be measured by examining responses to a set of eight policy-orientated questions in the survey, which replicated a set of questions in the British Election Study.

Respondents were asked whether they thought that government should or should not do various things. The indicators were: 'get rid of private education'; 'spend more money to get rid of poverty'; 'encourage the growth of private medicine'; 'put more money into the National Health Service'; 'reduce government spending generally'; 'introduce stricter laws to regulate trade unions'; 'give workers more say in the places where they work'; and 'spend less on defence'.

The Labour party can be identified as being broadly in favour of some of these policy positions and against others, although not all statements agree or disagree precisely with party policy. Generally, the party is in favour of spending more money to get rid of poverty, and to promote the National Health Service, and spending less on defence. It is also in favour of giving workers more say in the places where they work, but against promoting private medicine, against stricter laws on trade unions, and opposed to overall reductions in public spending. If a respondent feels strongly about all these issues, and has views which accord with Labour party preferences, they should have a greater incentive to participate in order to promote these goals.

Support for policies favoured by the Labour party is a positive incentive for involvement, and opposition to policies opposed by the party is a negative incentive for involvement. Accordingly, these various statements were aggregated into an overall scale so that highest scores went to those individuals whose views most closely accord with those of the Labour Party.[5] The resulting collective-outcomes scale is labelled *B*.

Turning next to the measurement of the costs of activism, this was done with four Likert-scaled items: 'attending party meetings can be pretty tiring after a hard day's work'; 'party activity often takes time away from one's family'; 'many people find party meetings rather boring'; and 'many people think party activists are extremists'. Highest scores went to those respondents who agreed with these statements, and the resulting scale was labelled C_i.

In the earlier discussion of incentive theory, it was argued that participation can be influenced by four classes of factors: selective incentives, collective incentives, altruistic concerns, and social norms. Equation (1) focuses entirely on collective incentives—the provision of collective benefits—and does not examine the influence of the other factors. Thus we need to extend this equation to consider the influence of these other variables.

The first additional factor relates to selective incentives, and as argued earlier, these can take the form of outcome-orientated incentives and process-orientated incentives for participation. To consider outcome incentives first, these were measured in the survey by two Likert-scaled items designed to indicate how ambitious the respondent is in developing a career as an elected representative on behalf of the Labour party. The statements were: 'a person like me could do a good job of being a local Labour councillor'; and 'Labour would be more successful if more people like me were elected to Parliament'.

This indirect approach to the measurement of political ambitions is used since pilot work showed that direct questions on personal ambitions in the party are not readily answered by most people, because such motives are not socially acceptable in the party. Individual responses to these questions were aggregated with the highest scores going to those respondents who strongly agreed with both

[5] The five point scale for each of the items was 1 'definitely should'; 2 'probably should'; 3 'doesn't matter'; 4 'probably should not'; 5 'definitely should not'. If respondents select the 'definitely should' category for the abolition of private education, spending more on poverty, and the NHS, giving workers more say, and spending less on defence, they score 5 points for each answer. If they select the 'definitely should not' category for encouraging private medicine, reducing government spending, and introducing stricter trade union laws, they also score 5 points for each answer, giving a total of 40 points. By the same reasoning the reverse answers to all these indicators gives a minimum possible score of 8 points.

statements.[6] The resulting scale is labelled $S(O)$. Again those individuals who are most ambitious to make a career in politics, have the greatest incentive to participate.

Process-orientated incentives are measured in two ways; firstly, three Likert-scaled statements were used to elicit the individual's attitude to political activism in general. The statements were: 'the only way to be really educated about politics is to be a party activist'; 'being an active party member is a good way to meet interesting people'; and 'Labour party members are part of a great movement of like-minded people who work together in solidarity'. Highest scores went to those individuals who most strongly agreed with the statements. The resulting scale is labelled $S(P)$.

A second way of measuring process incentives uses one of the nine point left–right ideology scales referred to in Table 5.6. The most left-wing respondents scored one, and the most right-wing respondents scored nine. To repeat the earlier point, left-wingers are more likely to be actively involved in politics because it gives them a chance to give expression to deeply-held views which are deviant from the dominant political values in society, and this is a process incentive for involvement. Accordingly, we use the left–right ideology scale for Britain, and this is labelled ID.

Another important factor in influencing activism is having altruistic motives for involvement. We argued in Chapter 4 that these were fundamentally different from the other type of incentive factors, since they were not outcome-orientated; individuals did not perform them in order to receive a reward of some kind, but rather for intrinsic motives of an idealistic kind.

Attempts have been made in the rational-choice literature to incorporate altruism into the analysis of decision-making in order to account for types of behaviour such as voting which are not easily understood without such an assumption. Margolis (1982), for example, in a discussion of the paradox of participation applied to voting suggests that there is a 'social value' of participating in a presidential election in the United States, where this refers to the social utility of making other members of society better-off. He argues that this social value is 'easily estimated in the billions (of dollars)' (1983: 89), which implies that when it is discounted by the minutely small probability p_i, the return from voting is still positive.

[6] An individual who strongly agreed with both statements would score 10, and an individual who strongly disagreed with them would score 2.

With this factor in the equation, rational actors have an incentive to vote.

Unfortunately this appears to be rather arbitrary, since Margolis gives no account of why such altruistic concerns should be important to individuals, in a model which otherwise assumes that motivations are dominated by self-interest. It is fairly clear why individuals pursue self-interest in rational choice models, but it is not clear why they should want to pursue group or collective interests, particularly when they can profit from free-riding on the efforts of others. Since, by definition, altruism departs from narrow assumptions of self-interest it cannot be explained by the same type of theoretical account which is used to explain selective or collective incentives.

An alternative approach, which we will take, is to see altruism as being a product of an entirely different kind of motivation. It will be viewed as being a product of affective or expressive motivations. Thus collective action emerges out of a sense of loyalty, affection, or emotional attachments to the party, not out of a calculation of costs and benefits. In this interpretation altruism is not disinterested, since activists get emotional returns from being involved. But they do not undertake altruistic actions based on a calculus of costs and benefits.

We measure expressive or altruistic concerns using a 'thermometer' scale, derived from a question which asked respondents to indicate how 'warm and sympathetic' their feelings were towards the Labour party, up to a maximum score of 100 (minimum score 0).[7] Highest scores went to those with the warmest feelings towards the party, and the scale is labelled E, for expressive concerns.

In their model of unorthodox political participation Muller and Opp (1987) modify the standard model of equation (1) in two ways; first, they argue from empirical studies of political participation that 'individuals actually have reported the belief that their participation matters' (1987: 562). This implies, contrary to the arguments of rational choice theory, that p_i is not negligible. They suggest that if individuals believe themselves to be influential, one should accept this and not just assume that this belief is irrational.

This approach has been criticized by one writer, who takes issue with the suggestion that p_i is non-zero, arguing that this is an

---

[7] The precise wording of the thermometer questions appears in question 39 in Appendix II.

'egregious miscalculation' (Klosko, 1987: 559). In his view since the probability that an individual will actually influence the outcome of an election, or some other type of collective action, is negligible anyone who believes themselves to be influential is simply mistaken.

A second modification to the standard model which they make is to introduce an additional term p_g into the equation, as another weighting factor to be applied to B, which measures 'the influence of the group on the provision of public goods' (1986: 474). In their analysis this is motivated by altruistic concerns for the interests of the group as a whole. They suggest that it is independent of p_i and provides an additional reason for participating in collective action.

This additional term accords closely with the idea introduced in Chapter 4 that members can 'think' at the group level, and not just at the level of the individual. In other words it is important to measure members' evaluations of the effectiveness of the Labour party as a whole in obtaining collective benefits, as well as the effectiveness of themselves as individuals.

Following this idea we incorporate a measure of the members' perceptions of the influence of the party p_g into the analysis by means of three Likert-scaled items: 'when Labour party members are united and work together they can really change Britain'; 'the party leadership doesn't pay a lot of attention to the views of ordinary party members'; and 'by and large, Labour MPs try to represent the views of ordinary party members'. High scores went to those who perceive the party members as a group to have most influence,[8] and the measure was transformed to range from zero to one, in the same way as p_i.

Given this, it is important to recognize that p_i and p_g are not independent of each other, but interact in interesting ways. When p_g is small, p_i must also be small, since it does not make sense for the individual to believe that he or she is very influential in obtaining the collective goods, when at the same time he or she thinks that the party as a whole is not very influential. Equally when p_g is large the individual member might react to this in two different ways.

One reaction would be to feel politically influential as an individual, because one is part of what is perceived as an influential group. If so then p_i and p_g will both interact with each other—as one

---

[8] Highest scores went to those respondents who strongly agreed with the first and third of these statements, and strongly disagreed with the second.

gets stronger so does the other—producing a multiplicative relationship between the variables. In other words a sense of individual efficacy reinforces a sense of group efficacy, and vice versa.

But another reaction might be to feel overshadowed as an individual by the perception that the party is influential, or alternatively to be tempted to free-ride on the efforts of others. A member might reason: 'The party is pretty influential, so I am unlikely to make a difference'; or 'The party is influential, so I don't need to get involved'. In both cases this reaction would make p_i small. If this kind of interaction exists between perceptions of individual and group influence then there will be a curvilinear relationship between p_i and p_g of the kind depicted in Fig. 5.2. We can test these alternatives below.

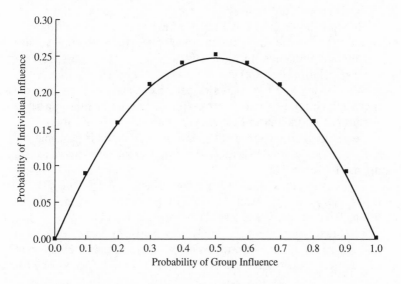

FIG. 5.2 A possible relationship between individual and group influence

Finally, we have suggested that social norms can influence activism, and that these are like altruistic motives in not being concerned with the outcomes of collective action. However, they are unlike altruistic motives in being strongly influenced by the opinions of other people. Thus they get their force from the attitudes and opinions of significant 'others'. To measure this factor we select out the respondents in the social-norms category of Table 4.5, which it will be recalled was created from the replies to an open-ended question about why people joined the Labour party in the first place; thus all members who joined the party because of the influence of other people such as relatives or friends score 1, and all others score 0. The resulting variable is labelled N.

In the light of this discussion the extended rational-actor model of activism can be written as follows:

$$A_i = (p_i) (p_g) (B) - C_i + S(O_i) + S(P_i) + E_i + N_i + ID_i; \quad (2)$$

or alternatively:

$$A_i = (p_i) (p_g - p_g^2) (B) - C_i + S(O_i) + S(P_i) + E_i + N_i + ID_i \quad (3)$$

In (2) we test the proposition that p_i and p_g interact multiplicatively with the benefits index, so that membership of what is perceived to be a powerful organization enhances the individual's sense of personal influence. In (3) we test the proposition that the curvilinear relationship specified in Fig. 5.2 applies, so that as p_g approaches 1.0 and the individual perceives the party to be increasingly influential, he or she feels personally less influential, possibly because of an inclination to free-ride on the efforts of others.

To get an overall picture of the various scales used in this analysis the means, standard deviations, and ranges of the different measures appear in Table 5.8.

To examine the relationship between activism and the various other factors in the model we begin by examining bivariate correlations between the variables.[9] These appear in Table 5.9.

The highest correlation in Table 5.9 is between the activism scale and selective outcome incentives or the ambition index (35 per cent of a perfect score). This means that there is a marked tendency for

---

[9] The correlation coefficient measures the strength of the association between two variables—in effect, the extent to which they vary together. As normally calculated the measure can vary from $+1.0$ to -1.0, the former denoting perfect positive association, and the latter perfect negative association. To illustrate, there is a high positive correlation between the heights and ages of schoolchildren (say $+0.90$), because tall children tend to be older than short children (with some exceptions). By contrast the correlation between heights and ages for adults is, if anything, slightly negative (-0.25), since young adults tend to have received better nutrition and thus grow taller than older people. To make the interpretation easier for those unfamiliar with these measures, we have multiplied the coefficients by 100, which allows them to be interpreted as percentages of a 'perfect' correlation, or score of 100.

TABLE 5.8. *Means, Standard Deviations, and Ranges of Variables*

Variable	Mean	Standard deviation	Range
Activism index (A)	20.6	6.2	1–32
Value of Collective Good index (B)	34.7	4.3	5–40
Personal Influence index (p_i)	0.65	0.15	0.07–1.0
Group Influence index (p_g)	0.70	0.12	0.07–1.0
Transformed Group Influence index ($p_g - p_g^2$)	0.20	0.05	0.00–0.25
Perceived Costs index (C)	7.6	1.4	2–10
Process Incentives S(P)	9.7	2.4	2–15
Outcome Incentives S(O)	6.3	1.9	1–10
Expressive Evaluations (E)	84.2	14.7	0–100
Left–Right Ideology index (ID)	4.3	2.0	0–9
Social Norms (N)	0.07	0.26	0–1.0

Note: Average N = 5037

those who are politically ambitious to be active in the party. Early research by Holt and Turner (1968) stressed the importance of political ambition in influencing party activism, and this is strongly confirmed by the present findings. Those seeking elective office in the party have to serve an 'apprenticeship' during which they are politically active, and clearly this provides an important selective incentive for participation.

The second highest correlation is between activism and the benefits of collective action index (24) which shows that the benefits side of the cost-benefit calculus significantly motivates activism.

TABLE 5.9. *Correlations between Activism, Incentives, Expressive Evaluations, Social Norms, and Ideology* (percentages of a perfect relationship of 100% defined as both variables being identical)

	Activism index
Value of Collective Goods index (B)	24*
Index of Personal Influence (p_i)	23*
Index of Group Influence (p_g)	−2
Index of Transformed Group Influence (p_g—p_g^2)	2
Perceived Costs of Involvement (C)	2
Process Incentives for Involvement (S(P))	13*
Outcome Incentives for Involvement (S(O))	35*
Expressive Evaluations (E)	8*
Social Norms (N)	−5*
Left–Right Ideology Scale (ID)	−17*

* denotes coefficient significant at the $p < 0.05$ level.
Note: Average N = 4991.

TABLE 5.10. *Models of the Effects of Incentives, Expressive Evaluations, Social Norms, and Ideology on Activism* (percentages of a perfect relationship)

	A	B	C	D
Collective Benefits times Personal Influence (B) (p_i)	28*	16*	—	—
Collective Benefits (B) times p_i times Group Influence (p_g)	—	—	9*	—
Collective Benefits (B) times p_i times Transformed Group Influence ($p_g - p_g^2$)	—	—	—	15*
Perceived Costs (C)	−2	−4*	−4*	−3*
Process Incentives (S(P))	—	11*	10*	12*
Outcome Incentives (S(O))	—	30*	32*	31*
Expressive Evaluations (E)	—	3*	3*	8*
Left–Right Ideology (ID)	—	−10*	−13*	−9*
Social Norms (N)	—	−2	−2	−2
Percentage of variance explained (R^2)	8	18	17	18

* All effects denoted thus are statistically significant at p < 0.05 or above.
Note: Average N = 4977.

Thus respondents who most closely accord with broadly defined Labour party policy positions on the health service, trade-union reform, and public expenditure, are more likely to be active than those who do not agree with these positions. We can see that the correlation between activism and the ambition index is about one-third larger or stronger than the correlation between activism and the benefits index.

The correlation between activism and perceptions of personal influence is about the same magnitude (23) as the correlation of activism with the benefits index, suggesting that these two variables are likely to have a significant interactive relationship with activism. This means that those who feel fairly influential in politics are more likely to be active than those who feel powerless.

There is a significant negative correlation between the ideology scale and activism (-17).[10] This coefficient summarizes the relationships in Table 5.7, the sign of the effect being purely an artefact of the coding of the ideology scale. The way the scales are coded means that inactive members who have a low score on the activism scale, are likely to be right-wing and have a high score on the ideology scale. This is consistent with the 'law' of curvilinear disparity discussed above, and implies that left-wing members are more active than right-wing members.

Process motives for involvement have a weak but significant positive correlation with the activism scale, as do expressive motives. This implies that members who enjoy politics for its own sake, and are warm and sympathetic towards the Labour party, are more active than members who do not have these characteristics.

Finally, the social-norms variable has a weak negative correlation with activism, which implies that those motivated to join the party by the influence of other people such as their spouse or friends, are likely to be less active than those motivated to join for other reasons.

Perceptions of group influence are not significantly correlated

[10] The term 'significant' has a specific meaning in this context. We are using sample data to try to make inferences about the population of all Labour party members, but a sample of 5,071 will very likely differ from the population of approximately 295,000 members. When a correlation coefficient is described as 'significant', this means that we can be fairly certain that the relationship in the sample also exists in the population; by contrast, a non-significant coefficient in the sample will very likely be non-existent in the population.

with activism either in their original or transformed form. This is also true of perceptions of costs. On the face of it this means that perceptions of group influence and costs have no reliable relationship with activism, but it would be unwise to draw any general conclusions about the influence of these variables, without examining multivariate models. Accordingly, we examine the multivariate specifications next.

Table 5.10 contains the regression analyses of the impact of various motives for participation on activism, as specified in models (1) to (3) above.[11] The first model in this table, A, contains the collective-benefits variable weighted by the probability of personal influence, together with the costs index. In this model the weighted-benefits variable has a highly significant impact on activism (28 per cent of a perfect score). Perceptions of costs, have a much weaker and non-significant negative impact on activism. Thus the combination of a strong sense of personal efficacy together with a high level of agreement with broad Labour policy goals stimulates members to be active. However, perceptions that activism has an unfavourable image, and can be tiring and boring as well, does not appear to inhibit involvement. The percentage of variance explained by this model is not large, at 8 per cent, but it is significant.[12]

Model B contains the other variables discussed above and the strongest effect is associated with selective outcome incentives—the ambition index—which has a regression coefficient of 30. This confirms the results of Table 5.9, and shows that ambition plays a very

[11] Regression analysis is concerned with finding the best fitting straight-line relationship between two or more variables. In this case the technique is being used to determine how well the different incentive measures predict variations in political activism. The interpretation of the coefficients in these tables is the same as the coefficients in Table 5.9, with one important exception. Each coefficient measures the relationship between the variable and activism, controlling for the influence of other variables. For example in model 1 we measure the impact of collective benefits times personal influence on activism, having taken into account the effect of costs. In Table 5.9 the correlations between benefits and activism does not take into account costs. For this reason regression is better than correlation analysis because it allows one to separate out the independent influence of the different variables on activism.

[12] This is measured by the R_2 statistic, which indicates how well it is possible to predict activism from the behaviour of the variables in the model. Typically, models derived from survey data of this kind are not very predictable, because there is a lot of variation in the data due to the idiosyncratic characteristics of individuals, as well as random 'noise' of various kinds. In an ideal world our models should be able to explain and predict, but in survey analysis researchers have to be content with explaining some of the patterns in the data without being in a position to predict how individuals will behave.

important role in explaining why some are active when others are not.

The second most important effect in model B after the ambition index is perceptions of collective benefits weighted by the personal-influence variable. It can be seen that the effect is rather weaker than in model A, something which is explained by the presence of controls for other variables in this model. Not surprisingly collective benefits have a weaker impact on activism when other factors are taken into account.

The third most important effect in model B is the measure of process incentives. Clearly, one of the reasons why members are involved is that they enjoy the political process for its own sake, and see participation as a way of becoming educated about politics, and as a means of meeting interesting people. It is noteworthy that two of the three strongest effects in the model are associated with selective incentives, those motives which do not face a collective-action problem.

Another interesting feature of model B is that perceptions of costs, though weak, have a statistically significant effect on activism. Again the change from model A can be explained by the presence of additional control variables in model B. Clearly, perceptions of costs play a role in inhibiting activism when all of the relevant variables are taken into account.

Expressive or altruistic motives, as measured by the thermometer scale, have a relatively weak though significant positive impact on activism. In a narrowly defined rational-choice model of participation these motives should not play a role at all, since the strength of the individual's attachment to the party does not alter the incentives for participation. An individual who is strongly attached to the party faces the same incentives to free-ride on the efforts of others as a someone who is weakly attached. The fact that expressive evaluations are important shows that such a narrowly cast model is not supported by the evidence. Expressive or affective evaluations cannot be ignored in any explanation of why people are active.

Social norms, as they are operationalized in this model do not have a statistically significant impact on activism in the presence of the various other control variables. This means that we cannot be sure that social norms have any influence on activism in the population of all Labour party members. Individuals who joined the party because of the efforts of other people like relatives and friends, do not appear to be more (or less) active than individuals who joined the party for other reasons.

Finally, in model B there is a significant negative relationship between activism and ideology. Again this implies that individuals who are on the left of the ideological spectrum in the party are more likely to be active than those on the right. This supports the findings in Table 5.9, and is consistent with the 'law' of curvilinear disparity, though the effect is not very strong.

Model C in Table 5.10 contains the same variables as model B except for the specification of the collective benefits variable, which has the specification of equation (2) in the text above. This postulates a multiplicative interaction between perceptions of individual and group influence, and the collective-benefits index. The specification tests the possibility that perceptions of group and individual efficacy reinforce one another when interacting with perceptions of collective benefits. In contrast model D in the table has the same specification as equation (3) above, which accords with the prediction that individuals are most likely to be active at intermediate levels of perceptions of group influence.

The results in the table suggest that model D is marginally better than model C. Thus the curvilinear specification is better than the multiplicative specification, if one takes into account perceptions of group influence in the model. This can be seen by comparing the standardized coefficients of these variables in the two models; the effect is significantly larger (15) in the curvilinear model in comparison with the multiplicative model (9). In addition the overall goodness of fit is slightly higher in the former case than the latter.

This suggests that if perceptions of the influence of the Labour party as a whole are incorporated into the model, then members who think that the party is very influential are likely to be less active than members who think the party is moderately influential. However, having said that model D has the same goodness of fit (R^2) as model B, which suggests that we can predict activism equally well by ignoring perceptions of group influence. As far as the other variables in model D are concerned their effects are similar to those in model B.

This finding implies that party members' sense of efficacy—the extent to which they think they can influence politics—does not readily distinguish between the influence of the individual and that of the group. As a consequence, personal efficacy will adequately measure this, without taking into account perceptions of the influence of the Labour party on outcomes.

To summarize this complex set of findings, since activism is costly, all the problems of collective action which have been extensively discussed earlier should apply with particular force in studying activists. The results show that considerations of individual and collective costs and benefits, do influence levels of individual activism within the Labour party. Perceptions of individual influence taken in conjunction with the value the individual attaches to the policy outputs resulting from collective action, have a significant impact on activism.

Equally, selective incentives associated with investing in a career in politics, and enjoying the political process for its own sake are important motives for action. Thus Labour party activists are responding to clear incentives when they become involved in day-to-day party activity.

A model of activism which focuses narrowly only on incentives is not the whole story, however, since expressive or altruistic motives which are unrelated to the outcomes of collective action play an important role in explaining participation. Even when the various incentive measures are included in the model, expressive attachments to the Labour party play an important role in explaining activism. Since this variable should have no impact at all in a narrowly cast model of rational participation, this finding indicates that altruism as measured by an affective attachment to the party is very important in influencing participation.

There is some support for the 'law' of curvilinear disparity in our findings. Even in the presence of controls for various types of incentives and expressive feelings, political ideology has a significant impact on activism; left-wing members are more likely to be active than right-wing members. Thus there is some support for the conventional wisdom that activists are more left-wing than passive members. However, this conclusion is based on only one measure of ideology—the self-assigned 'left–right' scale, and in any case it is not a very strong influence. Since this is such an important issue, it will be developed further in a more comprehensive analysis of ideology in Chapter 6.

6

Political Ideology and Party Membership

In Chapter 3 we examined in outline some of the political attitudes of party members in the survey. In general, our conclusions were that they regard political principles as being important; that they are critical of the market economy, and prefer more public intervention and the public provision of services; that they believe that the bargaining rights of trade unions should be maintained; and finally, that they dislike Britain's possession of nuclear weapons, and want to cut overall spending on defence.

In this chapter we will examine the attitudes and beliefs of the members in more detail, addressing the question of whether or not those attitudes are structured around a core set of beliefs which can be described as an ideology. The aim is to examine the extent to which political attitudes and beliefs are correlated with each other, or in the words of one influential writer, ideologically 'constrained' (Converse, 1964). Having done this we can examine the relationships between ideological beliefs and various social and political characteristics of the members. Finally, we will discuss the determinants of these relationships in a concluding section of the chapter.

The question of ideological structuring is important because the degree of attitude coherence among party members has significant implications for the way in which debates about policies and party strategies are conducted within the party. If, for example, members have a wide variety of attitudes about political issues, but these are not particularly coherent or interrelated, then it means that they will approach each political issue as a separate and discrete question; they will not, for example, make a connection between attitudes to nationalization and say, attitudes to nuclear weapons.

On the other hand if attitudes to most issues are closely interrelated to each other, for example, along a single 'left–right' continuum, then a debate about one issue becomes, in effect, a debate about all the other important political issues facing the party. For this reason attempts by the leadership to change policies are likely to face formidable barriers, since changing the opinions of party members on one issue involves changing them on many other issues at the same time. In other words, if beliefs are highly structured along a well defined left–right ideological continuum then considerable 'cognitive dissonance' (Festinger, 1957) will be created by an attempt to change any of those beliefs.

Ideological factionalism has been a perennial feature of internal Labour party politics over the years (Miliband, 1961; Drucker, 1979; and Shaw, 1988). Left–right conflicts have affected the Parliamentary Labour party (Norton, 1975), the National Executive Committee (Seyd, 1987) and the Party Conference (Minkin, 1978). This raises the interesting question of whether or not such divisions extend down to the grass-roots party. It may be that ideological factionalism is more a feature of the party at the élite level, as Janosik (1968) suggests, rather than at the local level. Alternatively, it may be that left–right divisions permeate the party at all levels.

The question of ideological structuring has been of some interest to academic researchers, but principally to those who have focused on the electorate as a whole. In their early analysis of voter attitudes, Butler and Stokes (1974: 316–37) showed that only 25 per cent of the electorate thought in left–right terms about the parties, and even those who did think in these terms did not have highly structured attitudes. However, more recent work using more sophisticated techniques of analysis has stressed the importance of ideological factors in explaining voting behaviour.

Himmelweit *et al.* (1981) argued that attitudes to issues among voters in their panel sample were quite well structured into two 'supra families' of issues, one centring on economic and political questions like public ownership and education, and the other on questions of law and order and social issues. Scarborough (1984) has suggested that ideological beliefs are at the centre of voting behaviour in Britain. Rose and McAllister (1990) in their 'lifetime of learning' model of electoral choice found that economic values were central to the explanation of voting behaviour. They defined such values as 'widely applicable and durable beliefs and goals about politics and society' (1990: 92), which encompassed attitudes to welfare, business power, privatization, centralization, and redistribution.

Research on the ideological beliefs of grass-roots Labour party members has not previously been carried out, except for a few early case-studies which suggested that ideological structuring at the local level was not very high (Donnison and Plowman, 1954; Berry 1970; and Hindess, 1971). However an analysis of the attitudes of Labour party conference delegates, the 'élite' of the party members, by Whiteley (1983) showed that their attitudes were fairly well structured around some general issues like perceptions of class politics, nationalization, trade-union rights, and attitudes to the European Community.

In the survey we asked a total of thirty-eight issue questions in order to elicit the members' opinions about all the major, and some minor, issues in British politics. In addition we include in the analysis the left–right scales introduced in Chapter 4, as measures of ideology. Thus the analysis of the ideological beliefs of party members begins with the responses to these questions.

ATTITUDE STRUCTURES IN THE MEMBERSHIP

We begin the investigation of attitude structures among Labour party members with a factor analysis of the thirty-eight indicators plus the two 'left–right' scales. Factor analysis is a statistical technique which enables us to examine whether or not there are underlying 'structures' of opinion on a wide range of issues. If two issues, such as attitudes to nuclear weapons and to immigration are highly related to each other, in the sense that respondents who agree with one tend to disagree with the other, then indicators of these attitudes will be highly correlated with an underlying factor; one will be negatively correlated, and the other positively correlated with the factor. If there is a broad left–right continuum underlying the attitudes of party members, then many different issue indicators will be correlated with this factor.

On the other hand, if attitudes to issues are not significantly related to one another, so that members tend to see issues as discrete questions, then no significant factor will underlie the issue indicators; in this case correlations between any factor and the issue indicators will be weak or non-existent. Accordingly, to investigate this question we begin with a factor analysis of all the issue indicators.

TABLE 6.1. *The Ideological Structure of Attitudes*

Attitude indicator	Factors			
	I	II	III	IV
Left–Right scale for Britain	−67			
Immigration too tight	−63			
Aid to the Third World	−61			
High tax deters hard work	59			
Capture the middle ground	59			
Free market is best	58			
Left–Right scale for party	−55			
Keep nuclear weapons	54			
Produce food at risk of countryside	53			
Risk pollution to create jobs	−52			
Nuclear energy essential	45			
Renationalize privatized industry		66		
Nationalization vs. privatization		58		
Class struggle in Britain		55		
Support secondary action		51		
Trade unions too much power in party		−50		48
Trade unions should have little power		−49		
Party stick by principles			63	
Party leader too powerful			59	
Support Poll Tax non-payment			59	
Constituencies select candidates			58	
Resist further EC integration			47	
Conference block vote disreputable				60
Farming methods damage countryside				55
One-person/one-vote for leadership				53
Introduce proportional representation				46
Variance explained by each factor (R^2)	20	11	7	5

Note:
  I. Left–Right Scale
  II. Class, Ownership, and Power
  III. The Politics of Principles and Localism
  IV. Party Democracy and Electoral Reform

The results of the factor analysis appear in Table 6.1,[1] and demonstrate that members' attitudes are significantly structured around a set of four underlying factors or dimensions. Each of these factors is independent of the others, and they have been labelled in the light of the correlations with the variables. The first is described as a general 'left–right' factor, the second as a 'class, ownership, and power' factor, the third as 'the politics of principles and localism', and the fourth as 'party democracy and electoral reform'.

The 'left–right' factor is labelled as such for two reasons; first, it encompasses many of the major issues debated within the party and in British politics in recent years. These include the role of the free market in the economy, immigration, nuclear weapons and nuclear energy, environmental quality and pollution, and Labour party strategy.[2] The second reason is that the factor contains the two 'left–right' scales introduced in Chapter 4, which related to the Labour party and to British politics as a whole.

While the first factor encompasses a wide variety of issues together with the left–right scales, it is important to note that a number of key issues, such as attitudes to public ownership, the trade-union movement and the European Community are not correlated with this first factor. Thus it does not encompass all the major political issues facing the party or British society.

To make the interpretation of this table clear, we can illustrate the meaning of the coefficients with two of the indicators: 'The Labour party should adjust its policies to capture the middle ground of politics' (abbreviated as 'Capture the middle ground'); and 'The production of goods and services is best left to a free market' (abbreviated as 'Free market is best'). These two issues have been central to British politics in recent years, the first relating to Labour's modernization strategy and the argument for electoral

---

[1] This table contains the factor loadings ($\times 100$) from a principal components analysis of the bivariate correlations between the issue indicators, transformed by a varimax rotation. The initial analysis used all forty issue indicators (including the two Left–Right scales) and identified four factors with eigenvalues greater than 1.5, and nine of the indicators were not significantly related to these factors. The latter were then omitted from the analysis and the factor analysis repeated. In this second analysis five significant factors were extracted, using Kaiser's criterion (i.e. eigenvalues > or = 1.0), but only the first four had any substantive meaning. All factor loadings greater than 0.45 were retained in this second analysis, and the results in Table 6.1 are derived from the factor analysis of these 25 indicators.

[2] The full wording of the issue indicators appears in Appendix II.

pragmatism which goes with it, and the second to the whole question of the role of the private market in the economy.

Both these indicators are strongly positively related to the underlying left–right scale. This means that there is a strong tendency for individuals who agree with the first statement to agree with the second. In contrast, members who agree with these statements are very likely to disagree with the proposition that immigration restrictions are too tight in Britain, and should be eased. For this reason the latter indicator is negatively related to this left–right factor. The same is true of attitudes to foreign aid, and the indicator of employment versus pollution.

The second factor is about class, public ownership, and the redistribution of power. In this case responses to a question about the importance of the class struggle between labour and capital are correlated with responses about the desirability of renationalizing privatized industries; the belief that the 'central question of British politics is the class struggle between labour and capital' goes with a belief that the party should renationalize 'public enterprises privatized by the Tory government'. Equally these beliefs go along with a conviction that the trade unions do not have too much power in the party or in British society.

The third factor is labelled 'The politics of principle and localism', because it links indicators which put principles before pragmatism in politics, and which oppose outside interference in local party politics, or EC interference in British politics. Thus members who believe that the Party Leader is too powerful also tend to support localism in party politics and oppose electoral pragmatism. The view that the party should stick to its principles 'even if this should lose an election' goes with a belief that the party should support individuals who 'refuse to pay the Poll Tax'.

The fourth factor is labelled 'Party democracy and electoral reform', since it is principally about matters of internal party democracy concerning the election of the Party Leader and the role of the trade-union block vote in the party conference, and electoral reform. Thus members who favour reforms to promote internal party democracy also favour the introduction of proportional representation for British elections. The same individuals tend to agree that the trade-union block vote brings the party into disrepute.

Overall, there is considerable structure to the attitudes and beliefs of members, but it would not be true to say that all the significant attitudes are structured around a single left–right continuum. It is true that the first factor encompasses a lot of contemporary issues, but it explains a relatively modest percentage of the variance,[3] and omits some major issues. Opinion differences within the party are more complex than is explained by a single left–right dimension.

In Table 6.2 we examine the variations in opinion within the party on the issues in Table 6.1. Most of the indicators used in the factor analysis were Likert-scaled items and these appear first; some of the indicators were measured by means of different scales and these appear subsequently. It can be seen that some of these were referred to earlier in Chapter 3, but they are all included in this table for ease of comparison with Table 6.1.

The percentages in Table 6.2 illustrate why it is necessary to factor-analyse the data in order to explore attitude structuring. It will be recalled that 'capture the middle ground' and 'the free market is best' were both positively related to factor one, the left–right scale. However, as Table 6.2 illustrates, some 57 per cent of the respondents agree or strongly agree with the first of these statements, and only 25 per cent do so for the second statement. The factor analysis shows that respondents who agree with the 'free market' indicator, also largely agree with the 'middle ground' indicator, even though the majority of opinions are on both sides of these issues. Thus a positive correlation in Table 6.1 does not mean that majorities favour both issues, only that individuals who favour one are likely to favour the other.

In general majorities of the members tend to disagree with the positively correlated items on factor one. This is true of the following indicators; 'high taxes deter work'; 'free market is best'; 'produce food at risk of the countryside'; 'keep nuclear weapons'; and 'nuclear energy is essential'. On the other hand, opinions are more mixed on the negatively related items such as 'immigration is too tight' and 'risk pollution to create jobs'.

As far as the 'class, ownership, and power' factor is concerned significant majorities favour more nationalization, secondary-strike action, and the proposition that the class struggle is the central question of British politics. With regard to the 'politics of principles

---

[3] This is a measure of how structured attitudes are; if, for example, factor one explained 90% of the variance it would mean attitudes were very highly structured around a single Left–Right dimension. As it is, there appears to be a modest amount of attitude structuring in the data.

TABLE 6.2. *The Distribution of Opinions on the Attitude Indicators*
(percentages)

Indicator	Strongly Agree	Agree	Neither	Disagree	Strongly Disagree
Immigration into UK too restricted	12	30	16	28	13
Government give more aid to the Third World	33	44	9	10	4
High Income tax deters hard work	13	22	11	38	16
Capture the middle ground of politics	19	38	10	22	11
Production best left to the free market	5	20	17	34	24
Farmers produce more food at risk of countryside	6	15	19	44	17
Nuclear energy development essential	4	9	8	36	44
Labour return privatized industries	45	37	10	7	1
Central question of politics is class	28	38	14	16	3
Workers should support secondary strikes	27	45	10	14	3
Trade unions have too much power in party	9	34	15	32	10
Trade unions should have little power	4	10	13	45	29
Labour should stick to principles	25	36	12	21	7
Labour leader too powerful	6	9	15	53	17
Labour support Poll Tax non-payers	21	21	14	32	12
Constituencies only select candidates	26	37	11	22	4
Labour resist further EC Integration	5	11	12	48	24
Conference block vote disreputable	23	49	12	13	4

TABLE 6.2. *Continued*

Indicator	Strongly Agree	Agree	Neither	Disagree	Strongly Disagree
Modern farming damages countryside	44	41	10	4	0
One-person/one-vote for leadership	37	44	7	9	3
Britain should have PR electoral system	21	37	11	21	10

Other indicators
Are you generally in favour of:

More nationalization of companies	71
Things left as they are now	27
More privatization	2
Britain should keep her own nuclear weapons	5
Britain should have nuclear weapons as part of Western defence	23
Britain should have nothing to do with nuclear weapons	72
Britain should continue as a member of the EC	89
Britain should withdraw from the EC	11
Government should create jobs even if this means more pollution	29
Government should cut jobs in order to reduce pollution	33
No opinion	38

and localism', factor members are relatively united in support of political principles and the right of local constituency parties to select parliamentary candidates. They are also relatively united in supporting further integration of the European Community, which is a fundamental change in the party compared with the 1970s (Whiteley, 1978). Finally, with regard to the last factor, majorities favour electoral reform both for choosing the leader of the party, and for general elections in Britain. They also agree that the trade-union block vote in the party conference tends to bring the party into disrepute.

Overall then, Labour party members do not hold completely unstructured beliefs, but nor do they divide solely on the basis of a left–right continuum in politics. Opinion differences within the party are more complicated than that, and centre on 'clusters' of issues relating to all the major debates in British politics about the role of the market, the environment and pollution, trade unions, and Labour party strategy.

In the next section we examine the correlates of these ideological variations in the party, in order to assess the influence of social background and other social characteristics on attitudes within the sample.

CORRELATES OF IDEOLOGICAL BELIEFS

A common stereotype is that left-wing party members are young, middle-class graduates, living in the south of England, who devote a good deal of their time to party activities. In contrast, those with more right-wing opinions are old, working-class individuals with minimal education, living in the north of England or Scotland, who do not attend party meetings either because they lack the time or have been driven away by the behaviour of the new left-wing activists. How accurate are these stereotypes? In this section we focus on the correlates of ideological variations within the party to see how valid these ideas are in practice. We begin by examining the first factor, the general left–right scale.

The left–right scale and social characteristics

We have seen that the self-assigned left–right scale for Britain has the highest correlation of any variable with the first factor in the analysis. Accordingly we can use this scale to represent the first factor in any examination of the socio-economic correlates of ideology. The distribution of members along the two left–right scales associated with factor one appear in Fig. 6.1.

It can be seen that the left–right scale applied to British politics is heavily skewed to the left, in comparison with the scale applied to the Labour party. This indicates that members broadly think of themselves as being to the left in British politics. The Labour party scale is also skewed to the left, but in this case the skewness is much less marked. For ease of interpretation, the nine-point British politics scale was recoded into five new categories: 'left', 'centre-left', 'centre', 'centre-right', and 'right'.[4] These categories contain approximately 42 per cent, 35 per cent, 11 per cent, 5 per cent, and 7 per cent of respondents respectively.

In Table 6.3 we examine the relationship between the British politics scale and various social-background characteristics. The

[4] In the recoded variable 'Left' refers to those coding themselves 1 or 2; 'Centre-left' 3 and 4; 'Centre' 5; 'Centre-right' 6 and 7; 'Right' 8 and 9.

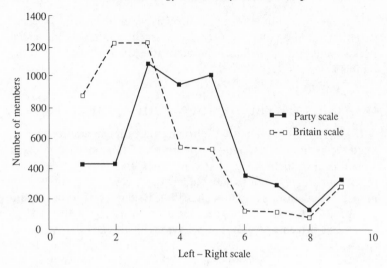

FIG. 6.1 The Left–Right ideology scales

table shows that as far as the age-variable is concerned, there is a clear tendency for young members to be on the left and old members to be on the right of the ideological spectrum. With respect to the left-wing category the important distinction appears to be between the young to middle-aged on the one hand and the middle-aged to old on the other. With regard to the right-wing category, the important distinction is between the retired members and the rest, since the former are significantly more likely to be on the right compared with the other members.

The relationship between ideology and class suggests that the middle-class members are significantly more likely to be on the left in comparison with the working-class members, who are quite likely to be on the right. The interesting distinction in the table is between the middle-class members and the others. Thus 50 per cent of the middle class are in the left-wing category, whereas the percentages of all the other occupational groups in the left-wing category are significantly lower than this figure. At the other end of the scale, some 7 per cent of respondents as a whole were in the right-wing category, but 13 per cent of the working class were in this category. Thus the working class are clearly more right-wing than the middle class.

TABLE 6.3. *Left–Right Placement by Social Characteristics* (percentages)

	Left	Centre-left	Centre	Centre-right	Right
All respondents	42	35	11	5	7
Age					
17–25	49	36	8	5	3
26–45	50	38	7	2	3
46–65	37	36	13	7	8
66+	33	28	15	7	17
Class					
Salariat	50	40	6	3	2
Routine non-manual	39	39	13	4	6
Petty bourgeoisie	39	37	9	8	7
Foreman and Technician	31	35	15	9	10
Working class	35	30	15	7	13
Gender					
Female	45	35	11	3	7
Male	40	36	10	6	8
Income					
Under £10,000	33	29	17	8	14
£10,000–£25,000	46	39	8	4	3
£25,000+	51	40	4	2	4
Graduate					
Yes	58	38	3	1	1
No	37	36	13	6	8

There is an interesting relationship between gender and the left–right scale, since it appears that female respondents are significantly more likely to be left-wing than male respondents. Some 40 per cent of males, and 45 per cent of females were in the left-wing category.

The relationship between income and ideology reinforces the conclusions derived from the class variable. It is clear that low-income respondents are much more likely to be right-wing, and much less likely to be left-wing than high-income respondents; this 'income' effect is fairly striking since 51 per cent of members with household incomes greater than £25,000 are in the left-wing category, compared with only 33 per cent of members with incomes under £10,000.

Finally in Table 6.3 there is the relationship between graduate

TABLE 6.4. *Left–Right Placement by Region* (percentages)

	Left	Centre-left	Centre	Centre-right	Right
Northern	36	32	16	7	9
Yorkshire	38	37	12	6	7
North-West	40	31	13	7	9
East Midlands	45	36	8	6	5
West Midlands	41	34	12	4	9
Eastern	41	39	10	4	7
Greater London	48	35	7	3	6
Southern	45	39	9	3	4
South-West	46	35	9	4	6
Wales	36	35	12	7	10
Scotland	42	36	9	4	9
All respondents	42	35	11	5	7

qualifications and ideology. This is probably the strongest relationship in the table, since graduates are very much more likely to be in the left-wing category than non-graduates. It is particularly noteworthy that non-graduates are eight times more likely to be in the right-wing category than graduates.

One interesting question is whether or not there are significant regional variations in ideology within the party. These could be due either to a local political culture, such as the 'hard leftism' associated with the London Labour party or with Merseyside. Alternatively it could be due to regional socio-economic differences, for example, if middle-class members are disproportionately located in the south of England and working-class members in the north, then this might translate into ideological variations within the party across the different regions of the country. This possibility is examined in Table 6.4 which examines the relationship between ideology and region of the country.

The results in Table 6.4 suggest that there is not much ideological variation across the Labour party regions, except possibly for the Northern region, Wales, and Greater London. The first two have a below-average percentage of members in the left-wing category, and the latter has an above-average percentage in this category. However, the relationships are not strong, and in addition there are no comparable deviations from the norm for these regions in the right-wing category, with the possible exception of Wales.

Since we have already shown that the left–right scale is highly correlated with the first factor, these findings will apply in varying degrees to the other issue indicators associated with factor one. Thus retired party members are likely to be on the right of the political spectrum on issues like nuclear disarmament, taxation, aid to the Third World, immigration, and environmental pollution. Overall, these results suggest that socio-economic characteristics of various types do help to explain ideological variations in the party of the type measured by factor one.

One important caveat to this conclusion is that the above tables examine only the bivariate relationships between attitudes and social backgrounds. These can be potentially misleading since they do not identify the influence of say, class on ideology independently of age, income, and the other social characteristics. In order to assess this question we carried out a regression analysis of the effect of class, age, income, graduate qualifications, gender, and region on the left–right scale. This showed that all of these variables had a statistically significant independent effect on ideology except region.[5] The strongest effect was due to age, followed by class, graduate qualifications, and income in that order. The weakest effect was due to gender. Overall, then it appears that attitudes to the range of issues summarized by factor one are influenced by various socio-economic characteristics, but are not influenced by geographical region of the country.

The class, ownership, and power factor

The second cluster of attitude indicators in the analysis centre around the questions of public ownership, trade-union rights, and perceptions of class politics. It is quite possible that the social characteristics of respondents could be related to these questions in a manner quite different from the left–right scale of factor one. This is because the two factors are quite independent of each other; a particular individual could be 'left-wing' on factor one, and 'right-wing' on this factor.

We examine the relationships between the class, ownership, and power factor, and socio-economic characteristics by taking a representative attitude indicator from this group of measures. The

[5] The different Labour party regions were incorporated into the analysis by means of dummy variables, excluding one region chosen arbitrarily to avoid statistical degeneracy.

TABLE 6.5. *Class, Ownership, and Power by Social Characteristics*
(percentages)
Question: Should privatized industries be returned to the public sector?

	Strongly agree/ agree	Neither	Strongly disagree/ disagree
All respondents	82	10	8
Age			
17–25	87	9	4
26–45	81	11	8
46–65	82	10	8
66+	82	10	8
Class			
Salariat	78	13	9
Routine non-manual	84	9	7
Petty bourgeoisie	81	14	5
Foreman and Technician	81	10	9
Working class	87	6	7
Gender			
Female	87	8	5
Male	77	12	10
Income			
Under £10,000	85	9	6
£10,000–£25,000	82	11	7
£25,000+	76	12	12
Graduate			
Yes	77	13	9
No	84	9	7

measure used has the highest correlation with the factor, a Likert-scaled item which stated: 'The public enterprises privatized by the Tory government should be returned to the public sector' (abbreviated in Table 6.1 to 'Renationalize privatized industry'). All of the social background measures in Table 6.5 proved to be statistically significant predictors of attitudes on this indicator in a multivariate analysis of the relationships.

The first point to make about the table is that a large majority of respondents in all social groups were in favour of nationalizing the industries privatized by the Conservative government. That aside, some interesting differences emerged in the table which contrast markedly with Table 6.4. It is fairly clear that young, low-income working-class members are more in favour of this policy, than old, high-income, middle-class members. Thus 78 per cent of the salariat support renationalization in comparison with 87 per cent of the working class. Similarly, 76 per cent of the high-income category support renationalization compared with 85 per cent of the low-income group. Interestingly enough females are more likely to agree with this policy than males, a similar result to that in Table 6.3. Finally, non-graduates are more likely to support this than graduates.

These results imply that since agreement with renationalization is a left-wing position, then on this issue the working class are clearly more left-wing than the middle class. This is of course in complete contrast with the issues associated with the left–right scale in Table 6.4. This further illustrates the heterogeneity of ideological beliefs within the party.

Given that the privatization–nationalization variable is highly correlated with factor two, we can infer that these findings also broadly apply to the other variables associated with this factor. Thus low-income working-class members are likely to be 'left-wing' on the question of the class struggle, secondary strike action, and the rights of trade unions.

THE POLITICAL PRINCIPLES AND LOCALISM FACTOR

In Table 6.6 we examine the relationship between various social characteristics and a key indicator in the 'political principles and localism' scale. Again, the indicator used has the highest correlation with that factor, an indicator of electoral pragmatism. Once again the results show that it is difficult to characterize Labour party ideology in terms of a single dimension which relates to all members. By journalistic conventional wisdom the left is the least pragmatic when it comes to electoral strategy, and the right is the most pragmatic among party members overall.

However, the results in Table 6.6 show that the 'leftist' middle-class members of Table 6.3 are significantly more pragmatic than the 'rightist' working-class members. Some 54 per cent of the salariat agree with the idea of sticking to principles regardless of the

TABLE 6.6. *Political Principles and Localism by Social Characteristics*
(percentages)
Question: Should Labour stick to principles even if this should lose an
election?

	Strongly agree/ agree	Neither	Strongly disagree/ disagree
All respondents	61	12	27
Age			
17–25	62	12	27
26–45	57	13	30
46–65	60	12	28
66+	70	9	21
Class			
Salariat	54	15	31
Routine non-manual	65	10	25
Petty bourgeoisie	60	8	32
Foreman and Technician	62	10	28
Working class	67	10	23
Gender			
Female	62	13	25
Male	60	11	29
Income			
Under £10,000	69	9	22
£10,000–£25,000	58	13	29
£25,000+	52	14	34
Graduate			
Yes	52	17	31
No	64	10	26

electoral consequences, in comparison with 67 per cent of the working class. In addition the young members are significantly more pragmatic than the old members, although in this case the real distinction appears to be between retired members who are very much against pragmatism, and the rest. The differences between graduates and non-graduates reinforce these conclusions. Graduates, who were very left-wing on the indicators associated with the first factor, are rather pragmatic with respect to this indicator.

Again, attitudes to the position of the Party Leader, the role of constituency parties in the selection of candidates, the Poll Tax, and European integration are all related to this factor, suggesting that a similar type of pattern of responses will exist for these measures. Thus middle-class members are less likely to believe that the leader is too powerful, that European integration should be resisted, and that the party should support non-payment of the Poll Tax.

The party democracy and electoral reform factor

The most highly correlated measure with factor four is the indicator of attitudes to the trade-union block vote. The results in Table 6.7 show that the middle-class high-income respondents are more likely to think that the block vote brings the party into disrepute than the working-class low-income respondents. In addition males are more likely to think this than females, and old respondents are more likely to think it than young respondents. Thus, if criticizing the trade-union block vote is a 'right-wing' position then the middle class are more right-wing than the working class.

In view of the correlation between other items and this factor, these results suggest that the middle-class members are more likely to support electoral reform, both for the election of the Party Leader and for Parliamentary elections in Britain, in comparison with working-class members.

Overall we can see that this exercise of 'mapping' ideological variations within the Labour party produces a heterogeneous set of results. It is fairly clear that all the major issues facing the Labour party and British politics do not fall into a single 'left–right' dimension, although it is also true to say that many important issues can be analysed in these terms. Indicators of environmental politics, nuclear disarmament, the role of the market in the economy, and aid to the Third World do group together into a left–right dimension quite well. However, nationalization, which is a traditional left–right issue in Labour party politics, is not significantly related to these other issues. The same could be said of the issues of electoral reform, party democracy, and electoral strategy.

One consequence of this heterogeneity is that middle-class members can be 'left-wing' on some issues and 'right-wing' on others, which indicates that the traditional journalistic concern to reduce Labour party politics to a battle of ideas between the left and the right, in which the social classes are type-cast in distinct

TABLE 6.7. *Party Democracy and Electoral Reform by Social Characteristics* (percentages)

Question: Does the trade-union block vote bring the party into disrepute?

	Strongly agree/ agree	Neither	Strongly disagree/ disagree
All respondents	71	12	17
Age			
17–25	55	24	21
26–45	64	15	21
46–65	78	9	13
66+	77	9	13
Class			
Salariat	73	13	14
Routine non-manual	65	16	19
Petty bourgeoisie	71	12	18
Foreman and Technician	76	6	18
Working class	70	9	21
Gender			
Female	66	16	18
Male	74	9	16
Income			
Under £10,000	71	10	19
£10,000–£25,000	70	13	17
£25,000+	74	14	13
Graduate			
Yes	72	14	14
No	70	12	18

ideological roles, is an over-simplification; who is left and who is right depends on the issue in question.

These results are interesting and raise the question as to why these variations in ideological beliefs exist. One key issue which stands out particularly is the question of class differences in attitudes; these are reflected in the relationships between attitudes, occupational status, income, and education. We consider this question next.

CLASS AND THE DETERMINANTS OF IDEOLOGICAL VARIATIONS

The various correlates of ideological variations discussed above throw important light on the question of why different members have different attitudes to the central issues in British politics. The relationship between ideology and social class in particular has been of interest to researchers ever since Parkin's pioneering work on 'middle-class' radicalism in the 1960s (1968). This touches on the debate concerning the hypothesized 'decline of working-class politics' within the Labour party, and the concomitant rise of middle-class politics (Hindess, 1971; Beackon, 1976; and Forrester, 1976).

We have observed interesting relationships between ideology and social class in the earlier tables, and these results parallel the relationships between class, membership, and activism discussed in Chapters 4 and 5. What could explain the patterns observed? Why should middle-class members tend to be relatively 'left-wing' on issues like the environment, nuclear weapons, and Labour party strategy, and relatively 'right-wing' on issues like nationalization and the role of trade unions?

We believe that the reason for this lies in the nature of the issues facing the Labour party in the 1990s in comparison with the issues which it faced earlier in this century. Essentially there are 'old' and 'new' left–right ideological issues (see Heath and Evans, 1988). The 'old' issues principally involve public ownership and the relationship between the party and the trade-union movement, and they go back to the early years of the Labour party. The 'new' issues are strongly related to the 'post-materialist' concerns discussed in Chapter 4; they concern environmental pollution, nuclear power, political participation, and democratic rights. To risk over-simplifying, the middle class tend to be left-wing on these 'new' issues, and right-wing on the 'old' issues. By contrast the working-class members tend to have the reverse priorities; they are right-wing on the 'new' issues and left-wing on the 'old' issues.

That public ownership is an 'old' issue can be seen by examining the early debates within the party about policy matters. The first comprehensive statement of Labour's socialist objectives appeared in *Labour and the New Social Order* written by Sidney Webb at the end of World War I (Labour Party, 1918). It was very influential and set the terms of the subsequent left–right debate within the party. In this document Webb set out four broad policy objectives; a national minimum income, democratic control of industry, reform of the tax system, and equality in education and social welfare (see Whiteley, 1983: 112–15).

Legislative action by subsequent Labour governments implemented many of the twenty-six resolutions passed at the 1918 Party Conference which translated these broad goals into specific policy objectives. Major gains have been made since that time on the issues of the minimum income, the reform of the tax system, and in the promotion of equality in society. These broad objectives are not controversial within the Labour party, although there are lively debates about the details of the implementation of these goals.

The one broad policy goal in the 1918 document which has clearly not been implemented effectively is the 'democratic control' of industry. For many people this is synonymous with nationalization, but the party has been very inconsistent over the years in the scope and nature of its plans for public ownership; some industries and services have appeared as candidates for nationalization in one election manifesto, only to be dropped in the next. Moreover, when the post-war Labour government did implement nationalization in certain key industries, it opted for the Morrisonian model of a public corporation, which by common consent has had little to do with the 'democratic control' of industry.

In addition, 'revisionist' writers like Anthony Crosland challenged the whole policy of public ownership. In his classic book, *The Future of Socialism* (1956), Crosland argued that the ownership and control of industry were two entirely different things, and that it was possible and desirable to control industry without state ownership. Thus public ownership is the archetypal 'old' left–right ideological issue within the Labour party, since it has been a controversial question from the beginning, and remains so today because the original policy goals are so far from being successfully achieved. A similar though lesser debate has taken place on the issue of the role of trade unions within the Labour party.

The common characteristic of the 'new' ideological issues is that they have become salient in British politics and within the Labour party only during the post-war years. Environmental pollution was not even discussed at that formative Party Conference of 1918, and for obvious reasons nuclear energy has only emerged onto the political agenda within the last twenty years.

These 'new' issues have post-materialist characteristics in many respects. As we pointed out in Chapter 4, the post-materialist thesis argues that relatively high-status individuals who have satisfied basic economic needs become concerned with values to do with self-esteem, self-expression, and intellectual satisfaction. As a consequence the middle class are preoccupied with post-materialist concerns in comparison with the working class. In this view attitude differences between the classes are a reflection of socio-economic differences.

However, there is a basic problem in describing 'old' issues as materialist, and 'new' issues as post-materialist. This is the fact that the 'old' issues of public ownership and trade-union rights are hard to characterize as being purely materialist questions. The original policy goal of the 'democratic control of industry' is, if anything, a post-materialist concern, since it is ultimately concerned with a desire for control over the impersonal forces of the market, and the power of corporate interests in society. Similarly our indicators of attitudes to trade unions are all about the power and influence of unions, rather than about their contribution to economic performance. Thus 'old' issues cannot easily be equated with materialist concerns, as distinct from the post-materialist 'new' issues.

A more promising explanation of the class differences in ideological beliefs is rooted in education, rather than in economic status. In this explanation, middle-class party members are likely to be more radical than working-class members on the 'new' issues, not because they have higher economic status, but because they have greater educational experience.

In their issue-evolution model Carmines and Stimson (1989) point out that political issues develop over time in a manner analogous to a Darwinian process of social evolution. With a multitude of potential issues vying for attention on the political agenda at any one time, those which survive and become really salient must address the real interests and concerns of a significant mass of the voters. In contrast, marginal issues are those which fail to address such concerns.

In the Carmines and Stimson model, political institutions, particularly parties and political leaders, as well as chance and contingency all play a role in explaining why issues rise and fall in saliency over time. Their discussion focuses principally on the long-running issue of race in American politics, and they were concerned to understand why it suddenly erupted on to the political agenda in the 1960s. In this view issue evolution is not a deterministic thing, but for issues to have the potential for surviving and growing they must be rooted in well established social or economic cleavages.

Given this, the 'new' issues of the type associated with factor one in Table 6.1, clearly do represent 'real' concerns to significant social groups. But these concerns are not necessarily class-based, since working-class people are as likely to be affected by environmental pollution or nuclear proliferation as middle-class people. Thus there is no reason to believe that the issues associated with factor one are of greater concern to the middle class than they are to the working class. But if we raise the question of who is likely to recognize the importance of newly emergent issues first, the answer is that highly educated individuals are more likely to do so than uneducated individuals. Thus in the process of issue evolution it takes time for newly emergent issues to get on to the agenda, and those individuals in society who have the conceptual framework to understand and see the significance of these new issues are likely to be the educated members of society. Such individuals will have more information about politics and society in general, and as a consequence will form more coherent judgements about what the issues mean and how they should be understood, in comparison with uneducated individuals.

Of course, this analysis says nothing about whether or not the educated will be more 'left-wing' or 'right-wing' in their response to newly emergent issues. But we can infer that if they have a predisposition for radical politics, which is true of Labour party members in general, then they will be more likely to take a radical stance on such issues.

Thus the explanation of why middle-class members are more radical than working-class members on some issues and less radical on others is rooted in education and in the evolution of issues over time. Radically disposed individuals who are educated will take up left-wing positions on newly emergent issues more rapidly than radically disposed individuals who are not educated. The educated have the conceptual framework and cognitive schemas for understanding and analysing these new issues.

Thus our explanation for the observed differences between middle-class and working-class respondents on the 'new' issues is based on cognitive and intellectual processes, not on basic conflicts of socio-economic interests between these groups. In this interpretation the close relationship between class and educational status explains much of the class differences we observe in attitudes. Middle-class members are generally more highly educated than working-class members, and education is the principal determinant of attitudes, rather than economic status.

Turning to the items in factor two, the 'old' political issues of nationalization and trade-union rights; as mentioned earlier these have been discussed within the party for most of the twentieth century. An 'old' issue does not require a sophisticated conceptual schema for it to be understood, since party members know what the debates are, and can well understand left and right positions on them because these have been staked out and argued since the time the party was founded.

Differences between middle-class and working-class members are smaller with respect to the 'class, ownership, and power' factor than with respect to the 'left–right' dimension of factor one. But once again the evolution of issues can explain why working-class members are more left-wing on the issues of nationalization and trade-union rights, than the middle-class members. This question is tied to the strategy of modernization of the party raised earlier and discussed more fully in Chapter 7.

The modernization strategy has by common consent been largely motivated by considerations of electoral pragmatism. As is widely recognized the strategy plays down the importance of nationalization as a policy goal, largely because the issue is politically unpopular among voters. In response to a question in the British Election Study of 1987, only 17 per cent of voters favoured more nationalization. In contrast, some 32 per cent favoured more privatization, and 49 per cent favoured the status quo.[6] Thus by any standards nationalization is not a popular policy. This is a relatively new development in British politics, since as recently as the October 1974 election significantly higher percentages of voters favoured nationalization over privatization (Heath *et al.*, 1991: 176).

We have seen that Labour party members support public

---

[6] Among Labour voters 37% favoured more nationalization, 6% favoured more privatization, and 55% favoured the status quo. Considering that these answers followed a period during which the Thatcher government actively reduced the public sector by privatizing industries, this marked preference for the status quo among Labour voters underlines how much of an electoral liability traditional nationalization has become.

ownership by big margins, but in so far as electoral pragmatism has influenced the attitudes of Labour's grass roots, it is likely to have influenced the educated members first, since they are the ones who are more able to see the link between party policies and electoral support. This is confirmed in Table 6.6, where 52 per cent of graduates opposed electoral pragmatism, when it was framed in terms of 'sticking to principles', in comparison with 64 per cent of non-graduates.[7] Thus when electoral pragmatism is seen to be in direct conflict with political principles majorities of all members oppose it, but significantly, the middle-class graduates are much less likely to oppose it than working-class non-graduates.

Thus the argument is that if the educated members are more responsive to newly emergent issues, then it is likely that they will be the first to recognize the fact that nationalization has become an electoral liability in recent years, and if they are interested in electoral success they will recognize that the party has an incentive to rethink it. In general, our argument is that educated members react to newly-emergent issues more quickly and more pragmatically than uneducated members, producing apparent class differences which actually reflect cognitive processes rather than economic differences.

This idea can of course be tested with data from the survey. If it is true, then education should override the influence of class as an explanation of the observed attitudinal differences. In other words, if educational differences explain these patterns, then class differences of the type we have observed should disappear or be reduced in significance, once we have controlled for the influence of education.

In Table 6.8 we examine the relationship between the left–right scale for Britain and social class, controlling for educational qualifications. The 'control' for education is achieved by selecting out two groups of respondents from the survey, and examining the relationship between class and ideology within these groups. The first group consists of respondents who reported that they had obtained no educational qualifications at all, and the second group is the respondents who reported that they obtained graduate qualifications from a university or polytechnic. Since there are no significant variations in education within these two groups, and if education

---

[7] Of course there need not be any conflict between electoral pragmatism and sticking to principles, but the wording of this indicator is designed to elicit reactions to this possibility among the party members.

TABLE 6.8. *Ideology and Social Class by Educational Qualifications*
(percentages)

	Left	Centre-left	Centre	Centre-right	Right	N
ALL RESPONDENTS	42	35	11	5	7	4974
No qualifications						
Salariat	31	34	17	12	6	174
Routine non-manual	31	33	21	6	9	207
Petty bourgeoisie	25	44	15	6	11	48
Foreman and Technician	17	36	16	15	15	105
Working class	32	27	18	7	15	618
ALL UNQUALIFIED RESPONDENTS	30	31	18	9	13	1152
Graduate qualifications						
Salariat	58	8	3	1	1	1121
Routine non-manual	54	44	1	0	1	102
Petty bourgeoisie	53	36	3	3	6	37
Foreman and Technician	49	16	16	0	19	7
Working class	63	29	2	3	3	44
ALL GRADUATE RESPONDENTS	58	38	3	19	1	1311

explains ideological differences, then middle-class respondents
should have the same ideological profiles as working-class respondents within each of the two tables. In other words by eliminat-
ing differences in education, this should eliminate or reduce ideological differences between the classes if education is primarily
responsible for such ideological differences in the first place.

The results in this table support the theoretical argument. To
examine the 'no qualifications' group first, it can be seen that no
significant differences exist between the middle-class and working-
class respondents in their representation in the left-wing category.
Thus when educational differences between the classes are removed,
the ideological differences observed in Table 6.3 disappear, at least
with respect to the left-wing category. It is true that differences
between the salariat and the working class still exist in the right-
wing category, but they are much less marked than those observed in
Table 6.3.

TABLE 6.9. *Attitudes to Public Ownership by Social Class and Educational Qualifications* (percentages)

Question: Should privatized industries be returned to the public sector?

	Strongly agree	Agree	Neither	Disagree	Strongly disagree	N
ALL RESPONDENTS	45	37	10	7	1	4970
No qualifications						
Salariat	46	33	12	7	2	172
Routine non-manual	48	36	6	8	2	204
Petty bourgeoisie	52	28	14	4	2	48
Foreman and Technician	46	33	10	10	1	105
Working class	56	33	4	6	1	621
ALL UNQUALIFIED RESPONDENTS	52	34	7	7	1	1149
Graduate qualifications						
Salariat	34	43	13	9	1	1110
Routine non-manual	43	39	14	5	0	102
Petty bourgeoisie	40	39	16	5	0	37
Foreman and Technician	67	16	16	0	0	7
Working class	36	45	11	8	0	43
ALL GRADUATE RESPONDENTS	35	42	13	8	1	1298

The relationships within the graduate group further support the hypothesis. Interestingly enough for graduates the working class are slightly more left-wing than the middle class, although the results for the former have to be interpreted with care since they are based on only forty-four cases. However, that aside, these findings support the inference that educational differences explain ideological differences among the party members.

In Table 6.9 we examine the relationship between attitudes to nationalization and social class, again controlling for education. It can be seen that among graduates in this table there again there is no significant difference between middle-class and working-class respondents on the issue of renationalizing privatized industries. Once again, apparent class differences are really educational differences. However among the group with no qualifications at all, class differences in responses to this question persist, which suggests that class plays a residual role in moulding attitudes for this group. This latter finding is consistent with the proposition that class differences arising from social processes are more likely to be important for uneducated members of the party in comparison with educated members, at least for this particular issue. Middle-class party members operate in a social milieu in which hostility to nationalization is considerably greater than for working-class members. In the 1987 British Election Study only 12 per cent of the salariat favoured more nationalization, and no less than 42 per cent of them favoured more privatization; for the working-class voters the comparable figures were 23 per cent and 22 per cent respectively.

Thus the social milieu of the party members has an important influence on their attitudes, in situations where a lack of education inhibits the development of a conceptual framework for interpreting and understanding issues. Moreover, this is particularly true for the issue of nationalization, which unlike the environmental concerns associated with factor one, is almost uniformly disliked by middle-class voters. Again, the reason for this class effect is not economic in character, as the post-materialist model would argue, but a product of the tendency for individuals to conform to the opinions of groups to which they belong.

It is important not to overstate this argument; the evidence indicates that clear majorities of the middle class are 'left-wing' on the issue of public ownership, and they oppose electoral pragmatism when it is framed in terms of abandoning principles, but nevertheless they do differ from the working class to a marked extent. In the long run the evolution of these issues over time may produce a situation where middle-class and working-class party members become less supportive of nationalization, if it remains very unpopular among the voters. This is particularly likely if the modernization strategy delivers electoral success. But only time will tell if this will actually happen.

In this chapter we have focused on the attitudes of party members to the major and some of the minor issues in British politics. In the next chapter we examine their attitudes to the Labour party, its leadership, and its place within the wider British political system.

7

Images of Party and Society

The analysis in Chapter 6 focused on most of the major, and some minor issues, which have been debated in British politics over the years. The discussion suggested that education plays an important role in influencing the responses of individual party members to new issues which arise on the political agenda. We also suggested that the electoral pragmatism which is one important aspect of the modernization strategy associated with Neil Kinnock's leadership, may have influenced perceptions of issues, particularly attitudes to nationalization among the educated members of the party.

The modernization strategy is a key issue facing the contemporary Labour party, so that the principal focus of this chapter is to examine the attitudes of party members to the strategy in the light of their perceptions of the nature and character of the Labour party. Electoral pragmatism about issues such as nationalization is an important aspect of the modernization strategy, but it goes beyond just rethinking the policy positions which the party takes up on any particular issue. It is also about changing the internal organization of the party by, for example, reducing the importance of the trade-union block vote at the party conference, and 'empowering' party members, with the aim of encouraging them to be more active.

The analysis in this chapter begins by examining the members' images of the party, or their beliefs about what the Labour party stands for and who it seeks to represent. An important component of this is the members' evaluation of the Labour leadership, including members of the front-bench team as well as Neil Kinnock.

This leads into a discussion of members' perceptions of the modernization strategy, focusing particularly on the differences between 'traditionalists', or opponents of the strategy and 'modernizers', the supporters of the strategy. We examine the social and political characteristics of the members in these two different groups, in order to throw light on the nature of the political divisions in the party over modernization.

In a third section we seek to develop a model to explain differences between 'modernizers' and 'traditionalists', and this turns out to be principally a function of ideological differences among the members.

Finally, we examine the attitudes of members to the other political parties and political institutions in Britain, addressing particularly the views of the membership about possible coalition partners in the future, and also the extent to which they can be characterized as deferential towards the institutions of the British state.

IMAGES OF THE LABOUR PARTY

What kind of party do the members think that the Labour party is? And in the light of this, is it possible to distinguish between reformers, who go along with the modernization strategy, and traditionalists who oppose it?

As we suggested earlier, party members are often discussed in contrary ways in the literature on the Labour party. Sometimes they are regarded as the reserve army of dedicated loyalists, who though inclined to grumble, usually rally around their party and leader, giving undeviating support and loyalty. At other times, they are seen as an 'awkward squad' who often embarrass the party and its leaders by making untimely and unappealing demands which undermine party unity.

The first interpretation refers to party members' record of loyalty and deference to their leaders, and suggests this is due, first, to a dominant trade-union value system of unity and solidarity and, secondly, to a working-class deference towards social superiors (Drucker, 1979). The second interpretation refers to numerous intraparty conflicts and suggests that members are assertive and questioning because they joined the party with distinct political opinions to express; also they are seen by nature to be rebels who inherently distrust authority since it is part of the 'establishment' that they are seeking to change.[1] This makes them aware of the corrupting nature of power, and they tend to distrust leaders who they are inclined to think will often 'sell out'. The spectre of Ramsay MacDonald still haunts the party.

---

[1] Dick Crossman is a good example of such rebelliousness. In his diaries he states 'my radical passions have never been based on a moral or egalitarian philosophy. It's been really an expression of my bump of irreverence, based on my conviction that governments and establishments are fools' (Crossman, 1976: 190).

Are the members loyalists or rebels? There is evidence over the past ninety years' history of the Labour party to sustain both interpretations. Now, however, we can examine the current attitudes of party members and discover to what extent they are loyalists or an 'awkward squad', and in more general terms how they see the role of the party in contemporary British society.

There are three important aspects of members' perceptions of the party. First, there are the members' general impressions of the image of the party in society. This concerns issues like the extent to which they think it is modern as opposed to old-fashioned, whether it is efficiently or badly run, and whether it is united or divided. To evaluate this we have taken some indicators from the British Election Study to facilitate comparisons between the members and Labour voters.

A second important aspect of perceptions of the party is the evaluations of the leadership. In earlier references to the party leadership, the focus has been almost exclusively on Neil Kinnock, but it is important to know what the members think of other prominent Labour parliamentarians, who make up the collective leadership. As a consequence we examine members' evaluations of some twelve prominent Labour politicians, as well as their evaluations of Neil Kinnock.

Finally, a third aspect of perceptions of the party focuses on the individuals and groups the party seeks to represent. To examine this we include a set of questions which asked members to assess the extent to which they perceive that the party looks after the interests of different social groups. To facilitate the analysis, a comparison is made with their perceptions of the role of the Conservative party in representing those groups.

When asked to score the Labour party on a thermometer scale from 0 to 100, members give it a high ranking with a mean score of 84.[2] This is the E_i index referred to in Chapter 5. No other institution or personality mentioned in the thermometer-scale questions gets a score as high as this, suggesting a considerable degree of warmth and support for the party among the members.

Table 7.1 contains the responses of members to a set of questions which asked them about the image of the Labour party. Some of these image questions were also asked in the British Election Study,

---

[2] The preamble to the thermometer scale questions can be seen in Appendix II.

TABLE 7.1. *Members' and Labour Voters' Attitudes to the Party* (percentages)

Those who think the party is very or fairly:	Members[a]	Labour voters[b]
Caring	81	94
Likely to unite nation	63	73
Moderate	54	71
United	56	43
Efficiently run	62	—
Modern	54	—
Left-wing	27	—
Uncaring	11	3
Likely to divide the nation	11	24
Extreme	6	22
Divided	27	51
Badly run	22	—
Old-fashioned	15	—
Right-wing	27	—
the party is neither:		
Caring nor uncaring	9	3
Likely to unite or divide nation	27	3
Moderate nor extreme	41	7
United nor divided	17	6
Efficiently nor badly run	16	—
Modern nor old-fashioned	31	—
Left-wing nor right-wing	47	—

[a] 1989 Members' survey
[b] 1987 British Election Study

and so it is possible to compare the responses of members as well as voters on these items.

It can be seen from Table 7.1 that Labour's strongest characteristic is that it is seen as a caring party. Interestingly enough, Labour voters are more likely to see the party in these terms than the party members. Very few members or voters see it as uncaring. Again, when comparing Labour voters and party members, the former are more likely to see the party as moderate and able to unite the nation than the latter, although majorities in both surveys see the party in these terms.

The one outstanding distinction between Labour voters and party members in the table relates to perceptions of party unity; whereas

TABLE 7.2. *Members' Perceptions of Labour Party Meeting Attended in Previous Year* (percentages)

Members who thought meeting was very or fairly:

Interesting	71
Friendly	73
Efficiently run	70
United	60
Easy to understand	77
Working class	40
Left-wing	35
Old-fashioned	29
Boring	20
Unfriendly	15
Badly run	19
Divided	26
Hard to understand	11
Middle class	33
Right-wing	20
Modern	38
neither:	
Interesting nor boring	9
Friendly nor unfriendly	12
Efficiently nor badly run	11
United nor divided	14
Easy nor hard to understand	12
Working nor middle class	27
Left- nor right-wing	45
Old-fashioned nor modern	34

Note: Approximately 58 per cent of members responded to this set of questions.

one-quarter of members see the party as divided, this rises to one half of Labour voters. As always, we have to qualify this finding by pointing out that the election study was conducted some two and a half years before the membership survey. But it seems reasonable to conclude that the party may still suffer to some extent from the image of being divided, an image it acquired in the early 1980s after all the internecine conflicts of that period.

With regard to other aspects of the party's image it is seen by the members to be efficiently run, moderate, and modern. However, some 22 per cent of party members see it as badly-run, and about 15 per cent see it as old-fashioned. In the context of this particular question we cannot probe further to examine what they mean by this, but the findings suggest that the modernization strategy of recent years is responding in part to a perception among some members that the party needs to be reorganized and brought up to date.

The results in Table 7.1 are interesting, but it is hard to know the origins of these images of the party, whether they derive from personal experience or from other sources such as the media. To avoid this problem, members were asked to give their impressions of the party obtained from direct personal experience. Members were asked to comment on their impressions of the most recent party meeting they had attended within the last year. Approximately 58 per cent of members replied to this question, indicating that only a minority of respondents had not attended a meeting within this period, and thus felt unable to comment on it.

The feelings among members about the last party meeting they had attended were very similar to their general impressions of the party set out in Table 7.1, with the exception of their views on the party's old-fashioned image. A majority of respondents regarded the party meeting as something which was interesting, friendly, efficiently run, and easy to understand. However, between one-fifth and one-quarter regarded the meeting as being divided, boring, and badly run. Almost one-third felt that the meeting was 'old-fashioned', double the proportion of those commenting on the party in general, perhaps suggesting that the standard Labour party meeting with its set-piece agenda and long-winded discussion is felt to be out of touch with modern conditions. In addition, the respondents who felt that the meeting was left-wing outnumbered the respondents who felt it was right-wing by almost two to one.

Overall, these results indicate that the members have a generally favourable impression of the way the party conducts its business, and that with the exception of the image of the party being 'old-fashioned', they are favourably impressed by direct personal contact with the party.

Turning next to the second aspect of the image of the party, concerning impressions of the party leaders, we asked a number of detailed questions about attitudes to Neil Kinnock as well as other members of the front-bench team. As regards images of Neil Kinnock, again it was possible to compare the attitudes of party members with those of Labour voters taken from the British Election Study, and the results of this appear in Table 7.3.

TABLE 7.3. *Members' and Voters' Images of Neil Kinnock* (percentages)

Those who think he is very or fairly:	Members[a]	Labour voters[b]
Caring	87	96
Likely to unite nation	64	79
Moderate	63	79
Strong leader	75	86
Likeable	86	93
Good at getting things done	79	84
Uncaring	5	1
Likely to divide nation	9	19
Extreme	7	20
Weak leader	15	1
Not likeable	7	6
Bad at getting things done	7	11
he is neither:		
Caring nor uncaring	8	3
Likely to divide or unite nation	27	3
Moderate nor extreme	30	2
Strong nor weak leader	10	13
Likeable nor unlikeable	8	1
Good nor bad at getting things done	14	5

[a] 1989 Members' survey
[b] 1987 British Election Study

Neil Kinnock has played a very prominent role in the party's renewal since 1983, and has made his views concerning policy reformulation and party reorganization clear and in such a manner as to arouse opposition among party members. Yet members remain strongly supportive and appear well satisfied with his leadership. Neil Kinnock has his critics but they are few. Those that do criticize him are among his old allies on the party's left. Kinnock's political roots are within the Labour left. He was a persistent left-wing critic of the Labour governments between 1974 and 1979, and was closely associated at the time with the *Tribune* newspaper and the Tribune Group in the PLP.

In the early 1980s, however, the Labour left fragmented and Kinnock's refusal to vote for Tony Benn in the 1981 deputy-leadership election distanced him from the 'hard' left. Since becoming Party Leader in 1983 his actions have distanced him further from his previous left-wing allies. As a consequence Kinnock's

TABLE 7.4. *Mean Popularity Scores and Saliency Measures for Senior Labour Personnel*

	Mean Score out of 100	Saliency*
Neil Kinnock	73	99
John Smith	73	84
David Blunkett	71	84
Gordon Brown	70	73
Robin Cook	69	87
Harriet Harman	67	78
John Prescott	66	86
Joan Ruddock	64	80
Dennis Skinner	63	86
Bryan Gould	63	89
Roy Hattersley	60	96
Tony Benn	59	96
Ken Livingstone	55	94

* Percentage of members responding, when asked to leave a score blank if they felt that they knew little about the person.

support today is drawn much more from the party's centre and right.

The results in Table 7.3 show that Neil Kinnock has a very favourable image both among party members and among voters. By large majorities both groups think he is 'caring', 'moderate', 'capable of being a strong leader', 'likeable', and 'good at getting things done'. Only one per cent of voters thought he was a weak leader, in comparison with 15 per cent of members. In complete contrast, some 20 per cent of voters thought he was 'extreme' in comparison with 7 per cent of members. Less than one party member or voter in ten regard him as 'not likeable as a person'. These results show that he has a fund of goodwill to draw on both within the party and among Labour voters.

However, members are not without criticism of the Labour leadership overall. This can be detected in response to a Likert-scaled proposition which stated 'The party leadership doesn't pay a lot of attention to the views of ordinary party members'. Some 40 per cent of members agreed or strongly agreed with this statement.

To assess opinions about other members of Labour's front-bench team, we asked members to score individuals using the thermometer scales referred to earlier. In addition, to get some idea of how salient a particular individual was in the mind of party members, we urged them not to score individuals 'if you feel you don't know enough about that person to rate them'.

The mean thermometer scores, together with the saliency measure for twelve prominent Labour party parliamentarians appear in Table 7.4. The lowest saliency score, for Gordon Brown, indicated that at least 73 per cent of the members felt able to score these individuals. So they are all fairly salient in the minds of party members. In view of the results in Table 7.3 the highest thermometer score was, not surprisingly, for Neil Kinnock. Interestingly enough, John Smith obtained the same mean score, which suggests that his formidable performances in the House of Commons, together with the favourable publicity this generates clearly influences the opinions of Labour party members. When asked to score their feelings towards all of the senior figures in the parliamentary party, members rate the younger personnel in the centre or 'soft' left higher than the older, more established figures and those on the 'hard' left.

Further analysis of these thermometer scores produced a surprising and intriguing finding; members essentially perceive that two Labour parties exist, in that they judge some prominent Labour politicians using different criteria from others. They judge members of the centre-left, centre and, right using the same criteria as they use to judge the Labour party itself, although as we saw above no individual receives a higher average score than the party as a whole. By contrast they judge members of the 'hard' left with different criteria, almost as though they perceive them to be in a different party. The evidence supporting this point appears in Table 7.5.

Table 7.5 shows the results of a factor analysis of the relationships between the thermometer scores for the prominent Labour party politicians. It can be interpreted in a similar way to Table 6.1. The analysis shows that there are two independent dimensions of evaluation for the individual politicians in the table. The first scale or dimension is labelled the 'mainstream' party, and includes all the leading front-bench politicians like Neil Kinnock, Roy Hattersley, and others. The evaluation for the Labour party also appears on this dimension. This means that an individual member who feels very warm and sympathetic towards the Labour party will also feel the same about the ten politicians associated with this scale.

The second dimension is termed the 'hard-left' party since it is associated with evaluations of three people: Dennis Skinner, Tony Benn, and Ken Livingstone, who are all linked with this wing of the

TABLE 7.5. *Members' Evaluations of 'Two' Labour Parties*
(correlation × 100)

	Mainstream party	Hard-left party
Labour Party	63	
Neil Kinnock	82	
Roy Hattersley	78	
John Smith	81	
Bryan Gould	82	
Harriet Harman	61	
David Blunkett	72	
Gordon Brown	69	
John Prescott	64	
Joan Ruddock	60	
Robin Cook	83	
Dennis Skinner		85
Tony Benn		84
Ken Livingstone		81
Variance explained (R^2)	46	19

party. These two dimensions are independent or uncorrelated, thus a 'typical' party member who is warm and sympathetic towards the mainstream party leaders, could equally be cold and unsympathetic, or warm and sympathetic towards these 'hard-left' politicians. In effect they are judged independently of members of the mainstream party as though they were members of a separate organization.

The reason for this is perhaps because there are two distinct Labour parties, personified by the personalities of Neil Kinnock on the one hand and Tony Benn on the other. The mainstream party exemplified by Kinnock is concerned to adapt party policies in order to win electoral support, to place considerable emphasis upon the party's media image, to distance the party from the trade unions, and to limit the powers of the party activists; the other, exemplified by Benn, is concerned to assert the party's distinct political ideals even though they may be electorally unpopular, to emphasize the party's links with the trade unions, to spend little effort or resources on developing a favourable media image, and to reward party activism with extended powers.

Given this, it is interesting to compare and contrast the social and political characteristics of individuals who rate Kinnock highly with those who rate Benn highly. This is done in Tables 7.6 and 7.7,

Images of Party and Society

TABLE 7.6. *Attitudes to Neil Kinnock by Social and Political Characteristics* (percentages)

	Cold	Cool	Warm	Hot
All respondents	4	12	35	50
Age				
17–25	7	13	40	40
26–45	6	15	38	41
46–65	3	10	32	55
66+	1	7	27	65
Class				
Salariat	4	14	40	42
Routine non-manual	5	11	35	49
Petty bourgeoisie	2	15	31	53
Foreman and Technician	2	9	25	64
Working class	4	9	26	61
Gender				
Female	4	14	36	46
Male	4	10	33	53
Income				
Under £10,000	3	10	27	60
£10,000–£25,000	5	13	37	46
£25,000+	4	13	41	43
Graduate				
Yes	6	16	43	35
No	3	10	31	56
Activism				
Inactive	2	11	31	55
Occasionally active	3	11	37	49
Fairly active	4	13	34	49
Very active	6	12	33	50
Ideology in party				
Hard left	14	23	32	31
Soft left	3	13	39	46
Centre	2	6	28	64
Soft right	1	5	37	58
Hard right	0	7	26	67

TABLE 7.7. *Attitudes to Tony Benn by Social and Political Characteristics* (percentages)

	Cold	Cool	Warm	Hot
All respondents	12	25	36	27
Age				
17–25	8	21	44	27
26–45	8	23	38	31
46–65	15	27	35	24
66+	17	29	29	25
Class				
Salariat	10	24	38	27
Routine non-manual	12	25	34	29
Petty bourgeoisie	9	19	40	33
Foreman and Technician	15	36	28	21
Working class	12	26	34	28
Gender				
Female	10	26	35	30
Male	13	25	36	26
Income				
Under £10,000	15	27	31	27
£10,000–£25,000	10	24	37	29
£25,000+	10	26	39	25
Graduate				
Yes	8	23	41	28
No	13	26	33	28
Activism				
Inactive	16	29	34	22
Occasionally active	10	26	37	27
Fairly active	12	23	37	28
Very active	12	25	32	30
Ideology in party				
Hard left	3	7	31	59
Soft left	6	22	42	30
Centre	18	35	35	12
Soft right	22	41	27	11
Hard right	28	37	26	10

where the thermometer scores for the two leaders have been recoded for ease of comparison.[3]

Table 7.6 indicates that while few are cool or cold towards Neil Kinnock, his support is drawn disproportionately from the old and, in particular, from the retired members, whereas Benn is rather disliked by this group. Benn has more of his support among the middle-aged group, in the generation educated in the 1960s and 1970s, who provided him with a good deal of the support for his bid for power in the party in the late 1970s. However, it is important not to overstate this since 32 per cent of this generation, i.e. the 26–45 year-olds, are 'cool' or 'cold' towards Benn, in comparison with 21 per cent who feel this way about Kinnock.

We might have expected that Kinnock would draw working-class and Benn middle-class support among the members. In fact, Kinnock's support is very strong among manual workers but also among the middle-class professionals. Interestingly enough, Benn's strongest support comes from the petty bourgeoisie, or the self-employed. But even among them, he is less popular than Kinnock. The poorest members and the non-graduates score Kinnock higher than average, and the richer members are inclined to give Benn above average support. Kinnock's support is stronger among men than women, the reverse being true for Benn.

Using the left–right ideology scale applied to the Labour party, Benn clearly outscores Kinnock in warmth of feeling on the thermometer scale among the 17 per cent of the 'hard left' on this scale. For all other ideological categories on this scale, however, Kinnock outscores Benn, and in the case of the 'centre' and 'centre-right' categories, by very large margins.

Finally, Kinnock is disproportionately likely to get support from the inactive as compared with the active, whereas the opposite is true for Benn. But once again it is important to note that more of the very active party members are 'cool' or 'cold' in their feelings towards Benn, than feel this way about Kinnock.

Overall, we can see that among Labour's traditional constituency of supporters, namely manual workers on low incomes with few educational qualifications, there is greater support for Kinnock and his new model Labour party than among other types of members. In the case of the middle-class members on high incomes with higher

---

[3] Scores from 0 to 25 are described as 'cold'; from 26 to 50 as 'cool'; 51 to 75 as 'warm'; and 76 to 100 as 'hot'.

educational qualifications there is rather more restrained support for Kinnock and his party.

Overwhelmingly members are loyalists; they are loyal to their leader and their general impressions of the party are complimentary. The 'awkward squad' is a very small proportion of the membership. Nevertheless, it is a very distinct group which displays the features of 'a party within the party'.

Before leaving the discussion of the party leadership there is one more issue to explore. At the time of writing Neil Kinnock is well established as Party Leader, nevertheless it is interesting to see who the members would like to see as his successor. We asked members to say who they would like to see elected party leader if Kinnock resigned. The strongest support was for John Smith; one-third opt for him and only three other individuals (Tony Benn, Gordon Brown, and Roy Hattersley) won the support of at least one in ten of the members. Runners-up were Bryan Gould (9 per cent), and John Prescott (4 per cent). Finally there was one vote for Glenys Kinnock!

One of the issues of dispute within the Labour party since the 1980s has been its sensitivity to the needs of specific groups in society such as women, blacks, and homosexuals. Many left-wing urban local authorities made distinctive efforts in the 1980s to advance the interests of such groups. Members were asked to assess how closely they thought the party looked after the interests of a wide range of groups in society. Their responses to these questions appear in Table 7.8.

Table 7.8 also includes members' responses to questions about the extent to which they felt the Conservative party looked after the interests of the same groups. These responses are included in this table for purposes of comparison. Members felt that the Labour party looks after the interests of the trade unions, the working class, the middle class, and the unemployed, but that it cares rather less for the interests of women, blacks, and homosexuals. In sharp contrast, members felt that the Conservative party looks almost exclusively after the interests of big business, and to a lesser extent, the middle class. Clearly, party members have a strong idea of the difference between the Labour party, and the Conservatives in this respect.

This chapter began with the assertion that the modernization strategy is the most important issue facing the contemporary Labour party. The contemporary party has changed significantly from the strife-torn party of the late 1970s and early 1980s. Today's 'new model' Labour party is one which has adapted its policies so that

TABLE 7.8. *Perceptions of party's Concern for the interests of Specific Groups*
(percentages)

Groups	Labour party		Conservative party	
	Close	Not close	Close	Not close
Working class	89	11	3	97
Middle class	83	17	76	24
Unemployed	82	18	1	99
Big business	39	61	99	1
Trade unions	90	10	2	98
Women	68	32	14	86
Blacks	67	33	7	83
Homosexuals	54	46	8	92

they are in closer accord with public preferences, and reformed its
internal party structures to give individual members a more direct
role in the party's affairs. The modernization strategy has allowed
the party leadership more influence in the selection of parliamentary candidates for by-elections, and it seeks to limit the voting
power of trade unions, and to reduce the policy-making powers of
the annual party conference.

This raises the interesting question of what the members think
about all these developments. Obviously, not all members approve
of these changes. We can distinguish between the 'modernizers',
namely those broadly in favour of the electoral strategy and the
structural changes introduced since 1983, and the 'traditionalists',
namely those opposed to this strategy and these changes. In the next
section we consider the distribution of opinions on the issues connected with the modernization strategy.

ATTITUDES TO THE 'MODERNIZATION STRATEGY'

There were a number of questions in the survey of Labour party
members which touched on the issue of party modernization. We
have already referred to one of them, the indicator of electoral
pragmatism examined in Chapter 6. Following the same approach
as in earlier chapters, we utilize several broad indicators of attitudes
to the reform of the party, which can be used to measure attitudes to
modernization in a single overall scale. A factor analysis revealed

that five Likert-scaled indicators relating to the question of modernization formed a single underlying dimension,[4] which can be interpreted as an 'attitudes to modernization' scale. The distribution of opinions on these items appear in Table 7.9.

The two themes which permeate these indicators of the modernization scale are, firstly, the conflict between principles and pragmatism and, secondly, the role of the party leader in initiating and promoting political change. A majority of members believe that 'the Labour party should adjust policies to capture the middle ground of politics'; that 'the party should always stand by its principles even if this should lose it an election'; and that 'the trade-union block vote at conference brings the party into disrepute'. But there were no majorities for the view that 'the Labour Party Leader is too powerful', and that 'the party leadership doesn't pay a lot of attention to the views of ordinary party members'. Responses to these questions were aggregated into an overall scale, and this was in turn recoded into three categories. Respondents were classified on this scale as 'traditionalists', 'intermediates', or 'modernizers'.[5]

In Table 7.10 we examine some of the social-background correlates of the traditionalism–modernization scale. Some 18 per cent of respondents fell into the 'traditionalists' category, 43 per cent into the 'intermediates' category, and 38 per cent into the 'modernizers' category. It can be seen that the modernizers are more likely to be older members whereas the traditionalists are younger members, especially those under the age of 25. The youngest group are almost twice as likely to be traditionalists as the retired group.

Class differences between traditionalists and modernizers are not significant with one exception; the foreman and technician group is more likely to be on the modernizing wing of the party. The lack of any difference on this scale between the members of the salariat and

[4] A factor analysis of the five items produced one significant factor, with an eigenvalue of 2.07 which explained 43% of the variance in the data. All factor loadings on these variables exceeded 0.47.

[5] A strong 'traditionalist' would strongly agree that the leader is too powerful, that the leadership does not pay much attention to the members, and that the party should stick to principles regardless of the electoral consequences. He or she would also strongly disagree that the party should try to capture the middle ground of politics, and that the block vote brings the party into disrepute. In the coding of the scale this profile of responses would receive a score of 5. A strong modernizer would have the exact opposite profile of responses to the traditionalist, and would score 25. Thus the overall scale ranges from 5 to 25. Individuals scoring from 5 to 12 are classified as 'traditionalists'; 13 to 17 as 'intermediate'; and 18 to 25 as 'modernizers'.

TABLE 7.9. *The Distribution of Opinions on the Party Modernization Indicators* (percentages)

Indicator	Strongly agree	Agree	Neither	Disagree	Strongly disagree
Labour should capture middle ground	19	38	10	22	11
Labour leader too powerful	6	9	15	54	17
Conference block vote disreputable	23	49	12	13	4
Leader ignores party members' views	10	29	17	39	5
Labour should stick to principles	25	36	12	21	7

TABLE 7.10. *Attitudes to Party Modernization by Social Characteristics*

	Traditionalists	Intermediates	Modernizers
All respondents	18	43	38
Age			
17–25	28	47	26
26–45	22	43	34
46–65	14	42	44
66+	15	44	41
Class			
Salariat	17	43	39
Routine non-manual	20	44	36
Petty bourgeoisie	23	40	37
Foreman and Technician	10	42	48
Working class	19	44	37
Gender			
Female	19	47	34
Male	18	41	41
Income			
Under £10,000	18	44	38
£10,000–£25,000	20	44	37
£25,000+	17	41	42
Graduate			
Yes	20	44	36
No	17	43	40

the working class is particularly interesting. In Chapter 6 we observed that middle-class, educated members were more in favour of electoral pragmatism than working-class, uneducated members. These results show that when the modernization strategy as a whole is examined, which involves attitudes to the reorganization of the party structure and to the party leadership as well as to electoral pragmatism, these differences disappear. Thus although the middle class are more electorally pragmatic, they are not necessarily more concerned about modernizing the party in general, than the working class. Clearly, support for the modernization strategy within the party is widespread and not specific to any one social group.

Another interesting point is that gender is not significantly related to attitudes to modernization. One of the aims of the leadership in reforming the party has been to provide greater opportunities for women to reach senior positions. Yet, if anything women are slightly less likely to be modernizers than men. Income is not a significant correlate of the modernization scale either, with the possible exception of the high earners who tend to be marginally more in favour than the other income groups. Similarly, the level of education also makes little difference to members' opinions on party reform. Thus overall, social characteristics are rather weakly related to attitudes to modernization, with the possible exception of age.

In Table 7.11 we examine the relationships between attitudes to modernization, political ideology, and party activism. The ideology scale is the left–right scale applied to the Labour party as set out in Fig. 6.1, and it shows one very significant effect.[6] Members of the 'hard-left' group are very much against the modernization strategy, and are very much more likely to be traditionalists in comparison with other party members. As mentioned earlier, they make up about 17 per cent of the sample. In the case of the 'soft left' who make up about 41 per cent of the sample, there is a slight tendency for them to be in the 'intermediate' rather than the 'modernizers' group, but they are no more likely to be 'traditionalists' than party members as a whole. In contrast members in the 'centre' or 'centre-right' are very supportive of the modernization strategy, rather more so than the 9 per cent of respondents on the right of the party.

[6] The nine-point ideology scale applied to the party was recoded so that individuals who scored themselves 1 or 2 are described as 'hard left'; 3 or 4 'soft left'; 5 'centrist'; 6 or 7 'soft right'; and 8 or 9 'right'.

TABLE 7.11. *Attitudes to Party Modernization by Ideology and Activism*
(percentages)

	Traditionalists	Intermediates	Modernizers
All respondents	18	43	38
Ideology in Party			
Hard left	51	36	13
Soft left	18	49	34
Centrist	5	44	51
Soft right	3	35	62
Hard right	8	43	49
Activism			
Inactive	15	44	41
Occasionally active	15	47	38
Fairly active	18	43	39
Very active	24	39	36

Finally, it is perhaps not surprising that among the very active in the party there are a greater number of traditionalists. It is the activists who won increased powers in the party in the late 1970s and early 1980s that Neil Kinnock wishes to restrain in order, he believes, to increase the party's electoral prospects. But the relationship between activism and the modernization scale is not particularly strong, certainly not as strong as the relationship with the ideology scale. It is also important to note that in the very active category the modernizers outnumber the traditionalists by a margin of three to two. Thus even though one of the objectives of the strategy is to restrict the power of the activists, it would not be true to say that very active members oppose the modernization strategy.

Overall, these results show that there is widespread support for the modernization strategy in the party, as measured by a willingness to 'adjust policies to capture the middle ground'. Moreover, this remains true even when the natural tendency of the members to want to stick to principles, and to be suspicious of the leadership is taken into account. Social differences between members appear to have little effect on their attitudes to modernization. The one group of party members who strongly oppose the strategy are the members of the 'hard-left' group. We consider the causal factors at work in explaining this finding next.

IDEOLOGY AND THE MODERNIZATION STRATEGY

In Chapter 6 it was suggested that educational differences accounted for the ability and willingness of party members to take on board new issues, even when those issues were important for all types of party member. A similar argument can be developed about the modernization strategy. In this case the thesis would be that in the interests of electoral success the party needs to modernize both its organizational structure and policy positions on a variety of issues. Educated members are more likely to appreciate this fact more quickly than uneducated members, and so we are likely to observe a difference between educated and uneducated members of the party in their attitudes to the strategy. If this is true, the educated members should be more in favour of the strategy than the uneducated members.

However, as the results in Table 7.10 show, there is no evidence that educated party members, as measured by graduate status, are more in favour of the modernization strategy than the others. Moreover, a more detailed analysis of relationships between educational qualifications and experience, and attitudes to modernization produces the same result; modernizers outnumber traditionalists in all educational categories, but there is no clear tendency for highly educated members to be more in favour of the strategy than less educated members.

This implies that the cognitive processes explaining issue evolution of the type discussed in Chapter 6 do not appear to be at work in this context. Thus once we go beyond the relatively narrow issue of electoral pragmatism and examine attitudes to party strategy, the reform of party organization and structure, and the role of the leader as well as electoral strategy, the educational differences noted in Chapter 6 disappear.

However, we have observed a strong tendency for the hard left to oppose the strategy in comparison with the rest. Thus it is possible that ideological differences are disguising educational differences, in the same way that in Chapter 6 class differences disguised educational differences. If, for example, members of the hard left tended to be under-educated in comparison with other party members, then it could mean that the ideological differences observed in Table 7.10 were to some extent explained by education.

However, an analysis of the relationship between education and the ideology scale shows no significant relationships between membership of the hard-left group and education. Some 17 per cent of graduates are members of the hard left, exactly the same proportion as non-graduates. Thus ideology is not disguising educational differences, but rather appears to be overriding them in comparison with the findings of Chapter 6. What then accounts for the fact that the only really significant influence on attitudes to the modernization strategy is ideology?

The answer to this question, which also explains why the issue evolution analysis does not apply in this case, is that members of the hard left have their own distinctive analysis of Labour party electoral strategy. They dislike the modernization strategy, not because they are slow to appreciate what it is trying to do, but because they fundamentally disagree with it as an electoral strategy. They have an alternative vision of how the Labour party should proceed in the task of building electoral support.

In Table 7.12 we examine the attitudes of the hard left and other party members in relation to five different indicators of electoral strategy. Two of these: 'capture the middle ground', and 'stick to principles even if this should lose an election', have already been used in building the modernization scale. But the other measures are independent of this scale.

It is notable that the hard left is six times more likely than other party members to strongly disagree with the idea that the party should try to capture the middle ground. The hard left is nearly three times more likely to agree strongly with the proposition that the party should stick to principles regardless of the electoral consequences. These findings merely underscore the earlier findings of Table 7.11. But the third and fourth indicators of Table 7.12 illustrate, in outline, their distinctive electoral strategy.

The hard left believes that British politics is fundamentally about class conflict, and that the correct electoral strategy for Labour is to adopt only those policies supported by a majority of working-class people. In comparison with other party members they are three times more likely to agree strongly that 'the central question of British politics is the class struggle', and about two-and-a-half times more likely to agree strongly that 'the Labour party should only adopt policies supported by a majority of working-class people'.

One of the problems of their approach to electoral strategy is, of course, that working-class people do not necessarily share the

TABLE 7.12. *Perceptions of Electoral Strategy by Hard Left and Other Party Members* (percentages)

Indicator	Strongly agree	Agree	Neither	Disagree	Strongly disagree
'Capture middle ground'					
Hard left	10	20	7	28	36
Others	21	42	10	21	6
'Stick to principles'					
Hard left	52	29	7	9	3
Others	19	37	13	23	8
'Central question: class struggle'					
Hard left	61	28	6	5	1
Others	21	40	16	19	4
'Adopt working class policies'					
Hard left	31	24	14	22	10
Others	13	27	18	37	6
'Coalition govt. is best'					
Hard left	1	3	8	31	57
Others	1	5	14	49	31

policy preferences of the hard left, and so this idea has some unpalatable policy implications for them.

But setting that issue aside, members of the hard left are much more hostile to the idea of a coalition government than other party members. Some 57 per cent strongly disagree with the proposition that 'coalition governments are best for Britain', in comparison with 31 per cent of the other members. One clear implication of a coalition government is that it involves co-operation between parties representing different social classes. The hard left vision of a fundamentally class-divided society makes them oppose class co-operation, and emphasize an electoral strategy based on a single class appeal.

In fact recent academic work by Przeworski (1985) and Przeworski and Sprague (1986) has argued that historically 'class-only' electoral strategies which appeal narrowly only to the working class, have been successful for left-wing parties in countries like Belgium, Germany, and France (Przeworski, 1985: 117). Their argument is that a class-only electoral strategy maximizes working-class electoral support, which can be eroded by a broader political appeal. This is of course the argument of the hard left.

However, these writers also suggest that 'supra-class' electoral strategies, in which left parties seek support from the middle class as well as the working class, have been successful in Denmark, Norway, and Sweden. As far as Britain is concerned they argue that the Labour party has pursued a supra-class electoral strategy since before World War II (Przeworski, 1985: 25–6). This type of electoral strategy is necessary, because:

> workers never were, and would never become a numerical majority in their respective societies and the political institutions of democratic countries are based on majority rule. Leaders of class-based parties must choose between a party homogenous in its class appeal but sentenced to perpetual electoral defeats or a party that struggles for electoral success at the cost of diluting its class orientation (Przeworski, 1985: 102).

The relevance of such a strategy in contemporary Britain is reinforced by the well-documented decline in the size of the traditional working class (Goldthorpe, 1980), which makes a class-only appeal more and more problematic for a party which seeks to win office.

Moreover, it is not clear that a 'class-only' electoral strategy has actually been successful in any democratic systems. As the above quote shows, Przeworski acknowledges that the working class have never achieved majority status in any Western European countries.[7] It is therefore something of a puzzle that he can argue that a class-only strategy based only on an appeal to the working class has been successful in some of these countries.

The validity of this claim depends crucially on the trade-off between working-class and middle-class support engendered by a supra-class electoral strategy. If middle-class support is 'purchased' at high cost in terms of a loss of working-class support, then a supra-class strategy is not worth it. These authors (Przeworski, 1985; Przeworski and Sprague, 1986) claim to have estimated this trade-off for a number of countries over time, but a close examin-

---

[7] These authors use a fairly narrow definition of the working class as 'manual wage-earners employed in mining, manufacturing, construction, transport, and agriculture, persons retired from such occupations, and inactive adult members of their households' (Przeworski, 1985: 104). They point out that this was the traditional definition used by Marx and others, and if salaried white-collar employees are incorporated into the definition, the concept becomes diluted to the point that it loses relevance.

ation of their modelling exercise suggests that their conclusions on this point are seriously flawed.[8]

Indeed a strong case can be made for the proposition that a narrow class-only strategy will produce recurring electoral defeat for any left party, in any type of democratic system. The only exception to this would be in a coalition system, where a left party might base its electoral appeal on the working class alone. But even in this case, the end result would not lead to public policies which favour the working class alone, making it problematic to define a class-only strategy in the first place.

Whatever the validity of different approaches to electoral strategy in Britain, it appears from the survey responses that a majority of party members have reached the conclusion that a single-class electoral appeal is most unlikely to win power for the Labour party. This is why they support the modernization strategy. None the less the hard left can claim that there is an alternative electoral strategy to the one implemented by Neil Kinnock, and it is this claim rather than any educational or other social background factors which explains their hostility to the modernization strategy.

These results show that the images that party members have of the Labour party are complex, though generally very favourable. In the final section of this chapter, we examine some of the images the members have of other political parties and institutions in Britain.

Attitudes towards the other parties

We referred earlier to the fact that party members are loyalists in terms of their voting record and their general support for party and leader. But what of their images of other parties and leaders? In the last few years there has been increasing talk in some circles of coalition government, either as a means of ensuring that Labour wins office or as a means of curbing executive powers in Britain. Whatever the reason the idea remains highly unpopular among Labour party members. We observed in Table 7.12 that few agreed with the propo-

---

[8] This is a technical point, but of some importance. They base their claim that a class-only strategy has been electorally successful in a variety of countries, from the results of estimating several structural equation models. However, as Przeworski admits these models are econometrically under-identified, and cannot therefore be estimated. This is the equivalent of saying that they are trying to infer too much from too little information. This means that the results really reflect the initial assumptions of the models, rather than any empirical reality. In effect they are simulating, rather than estimating the behaviour of the world. (See Przeworski, 1985: 99–132.)

TABLE 7.13. *Mean Popularity Scores for Political Parties and Leaders*

Party or Leader	Mean score out of 100
Labour party	84
Social and Liberal Democrats	30
Conservative party	8
Green party	43
Plaid Cymru	29
Scottish National party	32
Neil Kinnock	73
Margaret Thatcher	6
Paddy Ashdown	34

sition that 'coalition governments are the best form of government for Britain'. At the same time, and paradoxically, a majority support electoral reform. So they support political changes which are likely to produce coalition governments, but not the idea of a coalition itself.

The reality of electoral politics in Britain are that the only possible national party that the Labour party might enter into coalition discussions with would be the Liberal Democrats. Table 7.13 contains information on members' attitudes towards the other parties, particularly the Liberals, and towards other party leaders in Britain.

Not surprisingly, Table 7.13 indicates that the members really loathed both Margaret Thatcher and the Conservative party. By contrast, their attitudes to the Liberal Democrats and Paddy Ashdown can be described as 'cool', broadly the same as their attitudes to the Scottish and Welsh Nationalists. This finding does not rule out a Lab/Lib pact along the lines of the one which operated in the late 1970s, but it does make it unlikely that local Labour parties would agree to withdraw from parliamentary elections in favour of a strong local Liberal candidate, as a quid pro quo for the Liberals doing the same in Labour marginals.

The only party which the members show any degree of warmth towards, apart from the Labour party, is the Green party. In the absence of electoral reform the Greens will find it very difficult to achieve parliamentary representation in Britain. But if electoral reform takes place and the Labour party found itself in a similar position to that of the Social Democrats in Germany, where the Greens have significant parliamentary representation, party members would probably accept a Labour–Green coalition with equanimity. In addition they might be persuaded to arrange local election pacts with strong Green candidates, although that involves an inference about a situation which is radically different from the contemporary scene in British politics.

Attitudes to society

Members are party loyalists rather than party rebels. Is this also the case with their attitudes to society in general? Are they critics or supporters of the British state? It has been argued that the Labour party is very respectable (Drucker, 1979) and rather conformist in its attitudes to the institutions of the British state (Jones and Keating, 1985), and is committed to the basic civic values of the British political culture (Jessop, 1974). On the other hand, there has long been a radical dissenting tradition in Britain (Taylor, 1957) which historically has embraced republicanism, anti-colonialism, and pacifism among other things, and the Labour party has been one of the institutions around which dissenters have congregated.

The Conservative party has been very adept at identifying the Labour party as part of this dissenting tradition and as a nesting ground for critics of the British state. It claimed the Labour party was riddled with republicans and bolsheviks in the inter-war years, and anti-colonialists in the 1950s (McKenzie and Silver, 1968). During the 1980s it concentrated upon the anti-parliamentarian sentiment within the Labour party. So great was this Conservative attack that the Labour party leader, Michael Foot, felt bound to publicly dissociate the party from the supposedly anti-parliamentarian opinions of one prospective parliamentary candidate Peter Tatchell. During the Falklands War Mrs Thatcher took every opportunity available to identify the Labour party as weak on defending British interests and therefore, by implication, unpatriotic. There is no doubt that part of the reasoning behind Labour's close support of the British government's involvement in the Gulf War in 1991 was its desire not to be labelled as unpatriotic.

We asked party members what they thought of key state and non-state institutions and bodies such as the House of Commons, the police, the BBC, the TUC, the CBI, and the Stock Exchange.

Images of Party and Society

Table 7.14. *Mean Popularity Scores for Various Organizations*

Organization	Mean score out of 100
Trades Union Congress	63
European Community	58
BBC	57
House of Commons	56
Police	45
Confederation of British Industries	30
Stock Exchange	23
Sun Newspaper	5

They were also asked to score the *Sun* newspaper and the European Community. The results of this appear in Table 7.14.

A majority of members hold the House of Commons, the European Community, the TUC, and the BBC in reasonably high regard, giving them a thermometer score greater than 50. But neither the Stock Exchange nor the CBI are liked by party members. Nor are the police, since two-thirds of the members gave them a score of below 50. Finally, members positively detest the *Sun* newspaper, giving it a mean score below that of Margaret Thatcher and the Conservative party! This attitude is reflected in their newspaper-buying habits, since only one per cent of members subscribed to the *Sun* in comparison with 29 per cent who subscribed to its main rival, the *Daily Mirror/Daily Record*.

With regard to the attitudes of Labour supporters to the British state, the key institution to look at is the House of Commons, since this invokes long-standing debates about alternative roads to socialism other than the parliamentary road (see, for example, Miliband, 1961). A mean score for the House of Commons of 56 indicates that members are warm towards the institution, but hardly over-enthusiastic about it.

An analysis of the relationship between the social backgrounds of members and their attitudes to the House of Commons revealed no significant differences between the social class, gender, income, education, or even levels of activism of party members in relation to their attitudes. However, young members (i.e. 18 to 25 years old) and members of the hard left were significantly colder towards the

House of Commons in comparison with other members. In this respect attitudes are similar to those relating to the modernization strategy; individuals who dislike the House are largely those on the hard left who would object in some sense to the 'parliamentary road' to socialism.

In general these results suggest that Labour party members are supportive of the most important political institution of the British state, the House of Commons. But the strength of their support hardly demonstrates that members are very deferential to authority and constitutionality.

This concludes our discussion of the attitudes of members to the political parties and wider institutions in Britain. In the next chapter we change the focus of the analysis sharply from the close scrutiny of the characteristics of the members undertaken in the previous chapters, to an examination of the effects of party membership. This involves looking at the impact of party membership and campaigning on the Labour vote.

8

Membership, Activism, and the Labour Vote

Do party membership and political activism influence the Labour vote? This is a question which has intrigued academic political scientists as well as party managers and pollsters for many years. Recently there has been an increasing emphasis on the importance of centrally managed media campaigns in general elections. The focus is on prepared 'sound bites' and 'photo opportunities' for the party leaders, and 'hot' issues which can mobilize the voters. This image of the modern election campaign leaves very little room for the party member. Indeed in this view the individual member appears to have the role merely of a bystander, a supporting actor who will provide an appreciative audience in the set-piece election rallies whose chief purpose is to look good on TV.

If the centralized media campaign in the election dominates everything, then to put it bluntly the party members have no significant role to play in elections. If this is true, then a weak party organization might actually be an electoral asset, since a large number of independent-minded members and activists are likely to generate dissension and debate. Labour's experiences in the early 1980s demonstrate the electoral damage which can result from internal party strife, and so if members and activists are few in number and quiescent, that might help the media campaign. In this view members can, paradoxically, be influential in losing an election, but not particularly influential in winning one.

This question is central to debates about the kind of Labour party which might evolve in the future. One possible scenario for the future sees the party evolving into an American-style party organization in which the local members are increasingly irrelevant to electoral politics at the national level. US election campaigns have become increasingly independent of party organizations in recent years. Presidential and congressional candidates hire professional campaign managers and pollsters who are independent of the party organizations to run their campaigns, raise funds, and plan campaign strategies. As a consequence when they succeed, they owe few debts to the party which endorsed them in the first place (Goldman and Mathews, 1989). This fact coupled with a well documented decline of party identification in the electorate as a whole, has weakened the influence of local parties in the United States as never before (see Wattenberg, 1986).

The experience of one country never translates precisely into that of another, but if it can be shown that Labour party members play little or no role in winning elections, then that is likely to add to the pressures to move in the American direction and essentially marginalize the party members in the political process.

This 'media-dominated' view of elections has grown up largely because there has been little research into the role of local party members in election campaigns. The absence of evidence has made the members seem unimportant by default. However, the evidence of this chapter suggests that party members and political activists play a very important role in mobilizing the vote for the Labour party in general elections. Moreover, their influence is independent of other factors which determine voting behaviour. As a consequence, we can be confident that a thriving local constituency party is an electoral asset to the Labour party as a whole, in the sense that a significant number of Labour seats would not have been won in the 1987 General Election without active local campaigns. This implies that the party has every incentive to promote an active grass-roots membership, since it would probably be eliminated as a major electoral force without that membership.

The discussion in this chapter is divided into four sections; first, we review the evidence on the effects of local campaigns on voting behaviour. This is done for both Britain and the United States, since the literature for the latter country is much more extensive than for the former, and is relevant to the British case. Secondly we discuss the methodological approach needed to examine this question using the survey of Labour members in conjunction with electoral returns and aggregate data on the social characteristics of parliamentary constituencies compiled from the census.[1] Thirdly, we look at the results of a data analysis of the effects of membership and activism

---

[1] The constituency census information and the voting data for the 1983 election used in this chapter is taken from Crewe and Fox (1984), and the electoral data for 1987 is taken from Butler and Kavanagh (1988).

on the Labour vote using cross-tabulations as well as more complex multivariate models. Finally, we apply the models to the exercise of simulating the outcome of the 1987 election using varying assumptions about constituency party activism. The aim here is to examine the effects of different levels of party membership on the outcome of the election.

LOCAL CONSTITUENCY CAMPAIGNS AND ELECTORAL EFFECTS

The literature on the influence of constituency election campaigns on voting in Britain is very sparse, and for the most part effects have to be deduced from indirect evidence. However, in the United States research on this issue is rather more extensive. The US evidence has relevance for this discussion, since if local party campaigns influence the vote in a country with a weaker party system than Britain's, it is very likely that such campaigns have a significant effect in Britain.

There is one paper which provides direct evidence of a link between local campaigns and the vote in Britain. This is a study by Bochel and Denver (1972) of the relationship between campaigning and voting in a local government election in Dundee. They carried out an ingenious experiment to measure the effects of a local campaign, using two blocks of flats in a strong Labour ward in the city, both of which had very similar socio-economic characteristics. One of them acted as the experimental block and was subject to an intensive campaign of leafleting and canvassing; the other acted as the control block and was left untouched by the Labour campaign. A post-election survey showed that the campaign made a difference of about 10 per cent in the turn-out of Labour voters in the election.

One problem with this approach is that an intensive local campaign is likely to have a greater impact at a local election than at a general election, where the national campaign appears to overshadow local activities. However some 47 per cent of the respondents in the 1987 British Election Study reported that they had been canvassed by at least one of the political parties during the campaign.[2] Given that some election-study respondents may not have been at home or not answered the door when the canvasser

---

[2] Some 26% reported that they had been canvassed by the Labour party, and 26% by the Conservatives.

called, this probably understates the extent of canvassing at the election. Even on the minimal assumption that canvassing only mobilizes voters to actually turn out and vote, rather than to switch parties, this suggests that the local campaign may have had an important influence on the vote.

One piece of indirect evidence of the effects of local campaigns derives from the relationship between turn-out and the marginality or the 'winnability' of a constituency in general elections. Denver and Hands (1974, 1985) have shown that a clear relationship existed between turn-out and marginality, defined as the proximity of the first and second parties in the election, in the general elections between 1955 and 1979. Turn-out was significantly higher in marginal constituencies compared with safe seats. Moreover, their analysis shows that this relationship strengthened over time.

There are two possible theoretical explanations of this finding. The first is that voters are more likely to vote in marginal constituencies, since they perceive that their vote is more likely to 'make a difference' to the outcome. In terms of the model of Chapter 5, p_i is larger when the outcome of the election is closer. However, the weakness of this account, is that the probability of any voter being decisive in determining the winner is very small even in a marginal seat (see Margolis, 1982: 82–95). Thus it is hard to justify the perception that any one vote is likely to be influential.

The second explanation of this effect is more plausible; it is based on the fact that the parties concentrate more resources in marginal constituencies, because they have a better chance of winning in these seats. Thus the increased turn-out is due to the intensive local campaign, which implies that party activity has a significant impact on voting behaviour.

Another type of indirect evidence of local campaign effects derives from Miller's (1977) seminal analysis of the relationship between individual and constituency voting in Britain over the period of half a century. If constituencies are regarded as merely aggregations of atomistic individuals, then the relationship between social class and voting behaviour for each individual should be approximately the same as the relationship for the group of voters who make up a constituency. This means, for example, that if the probability that a working-class individual chosen at random from the country as a whole will vote Conservative is 0.30 or 30 per cent, then the same percentage of working-class voters should vote Conservative in all constituencies in the country.

However, Miller showed that the relationship between class and voting at the constituency level is very different from the relationship at the individual level. He showed that the probability that a working-class individual will vote Tory will vary according to the class characteristics of the constituency in which he or she lives. Thus a lower proportion of the working class vote Conservative in a very working-class constituency, and a higher proportion of them vote Conservative in a very middle-class constituency. Miller attributes this to environmental or ecological effects associated with each constituency. In other words constituencies are emphatically not simple aggregations of individuals, and the sum is greater than the individual parts.[3]

There are a number of factors which might explain these environmental effects. One is that a local political culture might exist in a constituency making both middle-class and working-class voters more Conservative (or Labour) than is true for the country as a whole. Another is that higher concentrations of middle-class voters in a constituency produces a situation in which working-class Labour voters come into frequent contact with Conservative middle-class voters on a day-to-day basis, which over the years makes them more Conservative-inclined. In other words conformity to a dominant local norm, produces environmental effects of this kind. The reverse would be true for middle-class voters in a strong working-class constituency; frequent contact with the working class would make them more Labour-inclined.

A third explanation of these effects relates to party activism and local election campaigns. If the Conservative party is strong in areas where there is a high Conservative vote, and the Labour party is strong in areas where there is a high Labour vote, then the most effective local election campaigns with the least opposition, will

---

[3] Miller (1977: 42) illustrates this point with an example from the 1966 British General Election. The British Election Study of that year suggested that about 30% of the working class voted Conservative. Thus nationally: Conservative vote = 0.73 middle class + 0.30 working class; or, Conservative vote = 0.30 + 0.43 middle class, since middle class vote = (1 − working class vote). However, an analysis done at the constituency level with census data showed that the relationship between class and Conservative voting was: Conservative vote = 0.16 + 0.93 middle class. The difference between these two equations reflects the fact that constituencies are not simple aggregations of individuals, but have their own ecological character which changes the relationship between class and voting.

occur in strong Conservative and strong Labour constituencies. Thus middle-class Conservative-incliners will be more likely to vote Labour in safe Labour seats, because they see a lot of their local Labour party and seldom, if ever, see their local Tory party. In these constituencies the impact of electioneering in terms of displays of election posters, the distribution of leaflets and canvassing is fairly one-sided in favour of the Labour party. The reverse is true for working-class Labour-incliners in safe Conservative seats.

By contrast, if both parties mount equally effective campaigns in marginal constituencies, these will tend to cancel each other out. Thus the heavy campaigning in marginal seats might make people more inclined to vote by drawing public attention to the election, but it will not make them more likely to switch parties.

The exact nature of these ecological effects is yet to be fully identified and measured, and so it is difficult to assess the precise role of local campaigns in all of this. But we do know that environmental effects are large, and that could mean that local party campaigns, both before and during elections, have a very significant influence on voting behaviour.

If the evidence on the effects of local political activism on electoral behaviour in Britain is largely indirect, the evidence in the United States is much more direct. This question has been a topic of considerable interest to researchers since the 1950s. One of the earliest papers by Cutright and Rossi (1958) in a study of Gary, Indiana, set out the methodological framework within which most subsequent research has been done. They pointed out that the main barrier to research on this issue is 'an inability to solve the problem of how to separate out the effects of party activity from those effects produced by the other factors at work in a particular election' (Cutright and Rossi, 1958: 151).

They combined the use of surveys of party activists, in this case precinct committeemen or the rough equivalent of Labour party ward chairpersons, with electoral returns and census data on the social characteristics of precincts, to determine the independent influence of party activism on election outcomes.

Their results showed, not surprisingly, that social characteristics, particularly the percentage of home owners and the ethnic origin of voters, explained a high percentage of the variance in the vote for the Democratic party in the 1956 Presidential Election. However, party activism as measured by various political activities undertaken by precinct committeemen made an important difference to the vote. Thus when a highly active Democratic committeeman faced a very inactive Republican committeeman this produced a gain of about 4 per cent for the Democrats in the vote, which was independent of the social and electoral characteristics of the precinct. At the other end of the scale when a highly active Republican committeeman faced a very inactive Democrat that produced a loss in votes for the Democrats of about 1.6 per cent.

In later work Cutright (1963) addressed the issue of trying to untangle the influence of a dominant local political norm, such as that generated by a heavy concentration of Democrats in an area, from the effects of party activism on the vote. His results showed that party activism improved the vote by about 4 to 5 per cent, after the environmental political norm had been taken into account (Cutright, 1963: 382).

With a slightly different research design Wolfinger (1963) found even stronger effects in New Haven, Connecticut, a city which traditionally had strong local party organizations. He examined the effects of activism on voting in a local referendum on an issue which had split the Democratic party, to do with the revision of the city's charter. The split meant that some Democratic precinct committeemen actively supported a revision of the charter, and others actively opposed it. By contrast, the Republican committeemen largely opposed it.

Wolfinger showed that demographic variables such as education, income, and ethnicity had virtually no influence on this issue, so it was easily possible to isolate the influence of activism on voting. In precincts where the Democratic committeemen actively supported the revision, 71 per cent of Democrats voted in favour. In precincts where Democratic committeemen actively opposed the revision, only 58 per cent of Democrats voted in favour (Wolfinger, 1963: 395). This neatly illustrates the effects of disunity within a party during an election campaign.

In a study which used a sophisticated statistical model applied to data from the American national election studies Kramer (1970) estimated the effects of canvassing at the precinct level on turn-out and voter preferences for candidates in four national elections from 1952 to 1964. This study was an improvement on the others in that it used national rather than local survey data, and examined effects for presidential, congressional, and local state candidates. It showed that canvassing had a significant effect on turn-out, but did not appear to induce voters to switch parties or candidates.

Another study by Crotty (1971) in North Carolina, with even more elaborate controls for voters' social and demographic characteristics, also showed that political activism had significant electoral effects. This was also true in a more recent study by Frendreis, Gibson, and Vertz (1990), which showed that the impact of party organizations on the vote at the county level for presidential and congressional elections between 1980 and 1984 was significant, but indirect. The party able to contest seats at all levels did much better than the party unable to do this, although the direct effect of organizational activism on the vote was limited. It is possible that the weakening of the US party system since the 1950s explains these more limited direct effects in comparison with the earlier studies.

Taken as a whole, the US results show that party activism has a significant effect on turn-out, and in the case of most studies, on the vote. When one recalls that the US party system is generally much weaker than in Britain, this suggests that similar or even stronger effects may be found in Britain. We turn to the question of developing a research design to test this next.

MODELLING THE RELATIONSHIPS BETWEEN ACTIVISM AND THE VOTE

To examine the relationship between party activism and the vote we have to look at the constituency level of analysis, since that is the level at which voting takes place in a general election. That means aggregating the individual responses from our sample of party members into constituencies. The 5,071 individual respondents in the sample were taken from a total of 480 parliamentary constituencies, which means that the average number of party members in each constituency sample was just under eleven people. With samples of this size, there are too few cases to do any significant analysis within constituencies, but it is possible to use the sample membership figures as an indicator of the total membership figures of a constituency party.

The methodological approach of this chapter is to compare two variables from the survey, aggregated by constituency parties, with voting data and measures of the social characteristics of those constituencies taken from census sources. The first variable is the number of party members in a particular constituency sample. As we point out in Appendix I, the research design used in the survey involved selecting a 1 in 30 sample of the Labour party membership, so that the number of respondents in the survey from each constituency should be roughly one-thirtieth of the total number of members in that constituency party. We can then compare the party membership in the sample with the Labour vote, to get a preliminary idea of the relationship between the vote and the organizational strength of the party.

The second indicator of Labour party constituency characteristics is a more direct measure of party activism than the number of party members. This is derived from the party activism scale discussed extensively in Chapter 5. It may be recalled from Table 5.4 that the activism scale was constructed from a set of eight indicators of party activities. For the purposes of the present chapter we require a measurement scale of activism which focuses specifically on elections. Four of the indicators in Table 5.4 were closely related to elections, i.e. 'displaying a poster'; 'delivering leaflets'; 'canvassing voters'; and 'standing for office'. Since only a small handful of individuals stood for office, we use the first three of these to build the aggregate activism scale.

The activism score for each constituency is then the total score on these three items for every respondent in that constituency sample.[4] This coding means that one constituency can have a higher activism score than another, either because it has more members (assuming that the average level of activism for each member is roughly the same), or because the existing members are more active, or both. The mean activism score for the 480 constituencies was 90, but there was a wide dispersion of scores on the scale. The minimum score was 4 and the maximum 404, with a standard deviation of 59.

The minimum score was very low because one or two of the constituency samples contained only one respondent, which raises questions about the validity of any generalizations based on such small numbers. Clearly, with an average sample size of ten, many of the samples may be too small to give an accurate picture of the constituency Labour parties they are supposed to represent. It is

---

[4] For example if a given constituency sample consists of 10 people, all of whom displayed an election poster frequently (scoring 4 × 10), all of whom delivered leaflets occasionally (3 × 10), five of whom canvassed occasionally (3 × 5), and five of whom canvassed rarely (2 × 5), the total score for that constituency would be 95.

necessary to have some external evidence that the activism measure is a valid indicator of political activity among constituency party members, notwithstanding the small numbers involved in its construction.

Fortunately this external evidence is provided by the British Election Study of 1987. Constituency identifiers were available to classify respondents in that study, and a total of 191 constituencies in the election study were the same as those used in the membership survey. Thus we can aggregate election-study variables for these constituencies, and compare them with aggregate measures from the membership survey.

We mentioned earlier that the election study asked respondents if they had been canvassed by anyone from a political party during the election campaign. Thus the percentage of voters in each of the 191 constituencies who reported being canvassed by the Labour party during the election campaign can be calculated. These figures can then be used to check the validity of the activism scale from the membership survey. If the relationship between the activism scale and the canvassing evidence from the election study is very weak, that means that the activism measure is a poor indicator of election activity. On the other hand if this relationship is strong, it implies that the activism scale is a good measure of election-campaign activity. The cross-tabulation of activism against canvassing appears in Table 8.1.

The activism and canvassing variables have been recoded into four categories in Table 8.1,[5] and there is clearly a strong relationship between them. Constituencies which, according to the membership survey are relatively inactive, appear to have done very little canvassing, according to the election survey. Thus 67 per cent of the relatively inactive constituency parties were to be found in constituencies where less than 20 per cent of the voters reported being canvassed by the party.

Equally, constituencies which the membership survey show to be very active, appear to have done quite a lot of canvassing. A total of 58 per cent of very active parties were found in constituencies where more than 40 per cent of the voters reported being canvassed by the

[5] In the case of the activism variable, scores from the lowest up to 50 are described as 'relatively inactive'; 50 up to 100 as 'somewhat active'; 100 up to 150 as 'moderately active'; and 150 up to the highest as 'very active'. Thus 26% of the sample of 191 constituencies were 'relatively inactive'; 39% were 'somewhat active'; 21% were 'fairly active'; and 14% were 'very active'.

TABLE 8.1. *The Relationship between Election-Related Activism and the Percentage of Voters who were canvassed by Labour in the General Election of 1987* (row percentages)

Activism of constituency party	Voters reporting being canvassed			
	Under 20	20–40	40–60	Over 60
Relatively inactive	67	29	4	0
Somewhat active	52	27	16	4
Moderately active	37	37	20	7
Very active	8	35	39	19
ALL CONSTITUENCIES IN THE SURVEY AND ELECTION STUDY	47	31	17	6

Note: N = 191.

party. The table shows that most of the very active local parties canvassed between 40 per cent and 60 per cent of households, which is consistent with an electoral strategy which targets Labour 'areas', rather than a strategy which targets all voters.

Thus the independent evidence from the British Election Study suggests that the aggregate activism scale is a good measure of constituency Labour party election activity, even though it is based on relatively small samples of party members within each constituency. In the light of these results we go on to examine the relationships between party activism and the Labour vote in the next section.

PARTY MEMBERSHIP, ACTIVISM, AND THE VOTE

We begin the analysis of the relationship between party membership, activism, and the vote with a look at some bivariate tables. This leads into a subsequent discussion of possible multivariate relationships between these and other aggregate variables.

The first relationship of interest is between the size of the party membership and the size of the Labour vote in the 1987 election. The simplest model of this relationship would suggest a straightforward linear relationship between these two variables. In other words really safe Labour seats should have large Labour parties, and at the other end of the scale safe Conservative seats should have small Labour parties.

However, it is possible that some safe Labour seats have

TABLE 8.2. *The Relationship between Party Membership and the Labour Vote in 1987* (row percentages)

Number of members	Labour percentage of constituency vote in 1987			
	Under 20	20–30	30–40	Over 40
Under 180	62	10	6	22
180–360	36	20	12	33
360–540	12	20	16	53
Over 540	4	16	19	61
ALL CONSTITUENCIES IN THE SURVEY	34	17	12	38

Note: N = 480.

moribund constituency party organizations. As we observed in Chapter 5, working-class party members tend to be rather less active than middle-class party members. Thus constituency parties in very safe Labour areas which consist almost exclusively of working-class members, might be less active in recruiting new members than more middle-class parties. For this reason we might observe a curvilinear relationship between the vote and membership, with the largest memberships found in marginal constituencies having many middle-class members.

The relationship between party membership and the Labour vote is set out in Table 8.2, where the membership figures represent the total number of members inferred from the constituency samples.[6] There is support in this table for the curvilinear hypothesis, since a number of both safe Conservative and safe Labour seats have relatively small memberships; thus 62 per cent of the small parties are found in constituencies in which Labour obtained less than 20 per cent of the vote; at the same time 22 per cent of these parties are found in constituencies where Labour obtained more than 40 per cent of the vote. However, it is important not to overstate this point since most safe Labour constituencies have large constituency parties; some 61 per cent of large parties are in constituencies with a Labour vote in excess of 40 per cent.

The most compelling figures in this table relate to the 34 per cent of constituencies in which the Labour party obtained less than 20 per cent of the vote, and the 38 per cent of constituencies in which it

[6] This is simply the constituency sample × 30.

obtained more than 40 per cent. In these two columns of the table there is a very strong relationship between the number of party members and the Labour vote; in the 'under 20 per cent' column, the percentage of constituency parties declines dramatically as one moves down the table from small parties to large parties. The reverse is true for the 'over 40 per cent' vote column in the table. Thus to a large extent Labour party membership mirrors the Labour vote.

The causal relationship between the size of the Labour vote and the number of party members is ambiguous, since it is possible that the vote influences the membership, rather than the other way round, in the sense that safe Labour seats are good places to recruit members. However if we examine the relationship between the change in the Labour vote between the 1983 and 1987 General Elections and membership, causality is much less ambiguous. In this case it is very likely that campaigning by the local party causes the swing to Labour, rather than the other way round.

This inference is plausible because an above-average swing to the Labour party can be achieved by an active local party, but the idea that a large swing to Labour will generate a large membership in the space of four years is much less credible. In the first interpretation there is a plausible mechanism for explaining the effect—campaigning influences the vote; in the second interpretation, there is no explanation as to why a large swing to Labour should have occurred in the first place, nor why that should necessarily influence party membership.

Accordingly in Table 8.3 we examine the relationship between membership and the change in the Labour vote between the two elections.[7] The evidence in this table supports the hypothesis that campaigning by the party membership influences the vote, since only 13 per cent of the small parties were in constituencies which experienced an increase in the Labour vote of 6 per cent or more. By contrast, some 37 per cent of large parties were in constituencies which experienced this above average increase in the Labour vote.

At the other end of the scale some 18 per cent of the small parties experienced a decline in the Labour vote, compared with only 7 per cent of large parties. The evidence clearly suggests that there is a

---

[7] The mean increase in the Labour vote between the 1983 and 1987 General Elections was 3.7% (see Curtice and Steed, 1988: 317).

TABLE 8.3. *The Relationship between Party Membership and the Change in the Labour Vote 1983–1987* (row percentages)

Number of members	Change in the Labour percentage of constituency vote, 1983–7			
	Under 0	0–3	3–6	Over 6
Under 180	18	52	17	13
180–360	14	42	23	21
360–540	17	24	20	40
Over 540	7	26	30	37
ALL CONSTITUENCIES IN THE SURVEY	15	39	22	25

Note: N = 480.

relationship between the size of the party membership and electoral performance.

One qualification to the last point is that a large party may not be very active, and equally a small party might be very active and make up for its lack of numbers by working very hard during a general election campaign. To examine this question we cross-tabulate the activism scale introduced in Table 8.1 with party membership in Table 8.4.

The results in Table 8.4 indicate that the relationship between the activism score and the number of party members is very strong, which indicates that there is little evidence to support the proposition that large inactive parties exist alongside small active parties;[8] some 92 per cent of small parties are 'relatively inactive' and some 95 per cent of large parties are 'very active'. This finding actually follows directly from the results discussed in Chapter 5, where it was shown that the 'average' party member was fairly active, and that most members played an important role in election campaigns by putting up posters and delivering leaflets.

This strengthens the interpretation of the findings in Table 8.3 that

---

[8] The bivariate correlation between the activism scale and the number of party members is 0.97, which is very strong. It is important to remember that one of the reasons for this is that the activism scale measures total election activity by a party, not 'per capita' election activity. This automatically means that large parties will have a higher activism score, compared with small parties. Activism is measured in this way because total activity is what influences the Labour vote, not 'per capita' activity.

TABLE 8.4. *The Relationship between Party Membership and Constituency Party Activism* (row percentages)

Number of members	Activism index			
	Relatively inactive	Somewhat active	Moderately active	Very active
Under 180	92	8	0	0
180–360	8	79	13	0
360–540	0	16	72	12
Over 540	0	0	5	95
ALL CONSTITUENCIES IN THE SURVEY	27	39	21	14

Note: N = 480.

TABLE 8.5. *The Relationship between Party Activism and the Labour Vote in 1987* (row percentages)

Aggregate activism of constituency party	Labour percentage of constituency vote in 1987			
	Under 20	20–30	30–40	Over 40
Relatively inactive	68	10	4	18
Somewhat active	35	23	11	32
Moderately active	11	12	18	59
Very active	3	18	20	59
ALL CONSTITUENCIES IN THE SURVEY	34	17	12	38

Note: N = 480.

large parties experienced a larger swing to Labour in 1987 than small parties, because election campaigning makes a difference. In Table 8.5 the relationship between the activism scale and the Labour vote is examined, which throws further light on this question.

It can be seen that the findings in Table 8.5 are very similar to those in Table 8.2. Some 68 per cent of relatively inactive parties were to be found in constituencies where Labour obtained less than

TABLE 8.6. *The Relationship between Party Activism and the Change in the Labour Vote 1983–1987* (row percentages)

Aggregate activism of constituency party	Change in the Labour percentage of constituency vote, 1983–7			
	Under 0	0–3	3–6	Over 6
Relatively inactive	20	50	18	12
Somewhat active	15	47	20	18
Moderately active	9	23	24	43
Very active	11	20	30	39
ALL CONSTITUENCIES IN THE SURVEY	15	39	22	25

Note: N = 480.

20 per cent of the vote. At the other end of the scale 59 per cent of very active parties were found in constituencies where Labour obtained more than 40 per cent of the vote.

Once again though, the relationship between the change in the vote between 1983 and 1987, and activism, is a much less ambiguous measure of the effects of campaigning on the vote, and this is examined in Table 8.6.

The results in Table 8.6 are very similar to those in Table 8.3 and confirm the point that highly active parties are very likely to be in constituencies which experienced an above-average swing to Labour. Equally, relatively inactive parties are likely to be in constituencies where the swing to Labour was below average or even negative between 1983 and 1987.

The analysis up to this point is encouraging to those who believe that local election campaigns can have a significant influence on the vote. But it is not conclusive evidence in favour of this hypothesis, since a number of other variables might be responsible for the relationships in the tables. If a variable influences both membership and the Labour vote, then it could be the hidden cause of the relationships observed in the tables. To deal with this problem it is necessary to control for the influence of such variables, in order to examine the effect this has on the link between membership and the vote.

One example of a variable which might influence both the vote and party membership is social class. The Labour party traditionally does well in constituencies with a high concentration of manual workers, and it is possible that this accounts for the relationships between membership and the vote. The earlier discussion of environmental or ecological variables suggested that a constituency with a high percentage of manual workers is likely to have a distinctively 'labourite' political culture.

It is possible that the relationship between the vote and membership only really exists in such constituencies, where the political environment for organizing a local party and mobilizing the vote is particularly favourable. If this is true then incorporating the percentage of manual workers in a constituency into the model as a control will significantly weaken or even eliminate the relationship between membership and the vote.

In general, we have to control for the influence of a number of other factors of this type in order to be sure that the relationship between party activism and the vote is genuine, and not merely the artefact of a relationship between these two variables and other omitted variables. We consider additional control variables in the next section.

A MULTIVARIATE MODEL OF MEMBERSHIP AND THE VOTE

In the earlier review of the US literature on the relationship between party activism and the vote, we observed that the standard approach to estimating effects is to examine the influence of activism on the vote after taking into account various constituency social characteristics. The basic idea is to include all the other variables in the model which might explain the relationship between activism and the vote, to see if the relationships still hold up in the presence of such controls. We have already suggested that the percentage of manual workers in a constituency might well account for a relationship between the vote and activism. Another possible control variable is the percentage of council housing in a constituency. Traditionally, the Labour vote has been higher among council tenants than among other working-class voters. So it is likely that constituencies with a high percentage of council tenants will have both a large Labour vote, and a high party membership because council estates are good places both to pick up Labour votes and to organize local parties. If so, the relationship between the vote and party membership might only exist in constituencies which have a large percentage of council housing. Accordingly, the percentage of council tenants in a constituency is included as a control.

A third variable discussed by Curtice and Steed (1988) in their analysis of the vote in the 1987 General Election is region. Regional variations in voting behaviour in Britain have become more and more marked in recent years, giving rise to distinct geographical cleavages in party support (see also Johnston, Pattie, and Allsop, 1988). Curtice and Steed point out that the swing to Labour was markedly stronger in the north and west of Britain than in the south and east (1988: 320). Again it is possible that the relationship between membership and the vote varies significantly by region, and may only exist in regions where the Labour party is strong.

On this interpretation, Labour party members may have a significant influence on the vote in Scotland, the north of England, and Wales, but a weak or non-existent influence in the south and east of England. Again, this is a product of the political environment within which the members operate. When Labour is the dominant local party, the environment is much more favourable, both to the party organization and to mobilizing the vote, than when it is weak. Accordingly, a control variable is included in the model which measures the effect of a constituency being in the north or west of Britain.[9]

A fourth possible explanation of the relationship between membership and the vote has been referred to earlier, and derives from the marginality or 'winnability' of a constituency. There are two different ways in which the marginality of a constituency might influence the relationship between activism and the vote.

First, the national party organizations will try to concentrate their resources on marginal constituencies, bringing in, for example, full-time organizers and outside volunteers to work intensively throughout the campaign. This heavy investment in campaigning in the marginals might well produce a relationship between party activism and the vote, which could otherwise be too weak to observe.

[9] Curtice and Steed (1988) distinguish between the North and West (i.e. Scotland, Wales and the North of England), the South and East (i.e. the South, East, and Midlands), and Devon and Cornwall. They point out that voting behaviour in these three regions varied markedly in 1987, with Labour being dominant in the North and West. The control for region in the model, scores one for constituencies in the Northern, Yorkshire, North-West, Wales, and Scottish Labour party regions, and zero elsewhere.

If this is true then a control for the marginality of a constituency should considerably weaken the relationship between activism and the vote.

The second interpretation reaches the same conclusion, that there is a relationship between marginality and the vote, but from the opposite direction. Since all the major parties try to concentrate their campaigning resources on marginal constituencies, this might have the effect of cancelling out the influence of the rival campaigns on the vote in these constituencies. Moreover, the heavy concentration of campaign resources in marginals implies that the national party organizations will invest few resources in what they regard as their opponents' safe seats, since these will be viewed as unwinnable. This implies that Labour party members have the best chance of influencing the vote in safe Labour seats, where rival campaigns are likely to be weak or non-existent.

In this interpretation the influence of local campaigns on the vote in marginal constituencies is much weaker than in safe Labour seats because all the other parties are campaigning in such constituencies at the same time, making the political environment too 'crowded'. Accordingly, a control for the marginality of the constituency in the model, will weaken or eliminate the relationship between activism and the vote, since by this argument, the relationship is only effective in safe Labour seats. The marginality of a constituency is measured by the absolute value of the difference between the Labour percentage of the vote, and that received by other parties.[10]

A fifth factor which might account for the relationship is the change in the turn-out. An increase in the turn-out in a constituency between 1983 and 1987 might well explain an above-average increase in the Labour vote. Thus if the change in turn-out is included in the model this might weaken or eliminate the relationship between activism and the vote. To be fair to the hypothesis, however, a rise in turn-out might itself be explained at least in part by campaign activity. Thus it is important to examine the influence of party activism on turn-out, if the latter proves to be significant in the vote model.

A sixth factor relates to the distinction between urban and rural

---

[10] If Labour won the seat then marginality measures the absolute difference between the Labour vote and the vote for the 2nd party; if Labour came 2nd or 3rd, marginality measures the absolute difference between Labour and the vote for the winning party.

constituencies. The Labour party has always been much stronger in urban areas in comparison with rural areas, something which can be observed by a casual examination of the social characteristics of safe Labour seats. If constituency Labour parties are weak in rural areas, this will tend to reduce their impact on the local election campaign, which for reasons discussed earlier would not be a high priority for the national party anyway. It is also the case that campaigning is more difficult in large rural constituencies where voters are scattered over a wide area, which implies that activism may only have a significant influence on the vote in urban areas. With these points in mind, the percentage of the work-force employed in agriculture is included as an additional control variable, in order to measure the extent to which a constituency is rural in character.

A final, general-control variable in the model is the Labour percentage of the vote in 1983. If there are any additional social or political characteristics of a constituency which might influence both the vote and party activism, then the 1983 Labour vote should measure the effects of such variables on the 1987 vote. An example of this is a variable like a local political culture which historically makes one constituency more Labour than another, something very hard to measure directly. A second might be a strongly organized local trade-union movement, such as existed in the old mining constituencies and still persists today in a weakened form. Both of these variables could influence the relationship between the vote and party activism.

Thus the 1983 Labour vote acts as a kind of general 'omnibus' variable which represents omitted or unmeasured factors which might possibly account for the relationship between activism and the vote. In the light of this discussion, we consider estimates of different versions of the vote models next.

ESTIMATES OF THE 1987 ELECTION MODEL

The multiple regression models of the influence of party membership and party activism on the vote, controlling for social background and election-related variables, appear in Table 8.7.

The first model in this table measures the influence of party membership, together with the control variables on the Labour percentage of the vote in 1987. The table contains standardized regression coefficients which are interpreted in the same way as in

TABLE 8.7. *The Influence of Party Membership and Activism on Labour Voting in 1987, controlling for other Variables*

Predictor variables	Labour vote 1987	Change in vote 1983–7	Labour vote 1987	Change in vote 1983–7
Party membership	2	7*	—	—
Activism scale	—	—	2*	8**
North and West regions	11**	55**	11**	55**
Change in turn-out 1983–7	−1	−5	−1	−5
Marginality of seat in 1987	2*	7*	2*	8*
Percent manual workers	2	13**	2*	13**
Percent council tenants	1	6	1	6
Labour vote in 1983	91**	—	90**	—
Percent agricultural workers	−2*	−11**	−2*	−11**
R^2	97	44	97	44

* significant $p < 0.10$.
** significant $p < 0.05$.
Note: N = 480.

Table 5.10. This model suggests that geographical region, marginality, the rural character of the constituency, and the Labour vote in 1983 all had a significant impact on the Labour vote in 1987. The goodness of fit of this model as measured by the R^2 statistic is excellent with 97 per cent of the variance explained. This indicates that all the significant variables that determine the vote have been included in the model, and that it is unlikely that any important factors are omitted which might influence the relationship between the vote and party membership.

The strongest influence on the 1987 vote in the first model, which easily outshines the other variables, is Labour's share of the vote in 1983. As we pointed out above, this summarizes the influence of a wide variety of social and political variables, some of which are hard to measure directly.

The second most important effect is region, which confirms the point that constituencies in the north and west of Britain had a higher vote share than elsewhere, even when the influence of the 1983 vote is taken into account.

The third strongest effect relates to the marginality of the constituency. The marginality of the seat has a positive impact on the vote, which implies that the larger the winning margin the higher the Labour vote. Substantively this means that safe Labour seats have a higher winning margin than safe Conservative seats,[11] although investigating this question was not of course the reason for incorporating the variable into the model.

The other significant variable in the model is the percentage of agricultural workers, the indicator of the extent to which a constituency is rural in character. As might be expected, this has a negative effect on the Labour vote, so that the Labour vote is lower in rural constituencies even when the other variables are taken into account.

Labour party membership is not a statistically significant predictor of the Labour vote in 1987, in the presence of all the controls. This is also true of the change in turn-out, the percentage of manual workers, and the percentage of council tenants. Clearly, the apparent relationship between the Labour vote and membership which appears in Table 8.2 can be attributed to the control variables.

However, it would be premature to infer that campaign activity does not influence the vote; for one thing, party membership is not the best indicator of campaigning, which is why the activism scale was developed in the first place. But secondly, as we argued earlier, the best evidence of campaign effects would be a relationship between membership and the change in the Labour vote between 1983 and 1987, rather than between membership and the level of the Labour vote in 1987. This is examined in the second model in Table 8.7.

In the second model of Table 8.7 there is a statistically significant and positive relationship between the size of the Labour membership and the change in the vote between 1983 and 1987, even with all the control variables included in the model.[12] This finding considerably strengthens the argument that members are electorally important. The magnitude of the relationship is about the same as the impact of marginality on the change in the vote. The effect is almost four times

[11] Since marginality is the difference between the Labour vote, and the vote for other parties it takes on large values in safe Labour and safe Conservative seats, and small values in marginal seats. This difference is larger in safe Labour seats than it is in safe Conservative (or other) seats, hence the positive relationship between marginality and the 1987 vote.
[12] The Labour vote in 1983 is not included as a control in this model, since it already appears in the definition of the dependent variable, the change in the vote from 1983 to 1987.

stronger in the second model than it was in the first. Moreover, this is true in the presence of the various controls which themselves have a stronger influence than in the first model. The finding suggests that parties with above-average memberships were able to obtain above-average swings to Labour during the election campaign. The only other difference between these two models is that a high percentage of manual workers in a constituency appeared to have a significant impact on the change in the Labour vote, something not true in model one.

The third and fourth models in Table 8.7 use the same specifications as the first two models, but include the party-activism variable as the measure of campaigning rather than the membership variable. The activism variable has a statistically significant impact on both the level of the vote in 1987, and on the change in the vote between 1983 and 1987. Since this is a better measure of campaigning than party membership this strongly reinforces the proposition that local campaigning has an important influence on voting behaviour. Again, the impact of activism on the change in the vote is four times greater than its impact on the level of the vote.

Table 8.7 contains standardized coefficients, so that the magnitude of the different effects can be compared with each other, but it is hard to interpret them in terms of estimating the quantitative impact of party activism on the vote. This is much easier to do with the unstandardized regression coefficients.[13] Since these multivariate models provide excellent fits to the data, it is possible to use the model to simulate the outcome of the election using different assumptions about the levels of party activism and the size of the Labour party membership. Within limits we can rerun the 1987 General Election to see what effect different numbers of activists and members would have had on the outcome.

SIMULATING THE 1987 GENERAL ELECTION

The models confirm that party activism and to a lesser extent, membership have a significant impact on the change in the Labour vote in 1987, and so this will be the focus of the simulations. The

---

[13] In the case of the first two models in the table, unstandardized coefficients measure the impact of one additional party member on the vote, whereas standardized coefficients measure the impact of a change of one standard deviation in the membership variable on the standard deviation of the vote variable.

best model of the effects is the fourth model in Table 8.7, and if the non-significant variables are deleted and the model re-estimated, the unstandardized estimates of the model are as follows:

Change 1983–87 = −2.330 + 4.459 Region − 0.130 Agriculture
                         (2.48)   (14.44)   (3.18)
+ 0.020 Marginality + 0.0057 Activism + 0.069 Manual Workers
   (2.11)   (2.24)   (4.35)

The interpretation of these coefficients can be best illustrated by focusing on the Region variable. The coefficient of this variable implies that each constituency in the North and West regions of the country had an increase in the Labour vote 4.459 per cent higher than constituencies elsewhere in the country. The figures in parentheses are t-statistics which indicate that all the coefficients are highly statistically significant.

The interpretation of the activism coefficient is similar to that of region. Each additional point scored on the activism scale by a constituency party increased the change in the vote by 0.0057 per cent. To make this meaningful, it is better to translate it into membership figures by calculating the average increase in the activism score created by the recruitment of additional members. The average activism score per member in the sample of constituency parties was approximately 8.5. This can be interpreted with reference to Table 5.5 and implies that, roughly speaking, the average member displays an election poster frequently, delivers leaflets occasionally, and canvasses rarely.[14] Given this, an extra 100 members in a constituency party would, other things being equal, produce an extra 4.85 per cent increase in the Labour vote between 1983 and 1987.[15]

The mean change in the Labour vote in the 480 constituencies sampled was 3.6 per cent.[16] Thus if every local party had recruited an additional 100 members prior to the 1987 election, and each of these increased the activism score by an average of 8.5 points then the mean change in the Labour vote between 1983 and 1987 would have

[14] For displaying an election poster frequently they would score 4, for delivering leaflets occasionally 3, and for canvassing rarely 2, which totals 9 points.
[15] That is 0.0057 × 8.5 × 100 = 4.85, or the size of the effect × the average activism score per member × 100.
[16] This is almost exactly the same as the mean increase in the Labour vote for all constituencies of 3.7% between 1983 and 1987.

been 3.6 per cent plus 4.85 per cent, which equals 8.4 per cent. In other words those extra members imply that the Labour party would have received about 35.7 per cent of the total vote in 1987, rather than the 30.8 per cent the party actually received.

The mean number of party members in the constituencies in our sample was just over 300. Thus these estimates imply that the party could have obtained nearly 36 per cent of the poll if it had been about a third larger in size, assuming that the new members were as active as the old ones. It is unlikely that this would have been enough to win the General Election of 1987 for Labour, but it would have made the difference to the outcome of the election in a number of key marginal constituencies.

Another way of looking at these estimates is to relate them to the historical record of support for the Labour party in general elections since the war. If these relationships had held during earlier elections, then almost certainly Labour would have lost the General Elections of 1964 and 1974, if the party membership had been significantly smaller than it was at the time. Of course without accurate data on membership during those years, this is a speculative conclusion, but it is broadly consistent with the evidence.

We can go further and try to determine the size of the party membership required to actually have won the 1987 General Election. This is a more tentative estimate, however, because the larger the membership figure assumed, the less plausible is the assumption that other things remain equal, an essential requirement for this exercise. In other words it is not advisable to project the model too far away from the data used to estimate it in the first place. There is also the point that this calculation says nothing about where these extra votes come from; an increase in the Labour percentage of the vote might only bring a marginal advantage in seats, if it mostly comes from non-voters or from Alliance voters. Thus a vote captured from the Conservatives is worth more in terms of seats, than a vote captured from elsewhere.

But with these caveats in mind, if the Labour party had been about twice its current size in 1987, with an average of 600 members per constituency, and assuming that the model accurately represents relationships, the party would have obtained about 45 per cent of the vote in the election. This is about 1 per cent more than it obtained in 1964 when it narrowly won an overall majority, and probably would have been enough to have won the 1987 General Election.

The model can also be used to discuss scenarios in which the Labour party is smaller. If the party had been about half its current size in 1987, with an average membership of about 150 in each constituency then the Labour share of the vote in the election would have been about 23.5 per cent, which means that it would almost certainly have been overtaken by the Alliance and pushed into third place in the poll. Undoubtedly, such an outcome would have had dire long-term consequences for the electoral prospects of the party.

As we have stressed more than once, the projections from these simulations have to be interpreted with care, but even with that in mind the results show that an active party membership is absolutely vital to the electoral performance of the Labour party. If the party becomes significantly smaller or significantly de-energized[17] over time, this will have serious implications for its electoral prospects.

These findings have some general implications for our understanding of electoral politics in Britain. One implication is that the ubiquitous emphasis on the centralized media campaign in discussions of electoral behaviour is far too one-sided, since it is clear that local campaigning plays a big role in influencing election outcomes. Interestingly enough, the importance of the local campaign is often acknowledged in by-elections, particularly when a large government majority is overturned. But the assumption has been that such campaigns are of little importance in general elections. These results show this is not the case.

A second implication relates to discussions of the decline in electoral support for the Labour party over time (see Whiteley, 1982). As we pointed out in Chapter 2, different writers have emphasized different factors as explanations of this decline, including changes in the social structure, changes in the political values of the electorate, and policy failures of incumbent Labour governments (Sarlvik and Crewe, 1983; Whiteley, 1983; Franklin, 1985; and Rose and McAllister, 1990). The present findings indicate that the decline in party membership over time is a relatively hidden, but powerful causal factor in explaining electoral decline. Obviously, electoral decline and the decline in membership interact in complex ways, but clearly one way in which the party can help to reverse its long-term electoral decline is to promote party membership.

A third implication from these results derives from the findings of Chapter 5 that the average party member is more active than the

---

[17] We have to thank Lewis Minkin for this expression.

conventional wisdom would suggest. We have seen that although the activism scale predicts the vote better than the membership data, the latter is still a statistically significant predictor of the change in the Labour vote over time in Table 8.7. This means that constituency party membership recruitment drives which succeed in obtaining many new members will tend to boost the Labour vote in a particular locality both in local and general elections. Moreover, this is true if members join as a result either of national or local membership recruitment campaigns. This suggests that the party can profitably invest resources in recruitment drives both at the national and local levels, and that these will not only help to raise money, but they will also help to boost votes for the Labour party.

This completes our discussion of the influence of party members on the vote. In the final chapter we tie in together many of the themes raised in the earlier chapters to discuss the prospects for Labour party membership in the future.

9

Conclusions

> We need a four year plan to at least double the membership of
> this party and increase the activism within this party.[1]

The above quote from Larry Whitty reflects one important aspect of
the modernization strategy, and an increasing awareness on the part
of the party leadership that promoting the growth of party membership is an important priority. However, as the figures in Table 2.1
indicate, there is no evidence that the objective of doubling membership and increasing the level of activism over the four years period
from 1987 to 1991 has succeeded. The number of individual party
members rose by only 25,000 (10 per cent) between 1987 and 1991.
Furthermore as we saw in Table 5.1, our survey reveals that four in
every ten members felt themselves to be *less* active today than they
were five years ago. Thus judged in terms of Larry Whitty's commitment it appears that the drive to promote membership and political
activism in the party has failed.

The party's organizing staff deserve credit, however, for stemming
the haemorrhage of membership which occurred in the 1980s. In just
four years (1984–8) 60,000 left the party and individual membership
stood at its lowest level for forty years. That downward spiral has
been arrested. To increase membership at all in an age when parties
have to compete with a large number of other organizations vying to
attract individual supporters, is praiseworthy. Moreover, it can be
argued that in today's individualistic consumer society people are
more interested in leisure activities than in party politics. It is also
the case that when many of the members and Labour voters see the
party as being 'old-fashioned', as the evidence in Table 7.1 suggests,
it is hard to attract people into the party.

We commented in Chapter 2 on Labour's historical lack of concern with membership and we noted Alan Ware's observation that
of all mass-membership parties the Labour party has been the one to

[1] Quotation from address by Larry Whitty, General Secretary of the Labour party,
to 1987 Annual Party Conference.

take membership recruitment least seriously. In the 1980s a major change occurred in the party leadership's attitude towards membership and it now wants to recruit members, to eliminate any difficulties individuals might face in attempting to join the party, and to involve them more directly in internal party affairs. There is now a professionalism surrounding recruitment, fund-raising, and communication which is entirely new. What is missing, however, is a clear sense of the political input this growing membership should make to the party.

There is a feeling that the Labour party at the time of writing appears to be increasingly 'de-energized', an organization in which members are increasingly passive rather than active, disengaged rather than engaged. Further research is needed to verify this fully, but there does appear to have been a decline in many traditional forms of activism; for example, constituency party meetings are increasingly inquorate and the number of resolutions sent by local parties to party headquarters have declined.[2] In addition, the party at national level often refrains from mounting any campaigns against particular features of Conservative government policies for fear that they may be dominated by 'ultra-left extremists'.

The discussion in this concluding chapter focuses on some of the reasons why the party has failed to achieve the growth in membership which it has sought over the last few years, and what can be done about it. If the party is to be 're-energized' and new members are to be recruited it is important to understand the reasons behind the decline in membership. It should then be clearer what, if anything, can be done to improve the situation. If the evidence in Chapter 8 is anything to go by, arresting the membership decline is an urgent priority from the point of view of electoral politics, if for no other reason.

THE DECLINE OF PARTY MEMBERSHIP

Since 1945 there has been a trend decline in individual membership of most socialist parties in Western Europe. Bartolini (1983) shows that a steady and quite dramatic decline in membership has occurred in Norway and Denmark, and a rather slower decline, subject to fluctuations, has occurred in Austria, Finland, and France. The only

[2] This conclusion is based upon discussions with senior members of the staff at Labour party headquarters.

unambiguous exception to this trend appears to be in Germany, where membership of the Social Democratic party has risen steadily since the 1950s.

These trends must be set against a background of large differences in the size of party memberships in different countries. The Swedish Social Democratic party, to take only one example, has well over a million members, but even in Sweden there appears to have been a long-term decline in the party membership (Sjoblom, 1978).

Students of political parties have speculated extensively about these trends, some of which we discussed in Chapter 2, but it is useful to review the kind of factors which are important in explaining this decline. Some of these factors are beyond the control of any party organization, though this is not true for all of them.

Social and cultural changes of various kinds are partly responsible for these developments, and these are obviously hard to influence. There has been a long-term decline in traditional electoral alignments in most Western democratic systems, and this has had an impact on electoral support for socialist parties and by implication on their membership over time (Dalton, Flanigan, and Beck, 1984). Voters in these systems are becoming more volatile, and less attached to traditional parties. Obviously, a weakening of partisan attachments among voters is very likely to produce a parallel decline in activism among party members. In the case of Britain the decline of partisan allegiance is now well documented (Sarlvik and Crewe, 1983). With fewer strong partisans around in Britain, it is likely that there will be fewer people motivated to join political parties.

One aspect of this is the decline of the traditional working-class communities and the growth of the service sector in the economy at the expense of the manufacturing sector. In Chapter 5 we noted that there had been a long-term decline in the influence of social norms as mechanisms for recruiting party members. Tightly-knit working-class communities of people who live and work in close proximity to each other, often produced this type of membership, but this is now largely a thing of the past.

Another aspect of the decline is the growth of educational opportunities, particularly in higher education which has occurred in all Western democracies. Over the past twenty-five years the proportion of the population attending colleges or universities has increased by 472 per cent in Britain, 347 per cent in the United States, and by no less than 815 per cent in Sweden (Dalton, Flanigan, and Beck, 1984: 6).

This development has had two effects; higher education has led to higher incomes and a rapid expansion in information processing of all types, particularly in the electronic media, and a greater demand for information-based leisure activities of various kinds. These provide attractive alternatives to political participation. Secondly, the rise of educational opportunities has produced a variety of alternative forms of political participation, many of which are rivals to party membership.

These alternative forms of participation include single-issue pressure groups, and new social movements of various kinds. The rise of single-issue pressure groups can be seen, for example, in the social-welfare field where in recent years a large number of new groups have come into existence (Whiteley and Winyard, 1987). These provide a more rewarding type of political participation for many people than membership of a political party.

There has also been a significant rise in new social movements which are political groupings concerned with a broad range of environmental, feminist, and peace issues, and they compete directly with traditional party organizations. A central tenet of the value systems of individuals involved in these movements, is often a mistrust of traditional forms of bureaucratic party organization (Dalton and Kuechler, 1990). They are acutely aware of Michels' (1962) 'iron law of oligarchy', or the tendency for political parties to become dominated by oligarchies over time, and to lose sight of their democratic roots.

In the words of one writer the new social movements prefer to 'rely on small local organized cores, surrounded by loosely affiliated sympathizers, and on weak national umbrella organizations that are called upon to co-ordinate a limited number of central protest events or political campaigns' (Kitschelt, 1990: 185). Thus their organizational structure and approach to campaigning are largely foreign to a traditional party organization like that of the Labour party.

In the area of environmental politics these new social movements have given rise to new political parties, the Green parties, which are now a feature of the party systems in most European democracies. Generally, Green parties have adopted a decentralized, loosely structured organization which serves them well in the recruitment of activists, but can cause severe problems when they get candidates elected to office. This has been the recent experience of the Greens in Germany where they have made the biggest electoral gains (Offe, 1990).

The Labour party can attract some of these people, particularly as their understanding of the political process matures. But it cannot attract others, simply because they are opposed to a traditional party organizational structure. In addition many would oppose Labour party policies for various reasons. For example, many members of environmental groups would disagree with party policies aimed at promoting economic growth, since they feel these are inconsistent with protecting the environment.

Changes in the social structure of this type have occurred in most advanced industrial democracies, and have served to produce a decline in party membership. However, in the case of the Labour party there are other reasons specific to British politics, for the decline.

One obvious factor is the Conservative dominance over British politics during the 1980s, which has induced a sense of demoralization and defeatism on the left. In particular, the defeat of the miners' year-long strike, and of the opposition to rate-capping by local authorities in 1985, were serious blows to activist resistance to Conservative policies.

Secondly, there is the decline in the status and powers of local government, something which goes beyond Conservative attacks on Labour local authorities in its impact. Local government in Britain has faced more than a decade of financial cuts, and a growing centralized control over policy-making. The abolition of the Greater London Council and other metropolitan authorities were only a very visible part of this process of centralization.

This trend was partly the product of a Thatcherite attack on consensus politics, which used the powers of the state to defeat political opponents. But more generally it reflects a decline in political accountability, which has been one of the main consequences of the spread of 'managerialist' ideologies in the public sector. These ideas which have been a constant theme in public administration in Britain since the time of the Fulton Report of the 1960s, implicitly hold that the elective principle subverts efficiency in government. They stress the importance of greater size in local government, of 'corporate planning', and 'professional management'. The hidden assumption is that local government works best when it is run like a business by professionals who are unencumbered by considerations of democratic accountability.

Another aspect of the same development is the denigration of the public sector, and the ethic of public service so common during the Thatcher era. The rhetoric of that period reinforced the idea that public provision and public service were inherently inferior to private market provision, and to private entrepreneurship. This has added to the overall decline in the status of the public sector in these years.

One of the main by-products of the decline in the status of local government, is that the incentives for political participation at the local level have been reduced. Some of these incentives concern the campaigning aspects of party activism. There is little point in campaigning within the local party or a local community group to change policies, if the local council is hamstrung by a non-responsive central government. Others involve the representational aspects of party activism. Fewer people will join the party with the aim of becoming involved in local government, if that government can do very little about bad housing, poor schools, and other types of local problems.

There is little that the Labour party can do to change the status and importance of local government until it achieves office. At the time of writing the party has drawn up plans for constitutional reform outlined in the policy document *Labour's better way for the 1990s* (Labour Party, 1991) for devolution of power from the centre. This document states that 'Labour is determined to pass power downwards and outwards from Westminster and Whitehall to the nations and regions of Great Britain' (Labour Party, 1991: 49). This should improve the incentives for political participation to some degree, but there is a danger that these reforms are too focused on the regional level.

As we have seen, one of the best incentives for political participation is the conviction that the individual can make a significant difference to outcomes in his or her own community. As the discussion in Chapters 4 and 5 indicates, a strong sense of personal efficacy is very important to political involvement, and that is likely to be strongest at the level of the local community. In other words the smaller the community, the larger the influence of any one individual. Thus in implementing constitutional reforms, the party should avoid the danger of introducing regional political institutions which might become as remote as Whitehall to the lives of ordinary people.

If the party must await office before it carries out the devolution of power from the centre, there are other things it might do to improve participation and membership in the meantime. Some people think that the 'new model' Labour party is rather 'sanitized', in the sense that all forms of politics which might create controversy are played down. There can be little doubt that the internecine conflicts of the early 1980s had damaging electoral consequences, but in their anxiety to avoid repeating that experience the party leadership may have gone too far in the opposite direction in discouraging debate and controversy.

The party leadership, quite rightly, has developed a long-term strategy designed to win an electoral majority. But there are two potential problems with this if it is taken to the point that the party becomes 'sanitized'. First, it is important to note that if disunity exacts an electoral price, then so does blandness. Blandness puts off voters who complain that they cannot see the difference between the parties, and it de-energizes the activists who are no longer inclined to mobilize the vote.

Labour's spectacular improvement in political communication in the 1987 election campaign in comparison with 1983 has focused attention on the national campaign. It is clear that the role of individual party members as envisaged by the shadow communications agency, which advised Peter Mandelson in the late 1980s, was very limited. The agency's principle of operation was that there should be a shift in party campaigning 'from "grass-roots" opinion-forming to influencing electoral opinion through the mass media' (Hughes and Wintour, 1990: 52).

The success of the media campaign in the 1987 election was however rather limited. The Labour vote increased by only just over 3.5 per cent between the 1983 and 1987 elections. Given that, it is hard to make the case that the national media campaign is the all-important determinant of electoral performance. Of course there are important factors in an election which are beyond the control of the Labour party when it is in opposition, not least the state of the economy (see Clarke and Whiteley, 1990). These can override the best-planned national campaign strategy. But our argument, developed in Chapter 8, is that the importance of local campaigns has been overlooked, and that party strategists need to take this fact into account in planning election strategies.

This means that, up to a point, dissension and debate is good for the party. The assumption that a unified, centrally controlled campaign is the way to fight elections, ignores the evidence that the effects of a good campaign in 1987 were really rather modest, and also the point that local members need to be motivated in order to organize effective constituency campaigns.

One weakness of the centralized, media-based approach to campaigning is that the national media, particularly television, have their own agenda which they pursue regardless of Labour party electoral strategy. In 1987 research has shown that television editors and producers decided to give equal prominence to issues of defence and security during the campaign, along with the usual array of domestic political issues. By contrast, both the public and the Labour campaign team wanted to focus on domestic social and economic issues, which are generally more favourable to the Labour party (Miller *et al.*, 1990: 196–232).

This point, coupled with the fact that the Conservatives received significantly more favourable election coverage than Labour by virtue of being the party of government, underlines the inherent limitations of a centralized national campaign strategy for the party. No matter how well it is run, a centralized strategy rapidly comes up against entrenched interests in the media who have their own agenda to pursue.

Having made this point, it is of course the case that nobody would advocate repeating the kind of shambles which occurred in the national Labour campaign of 1983, but election planning in 1987 was too centralized and dominated by national media concerns. More attention and resources need to be given to the local campaigns, which can be used to overcome the biases in the national media against the party.

Another problem with playing down internal debates is that it inhibits policy innovation, and this can have damaging long-term consequences for party support. In Chapter 1 we argued that parties had an important role to play in policy-making, and if this is weakened the danger arises that the party will become merely reactive. It is important to remember that parties can to some extent shape the political environments in which they operate. This is an argument convincingly developed by Przeworski (1985), and it has been a constant theme of debates on the left about the success of 'Thatcherism' (Hobsbawm, 1981).

The Conservative party under Mrs Thatcher sought to reshape the landscape of British politics in order to try to lock in long-term electoral support. It sought to do this with policy innovations like the programme of privatization and the sale of council housing to existing tenants at discounts. Research shows that the success of these policies in direct electoral terms has in fact been very limited. New shareholders and ex-council tenants do not appear to have switched to the Conservatives in large numbers, partly because most of them were Conservative-inclined anyway (see Heath *et al.*, 1991). But these initiatives may have had a more important indirect effect of making the government look 'dynamic' and the Prime Minister 'strong' and willing to take bold initiatives. Labour has had little new to say about these initiatives, and has appeared to be on the defensive on these questions.

A party which seeks to go on the offensive and take the initiative cannot be merely reactive. Thus the Labour party needs lively internal debates about future policy if it is to find these future policy innovations. In this way new ideas will emerge and support for specific policy commitments can be built over time. At present the party appears to lack the will to develop a distinctive, principled point of view on any matter if, as a consequence, it might attract hostile comment.

Some critics of the modernization strategy, like Eric Heffer (1986) have gone so far as to suggest that the 'new model' Labour party has become a 'mark two' version of the Social Democratic party. We have seen in Chapter 7, that this view is not shared by most party members. But nevertheless, it highlights a potential danger facing the party.

Another aspect of the point about the incentives for political participation, is that structural reforms have reduced the powers of the activists. Thus some of the incentives for attending local party meetings no longer exist. The constituency party's choice of parliamentary candidate and decision over whom to vote for in the election of Party Leader and Deputy Leader are no longer the sole prerogative of party delegates. Furthermore, the constituency party's choice over whom to vote for as its representatives on the NEC is also now decided by an individual ballot of local members.

Of course it is hard to argue that these powers are all that significant in making a particular individual active, since they are exercised only infrequently. But their removal sends a powerful signal to the 'contact' activists—the ones who attend meetings—that the party is less willing to listen to them and take account of their preferences than used to be the case.

The same point could be made about those activists who have been removed from office in recent years by the National Executive Committee. For example, in May 1991 the party instructed the Labour Group on Lambeth council to choose an alternative leader to Councillor Joan Twelves, whom the NEC decided was bringing the local party into disrepute. Another example of this occurred in 1988 when the NEC refused to approve the Vauxhall constituency party's choice of parliamentary candidate and instead imposed its own candidate, Kate Hoey, to contest the parliamentary by-election.

No doubt the NEC had good reasons for making these decisions. In the latter case, the intervention was probably prompted by the Greenwich by-election fiasco of February 1987, when a hard-left Labour candidate was rejected by a working-class electorate in a seat which had been Labour for many years. But the net result of this centralization of decision-making has been to send a message to the activists that their views may be overridden if the party headquarters decides that bad publicity will result from their actions.

The findings in Chapters 4 and 5 suggest that if the party wishes to increase its membership, and get many of the existing members to be more active it has to pay attention to the incentives facing ordinary party members. It is clear that inactive party members will respond to incentives designed to get them more involved, but only if power and influence are genuinely devolved down to the grass-roots level. In terms of the earlier discussion, the 'lumpiness' of the collective good is directly related to the ability of members to influence policy outcomes—the higher the threshold before the members can exercise influence the less incentive they have to be active.

The main purpose of these centralized curbs on the local parties is to prevent them making decisions which will attract adverse publicity and damage the party's image. Behind this is a hidden concern that party activists may be so different in their political attitudes from Labour voters, that the leadership cannot trust them to make sensible decisions. In other words if they are largely unrepresentative 'extremists', whose views on most questions differ quite markedly from the views of voters, then the leadership will have to curb their activities if the Labour party is to attract voters.

There are examples of local Labour parties which have been taken over by 'ultra-leftists' of the type associated with the Militant Tendency, and which have done things that have undermined support for the Labour party, particularly among working-class voters. But there is little hard evidence to support the argument that party activists in general are 'extremists' in comparison with voters. It is true that this image of party activists has been promoted in recent years by a virulent propaganda campaign by the Tory press against 'loony left' local authorities, and prominent individuals like Tony Benn and Ken Livingstone. But the evidence to support it is largely absent.

This is a question of some importance connected with the future strategy of the Labour party, so that it needs to be examined closely. Since the membership survey replicated a number of issue questions in the British Election Study, we can examine the extent to which this image is supported by the evidence.

AN ATTITUDE PROFILE OF MEMBERS AND VOTERS

In Chapter 3 we briefly touched on the question of whether or not party members radically differed from Labour voters in their attitudes to political issues. We saw that on the issues of unilateralism and nationalization members did differ substantially from voters, but that on several other issues there were great similarities in the opinions of the two groups. In this section we want to probe this question more deeply.

It will be recalled that in Chapter 5 we developed an index of collective benefits which, it was argued, would motivate individuals to become actively involved in politics. This index, B_i, was constructed from a set of issue indicators which also appear in the British Election Study. This means that we can examine the attitudes of party members, both active and inactive, and voters, both Labour and non-Labour, to a common set of issue indicators. This should provide a guide to how 'extremist' party activists are, in comparison with voters. This evidence is in Table 9.1, where we compare the opinions of Labour party activists, Labour party members, Labour voters, and finally all voters (including Labour voters) in relation to a set of nine issues.

Table 9.1. *The Opinions of Activists, Members, Labour Voters and All Voters on Political Issues* (percentages)

Issue		Definitely should	Probably should	Doesn't matter	Probably should not	Definitely should not
Get rid of private education	A	50	22	15	11	3
	M	41	23	18	14	5
	L	16	20	30	24	10
	V	7	11	22	30	30
Spend more money to get rid of poverty	A	93	6	1	0	0
	M	89	10	1	0	0
	L	73	24	2	1	1
	V	49	39	5	6	2
Encourage private medicine	A	2	1	3	10	84
	M	2	2	5	17	75
	L	6	14	13	34	33
	V	10	28	17	28	17
Spend more on the NHS	A	95	5	0	0	0
	M	94	5	0	0	1
	L	81	17	1	1	0
	V	57	35	3	5	1

Introduce stricter laws for trade unions	A	2	7	7	25	59
	M	3	9	10	29	50
	L	7	19	14	31	30
	V	22	31	12	23	12
Reduce government spending generally	A	5	11	5	25	54
	M	6	15	6	29	44
	L	14	30	12	25	19
	V	11	35	13	30	11
Give workers more say in places where they work	A	72	23	2	2	2
	M	64	30	3	2	2
	L	40	47	5	7	1
	V	29	50	7	12	3
Spend less on defence	A	64	22	2	6	5
	M	60	26	3	7	5
	L	14	30	12	25	19
	V	16	25	8	29	23
Pull troops out of Northern Ireland immediately	A	35	28	4	22	11
	M	35	28	4	22	11
	L	36	29	5	20	11
	V	26	26	5	26	17

A = Party activists; M = Party members; L = Labour voters; V = All voters

The Labour party activists in Table 9.1, are the very active party members, defined in the same way as in Table 5.6. In other words they are individuals who scored highly on the political activism scale developed in Chapter 5. The second group of Labour party members, consists of all respondents in the membership survey. Finally, the voters consist of Labour voters and all voters in the British Election Study of 1987.

The wording and format of the question in the membership survey was exactly the same as that of the election study, so there are no methodological differences between the two surveys except the fact that they were carried out more than two years apart.[3] As we suggest below, this probably makes a significant difference to responses only in the case of one question.

Responses by the four different groups can be classified into four types. The first type contains questions for which there are no significant differences between the four groups, in effect where there is a consensus of opinions. The second type consists of issues where there are differences between Labour supporters, i.e. party members, activists, and Labour voters on the one hand, and voters in general on the other. The third type contains issues in which members and activists differ significantly from Labour voters, and all voters. Finally, the fourth type are the issues where the activists differ significantly from everyone else.

The charge that members and activists are out of touch or 'extreme' in relation to voters applies only to the third and fourth types of issues. The fourth type, in particular covers the 'loony left' case, where the activists are out of touch with everyone else.

The evidence in Table 9.1 shows, surprisingly enough, that the first category, in which there is a broad consensus of opinions, contains most issues. No less than four out of the nine issue indicators are in this category. These are 'Spend more money to get rid of poverty'; 'Spend more on the NHS'; 'Give workers more say in the places that they work'; and 'Pull troops out of Northern Ireland immediately'. Clear majorities of Labour party activists, party members, party voters, and all voters, sometimes large majorities, think that the government should do these things. The only significant difference between party members and voters on these issues

---

[3] The preamble to the set of issue questions reads 'Please indicate whether you think the government should or should not do the following things, or doesn't it matter either way?'.

relates to the intensity of their preferences. With the exception of the Northern Ireland indicator, activists and party members are more likely to feel strongly than voters about these issues, but there is no difference between them in terms of a majority of opinions.

Two of the indicators in this first category are rather surprising, the indicators relating to industrial democracy and to Northern Ireland. Clearly, if a future Labour government introduced measures of industrial democracy, such as the idea of electing workers on to company boards, this would not only please the activists and party members, it would also command majority support among voters in general. The same could be said about withdrawing troops from Northern Ireland.

The other two issues of the first type are not surprising, since the popularity of the National Health Service has been apparent in many opinion surveys over the years, as is the widespread public concern about the growing problem of poverty.

The second category of issue, in which Labour supporters, members, and voters differ from voters in general, contains two issues: 'Introduce stricter laws to regulate trade unions'; and 'Encourage private medicine'. It is clear that voters in general are more likely to favour these policies than Labour supporters. However, even for these issues it would not be true to say that clear majorities of all voters support both policies. Some 38 per cent of all voters would encourage private medicine, but no less than 45 per cent of them would not.

Thus it seems plausible that a Labour government which actively supported the National Health Service and at the same time curbed many of the hidden subsidies to private medicine from the NHS, would please Labour supporters in general, and would not be opposed by a majority of other voters, particularly if the two policies were linked together into an overall package.

Thirdly, there is the type of issues which separates party members on the one hand from voters in general on the other. There are three of these: 'Get rid of private education'; 'Reduce Government spending generally'; and 'Spend less on defence'. There is, however, one problem for the defence issue which also applies to the question of unilateral nuclear disarmament discussed in Chapter 3. Reliable comparisons between Labour members and voters on these issues are problematic, since the international situation changed so dramatically between the time of the election study and the time of the membership survey.

At the time of the election study the cold war was thawing but still very much alive; but by the time of the membership survey it was dead. This means that voters were answering these questions in a very different political environment from members. Part of the reason why members are more enthusiastic about cutting defence in comparison with voters is because of this fact.

This means that differences between party members and voters cannot be reliably judged on the defence issue. Thus we must examine opinions on private education, and on public spending in general to get a picture of the differences between these groups. Opinions clearly differ on the question of private education. Party members are in favour of abolition, and voters are against it. However, Labour voters are less supportive of private education than voters in general.

On the issue of public spending party members are clearly more in favour of it than voters. However, there is no evidence that a majority of voters wants cuts in public spending. Some 46 per cent of all voters support the ideal of cuts in public spending, compared with 41 per cent who oppose this ideal. Labour voters are even less enthusiastic about the idea, since 44 per cent of them oppose it, exactly the same percentage who support it.

The other important point to make about the public-spending indicator is that it is inconsistent with the spending questions on the Health Service and poverty.[4] Voters may echo the Thatcherite rhetoric about the desire to cut spending in general terms, but they do not support it in the case of specific policies.

Finally, if we consider the fourth type of question, where party activists differ from everyone else, it is important to note that there are no examples of such questions in this battery of nine issue indicators. Thus the conventional wisdom which suggests that party activists are 'extremists', whose opinions in general do not reflect those of any other group, whether party members or voters, is quite wrong.

It is also wrong if it is extended to mean differences between party

[4] This particular version of the public-spending question can be criticized on the grounds that it offers people a costless alternative. If they are offered, in effect, something for nothing they are likely to accept it. For this reason the public-expenditure question in Table 3.10 is a superior measure, since it asks people to consider the trade-off between spending and cuts. It is noteworthy that differences between voters and members on that version of the public-expenditure question are relatively trivial.

members on the one hand and voters on the other. Many of the salient domestic political issues, such as support for the Health Service and anti-poverty policy produce a consensus of opinion in all groups. The only difference between party members and voters on these issues is that the former tend to feel more intensely about these questions than the latter. This is of course one of the reasons why they are party members in the first place.

The point that there are no really significant differences between party activists and party members is consistent with the discussion of Chapter 5. We observed in that chapter that activists are more left-wing than party members, but that differences between these two groups are not large. The results in Table 9.1 reinforce that conclusion.

It could of course be argued that the most important issue in which there are clear differences between party members and voters does not appear in Table 9.1. This is the issue of nationalization, which was examined in Table 3.10, where we observed very significant differences between the opinions of these two groups. However, within the Labour party the issue of nationalization is much more than a public-policy question about the role of the state in running British industry. It has become very much a symbolic question, because it has a long association with historic conflicts between the Left and the Right over Clause 4 of the party constitution. While the voters may see it in practical terms, to do with whether or not nationalized industries deliver a better service at a better price than the private sector, activists and members often see it as a fundamental touchstone measure of socialist values.

Interestingly enough, this has not always been the case. As we pointed out in Chapter 6, the founding fathers of the Labour party were more concerned about the 'democratic control of industry', than about nationalization on the Morrisonian model. Furthermore there has always been a strong tradition in the party, exemplified by the Co-operative party, which fundamentally disagrees with the idea that state monopolies run by political appointees brings about democratic control of industry.

It is not our purpose to argue the merits for and against nationalization in this discussion, although it does seem to be the case that the party has neglected other more popular methods of making private capitalism more accountable, as the responses to the question on industrial democracy in Table 9.1 indicate. Our main point is rather that nationalization is connected to so many other symbolic issues in the party, that it invokes many political values other than the narrow issue of public ownership. In other words party activists and Labour voters are really answering different questions when they are asked about nationalization. For this reason it provides poor support for the proposition that party members are unrepresentative extremists.

The opinion evidence suggests little support for the argument that party members and activists are unrepresentative extremists. It is true that they differ from voters on some issues, and in general they feel more intensely about issues than the voters, but the 'loony left' label is largely a myth. It should be recognized for what it is, namely a piece of cheap propaganda.

Overall then, the party has much to gain by promoting local activism and local campaigns of various kinds. 'Re-energizing' the party means devolving power to the grass roots, and aside from the issue of Trotskyite entryism which was a clear threat to the party but which has now been largely diffused by Neil Kinnock, there is much to be gained by promoting further democratization. There is every reason for the party headquarters to organize and support political campaigns of various kinds at the local level, since these promote participation and ultimately will help to sustain party membership. De-energized local Labour parties represent much more of a danger to the electoral future of the party, than vociferous campaigns on local and national issues.

CONCLUSIONS

We should end perhaps by posing the same question as that discussed in Chapter 1: Does the Labour party really need a thriving grass-roots party? If it is possible to raise sufficient funds from inactive supporters, particularly by means of computerized direct mailing, and if a future government introduces the state funding of political parties, it can be argued that there is less of a need for party members. If in the future political communication is conducted primarily through the media, and by means of advertising, there is less need for the party's foot-soldiers to knock on doors and represent the party at the local level.

There are those in the Labour party who envisage a reduced role for both members and activists. They may concede that members help to provide funds, and give the party a sense of political legitimacy. But there is a suspicion that members are also a nuisance because they intrude into the process of political packaging. It is easier to direct party activities from the top when the grass-roots members appear to have no legitimate role to play in politics. In this view a mass-membership party in which individual supporters are willing to affirm and provide money is acceptable, but one in which they play a role in policy formation and the selection of leading personnel is not.

We have discussed some of the reasons why grass-roots members are important at various different points in the book. First, local government although limited and further curtailed in the 1980s, remains an important feature of representative democracy. Party politics still predominate in local government and the Labour party, as one of the major parties, needs to recruit individuals willing to become local councillors.

In addition, local school governing-boards have local government representatives as part of their membership, and it is important for the Labour party to ensure that its point of view is represented on these boards, which now have enhanced powers over education. Local magistrates are also chosen from a wide range of personnel in the community but one of the nominating bodies from which these people are selected is the local Labour party. A membership party, in other words, acts as a net, trawling people into local public life.

Parties, however, act as more than recruitment agencies for public representatives. They still require members for the traditional electioneering functions of canvassing and leafleting voters and persuading supporters to go out and vote. Legal restrictions in Britain mean that, unlike in some other countries, local election campaigns cannot be purchased. For this reason members remain a significant force in constituency campaigning. Conventional academic wisdom has suggested that local electioneering has been superseded in importance by national campaigning in which parties are not bound by the same financial and legal restrictions. It has been argued that so long as the parties can raise enough money to sustain their national campaigns there is no need for active, local members. But as we show in Chapter 8 local members do have a very important role in general-election campaigns, perhaps even equally as important as the national campaign.

In addition, local-government elections should not be ignored in this emphasis on the local campaign in general elections. Academics disagree over the extent to which local elections are mini-general elections, won or lost on the basis of national parties' overall performance. Whether the local vote is determined by national factors or not, there is still a need for local volunteers to fight the campaigns.

Grass-roots parties provide elected representatives, they carry out electioneering, but thirdly they are 'opinion carriers'. They provide a voice in the community, often becoming key opinion-formers in the neighbourhood. In this respect they help to set the political agenda, and legitimize certain opinions in comparison with others. The exact processes of opinion formation in the local community about political issues are not known, but there is a 'spiral of silence' (Noelle-Neumann, 1984) in which issues can be pushed off the agenda when they have no effective advocates in the community. At its most general, the local Labour party gives voice to opinions and interests which would otherwise be crowded out of the political process.

Grass-roots party members are themselves aware of these things. They join the party because they hope that it will make a difference to themselves, their communities, and ultimately to Britain. Therefore it is perhaps appropriate to end this book with the words of one of the respondents. This 39-year-old Scot gave her reasons for joining the party as follows, reasons echoed by thousands of other respondents:

I felt that the Tory party did not care about local services, people or the 'ordinary person' and that the Labour party should be in power and would protect the NHS, local government, and try to eradicate poverty. In my job I do see so much poverty and it is getting worse while others get richer.

So we end with a question. How could the Labour party do without people like that?

APPENDIX I

The Design of the Survey

The empirical aspects of the project began in August 1989 with an extensive series of face-to-face interviews with Labour party members in Sheffield and Bristol using various versions of the questionnaire. The aim was to develop a set of indicators which would be both reliable and valid measures of the underlying theoretical ideas, using a mail-survey approach. The development phase of the questionnaire lasted about four months.

At the same time the sampling strategy was developed. The sample used was a two-stage systematic random sample of party members. The first stage involved selecting a total of 480 constituencies as sampling points, using a sampling frame stratified by Labour party regions. This ensured a representative regional distribution of constituencies. The second stage involved selecting a systematic random sample of party members from the national membership lists kept at the Labour party headquarters in Walworth Road.

The aim was to draw a sample of approximately one member in thirty from the constituencies selected in the first stage. In the event a total of 8,075 questionnaires were sent out to party members, and 5,065 were returned which represents a response rate of 62.5 per cent. Since some of the membership lists derived from 1988 rather than 1989, and there were some errors in their initial compilation, we believe this represents a higher response rate than this figure suggests. Overall, this is an excellent response rate for a survey using this type of design.

By conventional standards we have selected a large sample. This was done in order to facilitate regional analysis, although in the event regional variations in most of the important variables turned out to be small. We also required a large sample to estimate models of the effects of party activism on the vote at the constituency level. These are discussed in Chapter 8.

Each of the members in the sample received an initial letter from Larry Whitty the General Secretary of the Labour party explaining the nature of the study, and endorsing it on behalf of the Labour party. The questionnaire, together with a second letter from Larry Whitty and a letter from the research team was sent shortly after this first letter. Members in the sample were given a hotline number to call at the University of Sheffield, if they had any questions about the survey.

The first reminder to non-respondents was sent shortly after the daily response rate to the questionnaires had peaked, some three to four weeks after the initial mailing. This produced another upsurge in replies, and a second reminder, together with an additional questionnaire was sent to the remaining non-respondents about a month after that.

In order to investigate potential biases in the responses a short two-page questionnaire was designed and sent to a random sample of the remaining non-respondents, about two months after the second reminder. This questionnaire comprised social background questions on age, gender, social class, trade-union membership, and ethnicity. A sample of non-respondents was selected to ensure that the short questionnaire could be followed up vigorously by telephone and mail. A total of 150 short questionnaires were obtained.

The information from the short questionnaire suggested that respondents to the main survey were more likely to be middle class and members of a trade union, than Labour party members as a whole, though the biases were not large. Accordingly, information from the short questionnaire was used to design interlocking weights for social class and trade-union membership which were applied to the full survey. This was done by concatenating the file of 150 non-respondents, with a random sample of 245 respondents from the full study (i.e. to produce a combination of 38 per cent non-respondents, and 62 per cent respondents) to derive the weights. The weighted sample, which is used in all the analysis consists of 5,071 respondents.

The weighting and all data analysis was done using Releases 3 and 4 of SPSS (Statistical Package for the Social Sciences). The data is available from the ESRC archive at the University of Essex. The data consists of a data file, and an SPSS set-up file. Anyone using the data for secondary analysis should use the weight variable for consistent results.

As usual in this kind of survey the interpretation of the results is solely that of the authors, and does not necessarily represent the views of the ESRC or the Labour party.

APPENDIX II

The Questionnaire

INTRODUCTION

The questions inside cover a wide range of subjects, but each one can be answered simply by placing a tick (✓) or writing in a number in one or more of the boxes provided. In some cases you are asked to write in answers. No special knowledge is needed to fill in the questionnaire, and we are sure that everyone will be able to give an opinion on all questions.

We want all people to take part, not just those with strong views about a particular issue. The questionnaire should not take too long to complete and we think you will find it interesting and enjoyable. It should be completed only by the person to whom it was sent, so that responses will reflect all shades of opinion within the Labour party.

When you have filled it in, please place it in the enclosed postage paid envelope and post it back to us, as soon as you possibly can.

THANK YOU FOR YOUR HELP

1. Would you call yourself very strong Labour, fairly strong, not very strong, or not at all strong?

PLEASE TICK ONE BOX ONLY

Very Strong	54.9
Fairly Strong	38.0
Not Very Strong	6.0
Not At All Strong	1.1

2. Thinking back to the time you first joined the Labour Party, did you approach the Party to apply for membership, or did they approach you?

PLEASE TICK ONE BOX ONLY

I approached the local party	71.4
The local party approached me	20.9
I approached the regional party	1.5
I approached the national party	6.2
Don't Remember	

2a. IF YOU APPROACHED THE LOCAL PARTY
Did you find it easy or difficult to make contact with them?

PLEASE TICK ONE BOX ONLY

Very Easy	40.3
Easy	42.6
Difficult	13.2
Very Difficult	3.9

3. In which year did you first join the Labour Party?

PLEASE WRITE IN THE YEAR _____

4. Have you been a member continuously since that time?

PLEASE TICK ONE BOX ONLY

Yes   85.8

No   14.2

4a. If NO, how many years have you been a member altogether?

PLEASE WRITE IN   _____ Years

_____

5. What was your MOST important reason for joining the Labour Party? (feel free to explain in detail)

PLEASE WRITE IN

_____

_____

_____

_____

_____

_____

6. What annual membership subscription do you pay to the party?

PLEASE WRITE IN THE AMOUNT   £ _____

6a. What do you think the cost of the annual subscription for membership of the Labour Party should be for someone like yourself?

PLEASE TICK ONE BOX ONLY

Under £5   29.0

£5 up to £10   31.4

£10 up to £15   24.7

£15 up to £20   10.2

Over £20   4.7

_____

7. Have you responded to any of the national appeals for money by the Labour Party in the LAST YEAR?

PLEASE TICK ONE BOX ONLY

Yes	35.0
No	65.0

---

8. Thinking back over the LAST YEAR, how often have you had contact with people active in your local branch or Constituency Labour party?

PLEASE TICK ONE BOX ONLY

Not at all	9.6
Rarely	16.9
Occasionally	29.4
Frequently	44.1

---

9. Thinking back over the LAST YEAR, how often have you attended a Labour Party meeting?

PLEASE TICK ONE BOX ONLY

Not at all	36.0
Rarely	13.6
Occasionally	19.9
Frequently	30.4

9a. If you attended AT LEAST ONE meeting within the LAST YEAR, please indicate your reactions to it using the following scales.

If, for example, you found the meeting very interesting, you would tick the box on the left hand side. If you found it very boring, you would tick the box on the right hand side. If you found it neither boring nor interesting, you would tick the middle box.

If you attended more than one meeting, think about the LAST meeting you attended.

IF YOU DIDN'T ATTEND A MEETING WITHIN THE LAST YEAR, GO TO QUESTION 10.

PLEASE TICK ONE BOX ONLY
FOR EACH DESCRIPTION

	very	fairly	neither	fairly	very	
Interesting	22.2	48.8	9.4	14.0	5.7	Boring
Unfriendly	4.9	10.6	12.2	32.9	39.5	Friendly
Efficiently Run	26.8	43.4	11.0	12.6	6.2	Badly Run
United	21.2	39.1	14.3	15.3	10.1	Divided
Hard to Understand	2.4	9.0	12.4	30.6	45.6	Easy to Understand
Working Class	20.2	20.4	27.2	20.7	11.5	Middle Class
Left wing	6.2	29.1	45.4	13.7	5.5	Right wing
Old-Fashioned	9.7	19.3	33.5	28.0	9.5	Modern

10. Are you more active or less active within the party than you were five years ago, or about the same?

PLEASE TICK ONE BOX ONLY

More active	19.8
Less active	42.6
About the same	37.6

11. Do you at present hold any office(s) within the Labour party? (e.g. Branch Secretary, Constituency Treasurer, Branch membership Secretary)

PLEASE TICK ONE BOX ONLY

Yes	14.2
No	85.8

11a. If YES, which one(s)?   Since When?

PLEASE WRITE IN

_____   _____

_____   _____

_____   _____

_____

12. How much time do you devote to party activities in the average month?

PLEASE TICK ONE BOX ONLY

None	50.5
Up to 5 hours	30.3
From 5 up to 10 hours	9.6
From 10 up to 15 hours	4.0
From 15 up to 20 hours	2.0
More than 20 hours	3.7

_____

13. Before you joined the party were either your father or mother a Labour party member?

PLEASE TICK ONE BOX ONLY

Yes	30.2
No	69.8
Don't Know	

_____

14. Are you currently a local Labour councillor?

PLEASE TICK ONE BOX ONLY

Yes	5.8
No	94.2

14a. Do you currently represent the Labour party on any official bodies (e.g. as a school governor, or member of an area health authority)?

PLEASE TICK ONE BOX ONLY

	Yes	15.2
	No	84.8

14b. If YES, which is the MOST important one to you?

PLEASE WRITE IN

_____

_____

15. Are you currently a member of any of the following groups within the party?

PLEASE TICK AS MANY AS APPLY

	Yes		Yes
Young Socialists	0.7	Tribune Group	0.5
Co-operative Party	5.5	Black section	0.4
Fabian Society	2.7	Campaign Group	2.4
Women's Section	4.7	Campaign for Labour Party Democracy	1.1
Workplace Branch	1.2	Labour Co-ordinating Committee	0.9

None of These [ ]

Others (PLEASE WRITE IN)

_____

_____

_____

_____

_____

16. WITHIN THE LAST YEAR have you actively supported, (for exam-
    ple by signing a petition or attending a meeting) any political cam-
    paigns promoted by the Labour party?
    (e.g. the Poll Tax campaign, or the NHS campaign)

PLEASE TICK ONE BOX ONLY

Yes 81.7

No   18.3

17. Next there is a set of statements about important political issues. We
    would like to know if you agree or disagree with them.

PLEASE TICK ONE BOX
FOR EACH STATEMENT

	Strongly Agree	Agree	Neither	Disagree	Strongly Disagree
The central question of British Politics is the class struggle between labour and capital	28.2	37.8	14.4	16.2	3.3
The Labour Party should adjust its policies to capture the middle ground of politics	19.3	38.0	9.9	22.3	10.6
The Public Enterprises privatized by the Tory government should be returned to the public sector	44.7	37.2	10.2	6.8	1.1
The next Labour government should establish a prices and incomes policy as a means of controlling inflation	24.9	39.2	16.4	14.8	4.7
Modern methods of farming have caused great damage to the countryside	44.3	41.4	9.9	3.9	0.4

17. (Continued)

	Strongly Agree	Agree	Neither	Disagree	Strongly Disagree
The next Labour government should abolish private fee-paying education entirely	37.1	23.7	14.0	22.1	3.1
It is better for Britain when Trade Unions have little power	3.5	9.6	13.3	44.6	29.0
Income and wealth should be redistributed towards ordinary working people	46.0	41.8	7.7	3.8	0.8
The production of goods and services is best left to a free market	5.4	19.7	17.0	34.3	23.6
Workers in private industry should be encouraged to become shareholders in their firms	15.4	45.1	18.1	14.6	6.7
The Labour party should only adopt policies supported by a majority of working class people	16.2	26.1	17.4	33.9	6.4
The Labour party should support individuals who refuse to pay the Poll Tax	21.2	20.7	13.9	32.4	11.8
Further nuclear energy development is essential for the future prosperity of Britain	3.5	8.9	8.2	35.8	43.7

17. (Continued)

	Strongly Agree	Agree	Neither	Disagree	Strongly Disagree
High income tax makes people less willing to work hard	12.9	22.4	10.7	37.9	16.2
The Labour party should always stand by its principles even if this should lose an election	25.2	35.7	11.9	20.5	6.7

18. Are you a member of any of the following interest groups?

PLEASE TICK AS MANY AS APPLY

	Yes		Yes
Anti-Apartheid Movement	11.8	SHELTER	2.5
Amnesty International	6.8	OXFAM	7.0
Friends of the Earth	8.2	MIND	1.7
Campaign for Nuclear Disarmament	18.9	Child Poverty Action Group	2.4

National Council for Civil Liberties   3.1

None of these   ☐

18a. Are you a member of any other interest groups? (e.g. a local tenants group, community action group, women's group or charity)

IF SO, PLEASE WRITE IN

_____

_____

_____

19. Did you become a Labour party member as a result of campaign activity in an interest group? (e.g. such as CND, or a local campaign to prevent hospital closures in your area)

PLEASE TICK ONE BOX ONLY

Yes	8.6
No	91.4

20. Are you a member of a trade union or staff association?

PLEASE TICK ONE BOX ONLY

Yes—Trade Union	63.8
Yes—Staff Association	2.7
No	33.5

20a. If YES, what is the name of your trade union, or staff association?

PLEASE WRITE IN

21. Did you become a party member as a result of voluntary work in your trade union or staff association?

PLEASE TICK ONE BOX ONLY

Yes	14.2
No	85.8

22. What was your age last birthday?

PLEASE WRITE IN _____ Years

23. Please indicate your gender.

PLEASE TICK ONE BOX ONLY

Female	39.2
Male	60.8

24. Next we would like to ask you about political activities you may have taken part in during the last FIVE YEARS.

ACTIVITY How often have you done this?

PLEASE TICK ONE BOX FOR EACH ACTIVITY

	Not at All	Rarely	Occasionally	Frequently
Displayed an election poster in a window	10.2	3.8	20.8	65.3
Signed a petition supported by the party	6.0	4.6	30.1	59.3
Donated money to Labour party funds	18.4	15.0	33.9	32.8
Delivered party leaflets during an election	17.3	5.1	20.9	56.7
Attended a party meeting	18.1	13.8	25.6	42.4
Canvassed voters on behalf of the party	33.9	9.4	21.1	35.6
Stood for office within the party organisation	70.5	5.2	9.7	14.6
Stood for elected office in a local or national election	84.9	2.3	4.2	8.7

Other (Please specify)

_____

_____

_____

25. How old were you when you finished continuous full-time education?

PLEASE WRITE IN

_____ Years

26. Which of these descriptions applies to what you were doing last week, that is, in the seven days ending last Sunday?

PLEASE TICK ONE BOX ONLY

In full-time paid work	52.0
In full-time Education	3.0
On a government training/employment scheme (e.g. Youth Training Scheme)	0.4
In part-time paid work	8.1
Waiting to take up paid work already accepted	0.2
Unemployed and Registered at a benefit office	3.2
Unemployed and NOT Registered	0.8
Permanently sick or disabled	3.9
Wholly retired from work	19.1
Looking after the home full-time	4.8
In part-time voluntary (unpaid) work	1.4
Other (Please Specify)	3.0

26a. Which type of organisation do you work for? (If you are not working now, please answer about your LAST job)

PLEASE TICK ONE BOX ONLY

A private firm or company	36.6
Nationalised Industry/Public Corporation	9.6
Local Authority/Local Education Authority	27.1
Health Authority/Hospital	5.4
Central Government/Civil Service	5.0
Other (please specify)	16.2

26b. Are you self-employed, or do you work for someone else as an employee?
(If you are not working now, please answer about your LAST job)

PLEASE TICK ONE BOX ONLY

Self-employed	8.8
Employee	89.7
Never had a job	1.5

26c. In your job, do you supervise, or are you responsible for the work of any other people? (Again if you are not working now, please answer in terms of your LAST job.)

PLEASE TICK ONE BOX ONLY   Yes   44.2

                                            No   55.8

26d. If YES, how many people do you supervise?

PLEASE WRITE IN THE NUMBER

_____

26e. What is the title of your present job? (Again if you are not working now, please answer about your LAST job.)

PLEASE WRITE IN

_____

_____

26f. Would you describe in detail the type of work you do, being as specific as you can?

PLEASE WRITE IN

_____

_____

_____

_____

27. Do you ever think of yourself as belonging to any particular social class?

PLEASE TICK ONE BOX ONLY   Yes   72.5

                                            No   27.5

27a. If YES, which class is that?

PLEASE TICK ONE BOX ONLY

                            Middle Class   27.9

                           Working Class   69.5

                    Other (please specify)   2.6

_____

28. Which of these types of school did you LAST attend, FULL time?

PLEASE TICK ONE BOX ONLY

None—never attend any school [0.3]

Primary or Elementary school [16.1]

SECONDARY SCHOOL IN ENGLAND AND WALES:

Secondary or Secondary Modern [23.9]

Comprehensive (including sixth-form college) [11.9]

Grammar School [24.5]

Direct Grant School [2.6]

Independent fee-paying (i.e. Private or Public) [4.7]

Technical School [4.2]

SECONDARY SCHOOL IN SCOTLAND:

Junior Secondary [2.3]

Comprehensive (including sixth-form college) [2.3]

Senior secondary (6 year selective) [2.9]

Grant aided [0.6]

Independent fee-paying (private) [0.4]

Other (please specify) [3.2]

29. Have you ever attended (or are you now attending) a university, polytechnic or college to study for a degree?

PLEASE TICK ONE BOX ONLY

Yes—University [21.5]

Yes—Polytechnic or College [16.6]

Yes—both [5.4]

No [56.4]

30. When you were young, (i.e. a teenager) would you say that your family belonged to a social class?

PLEASE TICK ONE BOX ONLY

Yes		90.2
No		9.8

30a. If YES, which class was that?

PLEASE TICK ONE BOX ONLY

Middle Class		21.3
Working Class		76.7
Other (please specify)		2.0

---

31. Have you obtained any of the following qualifications?

PLEASE TICK AS MANY AS APPROPRIATE

None	28.8
CSE Grades 2 to 5	1.7
CSE Grade 1, GCE 'O' level, School Certificate	8.2
Scottish Ordinary/ Lower Certificate	1.1
GCE 'A'/'S' Level or Higher Certificate	5.4
Scottish Higher Certificate	1.3
Technical qualification (e.g. City and Guilds, B.TECH Ordinary/Higher)	10.6
Teachers training qualification	4.2
Nursing qualification	2.3
University or CNAA degree or diploma	28.9
Other British qualification (please specify)	7.6

32. Next there is another set of statements about various political issues. We would like to know if you agree or disagree with them.

PLEASE TICK ONE BOX FOR EACH
STATEMENT

	Strongly Agree	Agree	Neither	Disagree	Strongly Disagree
If farmers have to choose between producing more food and looking after the countryside, they should produce more food	5.8	14.9	18.5	43.5	17.4
The Trade Union movement has too much power over the Labour party	9.0	34.1	15.0	31.8	10.1
Labour should resist further moves to integrate the European Common Market	5.3	11.1	11.5	48.3	23.8
Restrictions on immigration into Britain are too tight and should be eased	12.4	30.0	16.4	27.9	13.4
Britain's present electoral system should be replaced by a system of proportional representation	20.7	36.9	11.4	20.6	10.3
Trade Unions do not get fair treatment in the press and broadcasting media	46.6	42.5	5.8	3.9	1.2
Constituency Labour parties should have the exclusive right to select their own Parliamentary candidates	25.8	36.6	11.3	21.9	4.4

32. (Continued)

	Strongly Agree	Agree	Neither	Disagree	Strongly Disagree
A problem with the Labour party today is that the leader is too powerful	6.0	8.9	14.6	53.5	17.0
Forty percent of the places on the National Executive Committee should be reserved for women	12.2	27.0	18.5	31.7	10.5
A future Labour government should introduce a directly elected Scottish Assembly with taxing powers	16.7	41.7	21.8	15.1	4.7
The Trade Union block vote at conference brings the party into disrepute	22.5	48.5	12.1	13.3	3.7
There is no need for a Bill of Rights in this country	3.5	8.0	10.7	40.6	37.2
Workers should be prepared to strike in support of other workers, even if they don't work in the same place	27.2	45.3	10.4	14.1	3.1
The Labour party leader should be elected by a system of one party-member, one-vote	36.7	44.2	6.7	9.4	2.9
Coalition governments are the best form of government for Britain	1.5	5.1	12.7	45.4	35.3
The government should give more aid to poor countries in Africa and Asia	32.9	44.2	9.1	9.9	4.0

32. (Continued)

	Strongly Agree	Agree	Neither	Disagree	Strongly Disagree
Neil Kinnock will stick to his principles even if this means losing a general election	11.8	25.9	16.4	33.4	12.6

33. In Labour party politics people often talk about 'the Left' and 'the Right'. Compared with other Labour party members, where would you place your views on this scale below?

PLEASE TICK ONE BOX ONLY

LEFT   RIGHT

8.5	8.5	21.7	19.1	20.2	7.0	5.9	2.6	6.5

33a. And where would you place your views in relation to British politics as a whole (not just the Labour party)?

PLEASE TICK ONE BOX ONLY

LEFT   RIGHT

17.7	24.6	24.5	10.9	10.5	2.5	2.3	1.6	5.6

34. At the last General Election, in 1987, some people didn't manage to vote. How about you? Did you manage to vote in the General Election?

PLEASE TICK ONE BOX ONLY

Yes   97.5

No   2.5

34a. IF YES,
Which party did you vote for in the 1987 General Election?

PLEASE TICK ONE BOX ONLY

Conservative   0.1

Labour   98.7

Alliance (SDP or Liberals)   0.7

Scottish National Party   0.1

Plaid Cymru   0.0

The Green Party   0.3

Other (please specify)   0.0

35. Was there any time during the General Election of 1987 when you seriously thought you might vote for another party?

PLEASE TICK ONE BOX ONLY

Yes	9.1
No	90.9

35a. If YES, which party was that?

PLEASE TICK ONE BOX ONLY

Thought of not voting	7.4
Conservative	3.2
Labour	18.1
Alliance (SDP or Liberals)	29.4
Scottish National Party	4.1
Plaid Cymru	0.8
The Green Party	34.5
Other (please specify)	2.6

36. Which party did you vote for in the 1989 European Election?

PLEASE TICK ONE BOX ONLY

Did not vote	4.1
Conservative	0.0
Labour	91.6
SDP or Liberal Democrats	0.2
Scottish National Party	0.2
Plaid Cymru	0.1
The Green Party	3.8
Other (please specify)	0.1

37. Have you always voted for the same party in General Elections?
PLEASE TICK ONE BOX ONLY

Yes	87.3
No	12.7

37a. If NO, which party or parties did you vote for previously?
PLEASE TICK AS MANY BOXES AS APPLY

Did not vote	6.3
Conservative	24.2
Labour	19.5
Alliance (SDP or Liberals)	31.6
Scottish Nationalist	2.8
Plaid Cymru	1.6
The Green Party	1.7
Other (please specify)	8.1

38. Next there are some statements about politics in Britain. We would like to know if you agree or disagree with them.

PLEASE TICK ONE BOX FOR EACH STATEMENT

	Strongly Agree	Agree	Neither	Disagree	Strongly Disagree
When Labour party members are united and work together they can really change Britain	46.4	45.6	5.4	2.3	6.3
The party leadership doesn't pay a lot of attention to the views of ordinary party members	10.1	29.3	16.9	38.6	5.0
By and large, Labour M.P.s try to represent the views of ordinary party members	9.5	64.2	12.5	11.9	1.9

38. (Continued)

	Strongly Agree	Agree	Neither	Disagree	Strongly Disagree
People like me can have a real influence in politics if they are prepared to get involved	17.5	56.4	12.1	12.0	2.0
Sometimes politics seems so complicated it is difficult for a person like me to understand what is going on	6.2	28.4	9.1	40.9	15.4
Parties in general are only interested in peoples' votes, not in their opinions	9.4	41.4	11.6	33.9	3.7
The only way to be really educated about politics is to be a party activist	10.7	33.3	9.2	39.8	6.9
Labour party members are part of a great movement of like-minded people who work together in solidarity	8.0	32.8	17.8	35.7	5.8
Many people find party meetings rather boring	16.9	58.5	13.0	10.1	1.5
A person like me could do a good job of being a local Labour Councillor	12.8	35.7	20.4	26.1	4.9
The people who are most active in the Labour party are the ones who have most say in deciding party policy	14.6	55.6	9.4	17.7	2.8

38. (Continued)

	Strongly Agree	Agree	Neither	Disagree	Strongly Disagree
Labour would be more successful if more people like me were elected to Parliament	10.2	24.8	31.9	28.5	4.6
Attending party meetings can be pretty tiring after a hard days work	14.4	57.7	12.4	13.8	1.7
Being an active party member is a good way to meet interesting people	12.3	55.8	20.4	9.4	2.1
Party activity often takes time away from one's family	19.1	63.1	11.6	5.6	0.5
Many people think party activists are extremists	17.5	56.7	10.3	13.3	2.1
The amount of work done by ordinary party members is very often unrecognized	27.0	58.3	8.7	5.7	0.4

39. Please think for a moment of a thermometer scale that runs from zero to 100 degrees, where 50 is the neutral point.

If your feelings are warm and sympathetic towards something or someone, give them a score higher than 50; the warmer the feelings the higher the score.

If your feelings are cold and unsympathetic, give them a score less than 50; the colder your feelings the lower the score.

A score of 50 means that your feelings are neither warm nor cold.

PLEASE WRITE IN

First, please give a rating to EACH of the party leaders.

39. (Continued)

	rating out of 100
Neil Kinnock	73.5
Paddy Ashdown	34.1
David Owen	19.8
Margaret Thatcher	5.7

Next, please give a rating to some Labour party politicians. (Leave a blank if you feel you don't know enough about that person to rate them).

	rating out of 100
Roy Hattersley	60.2
Tony Benn	59.6
Bryan Gould	63.2
Harriet Harman	66.5
David Blunkett	70.7
Dennis Skinner	63.1
John Smith	73.3
Ken Livingstone	54.9
Gordon Brown	70.1
Joan Ruddock	64.4
John Prescott	65.9
Robin Cook	68.7

Next, please give a rating for the political parties

	rating out of 100
The Labour Party	84.2
The Social and Liberal Democrats	29.9
The Social Democratic (Owenite) Party	16.8
The Conservative Party	8.1
The Green Party	43.1
Plaid Cymru	28.9
The Scottish National Party	31.9

Finally, please give a rating to the following people and organisations. (Again, leave a blank if you feel that you don't know enough about them to give a rating)

	rating out of 100
George Bush	39.7
Mikhail Gorbachev	76.1

39. (Continued)

The Sun Newspaper	4.9
The BBC	57.1
The Stock Exchange	23.1
The European Economic Community	57.8
The Trades Union Congress	62.9
The Police	45.1
The House of Commons	56.2
The Confederation of British Industries	30.3

40. If Neil Kinnock resigned the leadership of the Labour party whom would you like to see elected as leader?

PLEASE WRITE IN

41. And if Roy Hattersley resigned the deputy-leadership of the Labour party whom would you like to see elected as deputy leader?

PLEASE WRITE IN

42. Are you generally in favour of ...

PLEASE TICK ONE BOX ONLY

More nationalisation of companies by government   71.1

More privatization of companies by government   1.5

– or should things be left as they are now?   27.4

43. Please think about your general impressions of the LABOUR PARTY, and describe them using the following scales.

If for example, you think the party is very modern you would tick the box on the left hand side.

If you think it is very old-fashioned, you would tick the box on the right hand side.

If you think it is neither old-fashioned nor modern, you would tick the middle box.

43. (Continued)

PLEASE TICK ONE BOX ONLY FOR EACH SCALE

	Very	Fairly	Neither	Fairly	Very	
Modern	7.5	46.8	30.7	13	2.1	Old-fashioned
Extreme	0.4	5.0	40.6	38.4	15.5	Moderate
Efficiently Run	7.6	54.4	16.4	18.1	3.5	Badly run
United	6.1	49.6	17.2	22.7	4.4	Divided
Uncaring	2.3	8.3	8.5	44.1	36.8	Caring
Good for one Class	2.1	7.4	20.4	44.2	25.9	Good for all
Middle Class	2.6	15.0	44.8	26.2	11.5	Working Class
Likely to unite the nation	16.6	46.0	26.5	9.2	1.6	Likely to divide the nation
Left wing	1.3	25.6	46.5	21.3	5.3	Right wing

44. Please think about your general impressions of NEIL KINNOCK, and describe them using the same type of scale.

PLEASE TICK ONE BOX ONLY FOR EACH SCALE

	Very	Fairly	Neither	Fairly	Very	
Good at getting things done	22.3	56.5	14.2	5.3	1.7	Bad at getting things done
Extreme	1.4	5.8	30.2	43.3	19.4	Moderate
Capable of being a strong Leader	32.9	42.4	10.4	9.7	4.4	Not capable of being a strong Leader
Likeable as a person	51.1	34.6	7.5	4.3	2.7	Not likeable as a person
Uncaring	1.7	3.4	7.6	35.9	51.3	Caring
Looks after one Class	1.2	7.2	31.3	45.1	15.2	Looks after all Classes
Left wing	1.0	19.4	48.3	23.7	7.6	Right wing
Likely to unite the nation	18.4	45.4	26.7	7.6	1.8	Likely to divide the nation

45. Some people say that all political parties look after certain groups and are not so concerned about others. How closely do you think the LABOUR PARTY looks after the interests of ...

PLEASE TICK ONE BOX ONLY FOR EACH GROUP

	Very closely	Fairly closely	Not very closely	Not at all closely
Working class people	31.7	53.1	9.8	1.4
Middle class people	9.4	73.2	16.6	0.9
Unemployed people	37.0	45.3	14.4	3.3
Big business	4.5	34.2	48.2	13.2
Trade unions	28.7	61.2	8.8	1.3
Women	16.5	51.6	27	4.9
Black people and Asians	16.1	51.3	25.9	6.7
Homosexuals, that is gays and lesbians	9.1	44.7	33.3	12.9

45a. How closely do you think the CONSERVATIVE PARTY looks after the interests of ...

PLEASE TICK ONE BOX ONLY

	Very closely	Fairly closely	Not very closely	Not at all closely
Working class people	0.5	1.7	23.1	74.8
Middle class people	25.5	50.0	20.2	4.3
Unemployed people	0.3	1.1	14.7	83
Big business	93.8	4.7	0.7	0.8
Trade unions	0.8	0.8	8.5	90.0
Women	1.2	13	42.7	43.1
Black people and Asians	1.3	5.6	31.4	61.7
Homosexuals, that is gays and lesbians	2.4	5.8	19.4	72.4

46. Which of the following statements comes closest to what YOU feel should be done? (If you don't have an opinion just indicate).

PLEASE TICK ONE BOX ONLY

Britain should keep her own nuclear weapons, independent of other countries   5.4

46. (Continued)

Britain should have nuclear weapons as part of a western
defence system

$\boxed{22.8}$

Britain should have nothing to do with nuclear weapons

$\boxed{71.8}$

No opinion

$\boxed{}$

---

47. Please indicate whether you think the government should or should not
do the following things, or doesn't it matter either way?

PLEASE TICK ONE BOX ONLY FOR EACH
STATEMENT

	Definitely should	Probably should	Doesn't matter	Probably should not	Definitely should not
Get rid of private education	40.7	22.9	18.1	13.6	4.1
Spend more money to get rid of poverty	88.5	10.3	0.5	0.4	0.4
Encourage the growth of private medicine	1.6	2.3	4.6	16.5	75.1
Put more money into the National Health Service	94.2	4.8	0.2	0.2	0.6
Reduce government spending generally	6.1	15.2	6.4	28.8	43.5
Introduce stricter laws to regulate trade unions	2.8	9.2	9.9	28.6	49.5
Give workers more say in the places where they work	63.9	29.9	3.3	1.5	1.5
Spend less on defence	59.9	25.8	2.8	6.7	4.8
Pull British troops out of Northern Ireland immediately	34.7	28.0	4.2	22.4	10.8

---

48. Do you think Britain should continue to be a member of the EEC—
the Common Market—or should it withdraw?

48. (Continued)

PLEASE TICK ONE BOX ONLY

Continue $\boxed{89.3}$

Withdraw $\boxed{10.7}$

---

49. And do you think Britain should continue to be a member of NATO
    – the North Atlantic Treaty Organisation – or should it withdraw?

PLEASE TICK ONE BOX ONLY

Continue $\boxed{71.4}$

Withdraw $\boxed{28.6}$

---

50. Suppose the government had to choose between the following three options. Which do you think it should choose?

PLEASE TICK ONE BOX ONLY

Reduce taxes and spend less on health, education and social benefits $\boxed{1.9}$

Keep taxes and spending on these services at the same levels as now $\boxed{6.4}$

Increase taxes and spend more on health, education and social benefits $\boxed{91.7}$

---

51. Think of the accommodation where you live now. Do you ...

PLEASE TICK ONE BOX ONLY

Own the property $\boxed{70.9}$

Rent it from the council $\boxed{17.0}$

Rent it from a private landlord $\boxed{4.1}$

Rent it from a housing association $\boxed{2.0}$

Or are you living with family/friends $\boxed{4.6}$

Other (please specify) $\boxed{1.3}$

51a. IF YOU OWN YOUR PROPERTY, were you a council tenant in your present accommodation before you purchased it?

PLEASE TICK ONE BOX ONLY

Was previously a council tenant	17.0
Was not previously a council tenant	83.0

52. Do you, or does anyone in your household, own or have the use of a car or a van?

PLEASE TICK ONE BOX ONLY

Yes—one	53.1
Yes—two or more	23.9
No	23.0

53. Do you regard yourself as belonging to any particular religion?

PLEASE TICK ONE BOX ONLY

No	41.2

IF YES AND CHRISTIAN:

Roman Catholic	11.4
Church of England/Wales, Anglican, Episcopalian	25.8
Church of Scotland/Presbyterian	2.8
Methodist	5.4
Baptist	1.5
United Reform Church, Congregational	1.3
Christian, but no denomination	6.4
Other Christian (please specify)	1.3

IF YES AND NON-CHRISTIAN:

Jewish	0.9
Hindu	0.4
Islamic/Moslem	0.9
Sikh	0.3
Buddhist	0.2
Other non-Christian (please specify)	0.4

54. Please indicate your ethnic origins

PLEASE TICK ONE BOX ONLY

White/European	96.3
Asian (for example Indian or Pakistani)	1.8
Black (for example West Indian)	0.8
Other (please specify)	1.1

---

55. Which of the following statements comes closest to what you feel should be done by the next Labour Government?

PLEASE TICK ONE BOX ONLY

The government should contribute to the funding of Islamic schools in Britain	17.9
The government should make no contributions to Islamic schools	56.2
No opinion	23.7

---

56. Which of the following categories represents the total income of your household from ALL sources before tax?

PLEASE TICK ONE BOX ONLY

Under £5,000	16.5
£5,000 up to £10,000	21.2
£10,000 up to £15,000	18.2
£15,000 up to £20,000	14.7
£20,000 up to £25,000	9.7
£25,000 up to £30,000	7.5
£30,000 up to £35,000	5.2
£35,000 up to £40,000	3.1
£40,000 plus	3.9

57. Which daily MORNING paper do you read MOST?

PLEASE TICK ONE BOX ONLY

I don't read a daily paper	13.2
Daily Express/Scottish Daily Express	1.0
Daily Mail	1.4
Daily Mirror/Record	29.1
Daily Star	0.9
The Sun	1.3
Today	1.1
Daily Telegraph	1.7
Financial Times	0.5
The Guardian	35.4
The Independent	7.0
The Times	0.7
Morning Star	0.9
Other (please specify)	2.9

58. Suppose the government had to choose between the following two options; which should it choose?

PLEASE TICK ONE BOX ONLY

The Government should create more jobs even if this means more industrial pollution	29.2
The Government should cut jobs in order to reduce industrial pollution	32.7
No opinion	38.1

59. We would like to ask you how EFFECTIVE you think various political activities are in helping the Labour party to achieve its goals.

59. (Continued)

PLEASE TICK ONE BOX FOR EACH
ACTIVITY

	Very effective	Effective	Not very effective	Not at all effective
Displaying an election poster in a window	18.3	49.3	28.8	3.6
Signing a petition supported by the party	14.7	49.3	32.5	3.4
Donating money to Labour party funds	33.2	54.4	11.1	1.3
Delivering party leaflets during an election	35.3	51.7	12.3	0.7
Attending a party meeting	17.9	45.1	31.8	5.2
Canvassing voters on behalf of the party	44.8	44.2	10.0	1.0
Standing for elected office within the party organisation	22.4	52.6	21.5	3.5
Standing for elected office at a local or national election	32.0	50.6	14.8	2.7

60. Finally, what in your opinion are the main issues which the Labour party needs to face up to at the present time?

PLEASE WRITE IN

_____
_____
_____
_____
_____
_____
_____

END OF THE QUESTIONNAIRE

PLEASE CHECK THAT YOU HAVE ANSWERED ALL THE
QUESTIONS

THANK YOU VERY MUCH FOR YOUR HELP

REFERENCES

BARKER, M., CHANDLER, J., and MORRIS, D. (1978), *The Labour Party Ward Secretary* (Sheffield: Sheffield City Polytechnic Occasional Paper).

BARNES, S. and KAASE, M. (1979), *Political Action; Mass Participation in Five Western Democracies* (Beverly Hills, Calif.: Sage).

BARRY, B. (1970), *Sociologists, Economists and Democracy* (London: Collier-Macmillan).

BARTOLINI, S. (1983), 'The Membership of Mass Parties: The Social Democratic Experience, 1889–1978', in H. Daalder and P. Mair, *Western European Party Systems* (London: Sage).

BEACKON, S. (1976), 'Labour Party Politics and the Working-class', *British Journal of Political Science*, 6: 231–8.

BEALEY, F., BLONDEL, J., and MCCANN, W. (1965), *Constituency Politics: A Study of Newcastle under Lyme* (London: Faber).

BERRY, D. (1970), *The Sociology of Grass-roots Politics* (London: Macmillan).

BOCHEL, J. and DENVER, D. (1972), 'The Impact of the Campaign on the Results of Local Government Elections', *British Journal of Political Science*, 2: 239–43.

—— —— (1983) 'Candidate Selection in the Labour Party: What the Selectors Seek', *British Journal of Political Science*, 13: 45–69.

BRAND, J. (1973), 'Party Organisation and the Recruitment of Councillors', *British Journal of Political Science*, 3: 473–86.

BUTLER, D. and KAVANAGH, D. (1988), *The British General Election of 1987* (London: Macmillan).

—— and PINTO-DUSCHINSKY, M. (1971), *The British General Election of 1970* (London: Macmillan).

—— and ROSE, R. (1960), *The British General Election of 1959* (London: Macmillan).

—— and STOKES, D. (1974), *Political Change in Britain* (London: Macmillan).

BYNNER, J. and ASHFORD, S. (1990), *Youth Politics and Lifestyles* (London: Social Statistics Research Unit, Paper 25).

CARMINES, E. and STIMSON, J. (1989), *Issue Evolution: Race and the Transformation of American Politics* (Princeton, NJ: Princeton University Press).

CLARKE, H. and WHITELEY, P. (1990), 'Perceptions of Macroeconomic Performance: Government Support and Conservative Party Strategy 1983–1987', *European Journal of Political Research*, 18: 97–120.

COLE, G. D. H. (1948), *A History of the Labour Party from 1914* (London: Routledge & Kegan Paul).

CONVERSE, P. (1964), 'The Nature of Belief Systems in Mass Politics', in D. Apter, *Ideology and Discontent* (New York: Free Press), 206–61.

CREWE, I. (1983), 'Why Labour Lost the British Elections', *Public Opinion*, June–July, 7–9 and 56–60.

—— and FOX, A. (1984), *British Parliamentary Constituencies: A Statistical Compendium* (London: Faber & Faber).

CROSLAND, A. (1956), *The Future of Socialism* (London: Jonathan Cape).

—— (1960), 'Radical Reform and the Left', repr. in *The Conservative Enemy* (London: Jonathan Cape).

CROSSMAN, R. H. S. (1976), *Diaries of a Cabinet Minister*, ii (London: Jonathan Cape).

CROTTY, W. (1971), 'Party Effort and Its Impact on the Vote', *American Political Science Review*, 65: 439–50.

CURTICE, J. and STEED, M. (1988), 'Appendix 2 Analysis' in Butler and Kavanagh, *The British General Election of 1987*, 316–62.

CUTRIGHT, P. (1963), 'Measuring the Impact of Local Party Activity on the General Election Vote', *Public Opinion Quarterly*, 27: 372–85.

—— and ROSSI, P. (1958), 'Grass-roots Politicians and the Vote', *American Sociological Review*, 23: 171–9.

DALTON, R. and KUECHLER, M. (1990), *Challenging the Political Order: New Social Movements in Western Democracies* (New York: Oxford University Press).

—— FLANIGAN, S., and BECK, P. (1984), *Electoral Change in Advanced Industrial Democracies* (Princeton, NJ: Princeton University Press).

DENVER, D. and HANDS, G. (1974), 'Marginality and Turnout in British General Elections', *British Journal of Political Science*, 4: 17–35.

—— —— (1985), 'Marginality and Turn-out in General Elections in the 1970s', *British Journal of Political Science*, 15: 381–98.

DONNISON, D. and PLOWMAN, D. (1954), 'The Functions of Local Labour Politics: Experiments in Research Methods', *Political Studies*, 2: 154–67.

DOWNS, A. (1957), *An Economic Theory of Democracy* (New York: Harper and Row).

DRUCKER, H. (1979), *Doctrine and Ethos in the Labour Party* (London: Allen & Unwin).

DUVERGER, M. (1954), *Political Parties* (London: Methuen).

ELSTER, J. (1983), *Sour Grapes: Studies in the Subversion of Rationality* (Cambridge: Cambridge University Press).

—— (1989), *The Cement of Society* (Cambridge: Cambridge University Press).

EPSTEIN, L. (1967), *Political Parties in Western Democracies* (London: Pall Mall Press).

EWING, K. (1987), *The Funding of Political Parties in Britain* (Cambridge: Cambridge University Press).

FESTINGER, L. (1957), *A Theory of Cognitive Dissonance* (Palo Alto, Calif.: Stanford University Press).

FINKEL, S., MULLER, E., and OPP, K. (1989), 'Personal Influence, Collective Rationality, and Mass Political Action', *American Political Science Review*, 83: 885–903.

FORRESTER, T. (1976), *The Labour Party and the Working Class* (London: Heinemann).

FRANKLIN, M. (1985), *The Decline of Class Voting in Britain: Changes in the Basis of Electoral Choice 1964–1983* (Oxford: Clarendon Press).

FRENDREIS, J., GIBSON, J., and VERTZ, L. (1990), 'The Electoral Relevance of Local Party Organizations', *American Political Science Review*, 84: 225–35.

GOLDMAN, P. and MATHEWS, T. (1989), *The Quest for the Presidency: The 1988 Campaign* (New York: Simon Schuster).

GOLDTHORPE, J. H. (1980), *Social Mobility and Class Structure in Modern Britain* (Oxford: Clarendon Press).

GORDON, I. and WHITELEY, P. (1979), 'Social Class and Political Attitudes: The Case of Labour Councillors', *Political Studies*, 26: 99–113.

GOSS, S. (1988), *Local Labour and Local Government* (Edinburgh: Edinburgh University Press).

Hansard Society (1981), *Paying for Politics* (London).

HARMAN, H. (1967), *Modern Factor Analysis* (Chicago: Chicago University Press).

HEATH, A., and EVANS, G. (1988), 'Working-Class Conservatives and Middle-Class Socialists', in R. Jowell, S. Witherspoon and L. Brook (eds.), *British Social Attitudes: The 5th Report* (Aldershot: Gower), 53–66.

—— JOWELL, R. and CURTICE, J. (1985), *How Britain Votes* (Oxford: Pergamon Press).

—— —— —— (1991), *Understanding Political Change* (Oxford: Pergamon Press).

HEFFER, E. (1986), *Labour's Future: Socialist or SDP Mark 2?* (London: Verso).

HIMMELWEIT, H., HUMPHREYS, P., JAEGER, M., and KATZ, M. (1981), *How Voters Decide* (London: Academic Press).

HINDESS, B. (1971), *The Decline of Working Class Politics* (London: Mac-Gibbon & Kee).

HOBSBAWM, E. (1981) (ed.), *The Forward March of Labour Halted?* (London: Verso).

HOLLANDER, H. (1990), 'A Social Exchange Approach to Voluntary Co-operation', *American Economic Review*, 80: 1157–68.

HUGHES, C. and WINTOUR, P. (1990), *Labour Rebuilt* (London: Fourth Estate).

HOLT, R. and TURNER, J. (1968), *Political Parties in Action: The Battle for Barons Court* (New York: Free Press).

INGLEHART, R. (1977), *The Silent Revolution: Changing Values and Political Styles Among Western Publics* (Princeton, NJ: Princeton University Press).

—— (1982), 'Changing Values in Japan and the West', *Comparative Political Studies*, 14: 445–80.

JANOSIK, E. (1968), *Constituency Labour Parties in Britain* (London: Pall Mall).

JESSOP, R. (1974), *Traditionalism, Conservatism and the British Political Culture* (London: Allen & Unwin).

JONES, B. and KEATING, M. (1985), *Labour and the British State* (Oxford: Clarendon Press).

JOHNSTON, R., PATTIE, C., and ALLSOP, J. (1988), *A Nation Dividing? The Electoral Map of Great Britain 1979–1987* (London: Longman).

KITSCHELT, H. (1989), 'The Internal Politics of Parties: The Law of Curvilinear Disparity Revisited', *Political Studies*, 37: 400–21.

—— (1990), 'New Social Movements and the Decline of Party Organization', in Dalton and Kuechler, *Challenging the Political Order*, 179–208.

KLOSKO, G. (1987), 'The Rationality of Collective Action', *American Political Science Review*, 81: 557–61.

KOGAN, D. and KOGAN, M. (1983), *The Battle for the Labour Party* (London: Kogan Page).

KRAMER, G. (1970), 'The Effects of Precinct-Level Canvassing on Voter Behavior', *Public Opinion Quarterly*, 34: 560–72.

Labour Party (1918), *Labour and the New Social Order* (London: Labour Party).

—— (1988), *A Statement of Democratic Socialist Aims and Values* (London: Labour Party).

—— (1989), *Meet the Challenge, Make the Change* (London: Labour Party).

—— (1990), *Looking to the Future* (London: Labour Party).

—— (1991), *Labour Opportunity Britain: Labour's Better Way for the 1990s* (London: Labour Party).

McKENZIE, R. (1964), *British Political Parties*, 2nd rev. edn. (London: Mercury).

—— (1974), 'Parties, Pressure Groups and the British Political Process', in R. Kimber and J. Richardson, *Pressure Groups in Britain* (London: Dent).

—— (1982), 'Power in the Labour Party: The Issue of Intra-Party Democracy' in D. Kavanagh, *The Politics of the Labour Party* (London: Allen & Unwin): 191–201.

McKenzie, R., and Silver, A. (1968), *Angels in Marble* (Chicago: Chicago University Press).

McKibbin, R. (1974), *The Evolution of the Labour Party 1910–1924* (Oxford: Oxford University Press).

Margolis, H. (1982), *Selfishness, Altruism and Rationality* (Cambridge: Cambridge University Press).

Marsh, A. (1977), *Protests and Political Consciousness* (Beverly Hills, Calif.: Sage).

Maslow, A. (1962), *Towards a Psychology of Being* (Englewood Cliffs, NJ: D. Van Nostrand).

May, J. (1973), 'Opinion Structure of Political Parties: The Special Law of Curvilinear Disparity', *Political Studies*, 21: 135–51.

Michels, R. (1962), *Political Parties: A Sociological Study of the Oligarchical Tendencies of Modern Democracy* (New York: Free Press).

Miliband, R. (1961), *Parliamentary Socialism* (London: Allen & Unwin).

Miller, W. L. (1977), *Electoral Dynamics* (London: Macmillan).

Miller, W., Clarke, H., Harrop, M., LeDuc, L., and Whiteley, P. (1990), *How Voters Change: The 1987 British Election Campaign in Perspective* (Oxford: Clarendon Press).

Minkin, L. (1978), *The Labour Party Conference* (London: Allen Lane).

Moran, M. (1985), *Politics and Society in Britain* (Basingstoke: Macmillan).

Muller, E. and Opp, K. (1986), 'Rational Choice and Rebellious Collective Action', *American Political Science Review*, 80: 471–89.

——— (1987), 'Rebellious Political Action Revisited', *American Political Science Review*, 81: 561–4.

Noelle-Neumann, E. (1984), *The Spiral of Silence* (Chicago: Chicago University Press).

Niemi, R. (1976), 'Costs of Voting and Non-Voting', *Public Choice*, 27: 115–19.

Norton, P. (1975), *Dissension in the House of Commons 1945–1974* (London: Macmillan).

Offe, C. (1990), 'Reflections on the Institutional Self-Transformation of Movement Politics: A Tentative Stage Model', in R. J. Dalton and M. Kuechler, *Challenging the Political Order: New Social Movements in Western Democracies* (Oxford: Oxford University Press).

Olson, M. (1965), *The Logic of Collective Action* (New York: Schocken Books).

Opp, K. (1990), 'Postmaterialism, Collective Action, and Political Protest', *American Journal of Political Science*, 34: 212–35.

Parry, G. and Moyser, G. (1990), 'A Map of Political Participation in Britain', *Government and Opposition*, 25: 147–69.

Parkin, F. (1968), *Middle Class Radicalism* (Manchester: Manchester University Press).

PARKIN, F. (1971), *Class Inequality and Political Order* (London: MacGibbon & Kee).

PELLING, H. (1965), *Origins of the Labour Party* (Oxford: Oxford University Press).

PINTO-DUSCHINSKY, M. (1981), *British Political Finance* (London: American Enterprise Institute for Public Policy Research).

PRZEWORSKI, A. (1985), *Capitalism and Social Democracy* (Cambridge: Cambridge University Press).

―― and SPRAGUE, J. (1986), *Paper Stones: A History of Electoral Socialism* (Chicago: Chicago University Press).

Report of the Committee on Financial Aid to Political Parties (1976) (London: HMSO).

RIESMAN, D. (1961), *The Lonely Crowd; A Study of the Changing American Character* (New Haven, Conn.: Yale University Press).

ROSE, R. (1976), *The Problem of Party Government* (Harmondsworth: Penguin).

―― and MCALLISTER, I. (1990), *The Loyalties of Voters* (London: Sage).

SAMUELSON, P. (1954), 'The Pure Theory of Public Expenditure', *Review of Economics and Statistics*, 36: 387–9.

SARLVIK, B. and CREWE, I. (1983), *Decade of Dealignment* (Cambridge: Cambridge University Press).

SCARBOROUGH, E. (1984), *Political Ideology and Voting* (Oxford: Clarendon Press).

SCARROW, S. (1990), 'The Decline of Party Organization? Mass membership parties in Great Britain and West Germany', paper to American Political Science Association, San Francisco.

SCHATTSCHNEIDER, E. E. (1960), *The Semi-Sovereign People* (Hillsdale, Ill.: Dryden Press).

SEYD, P. (1987), *The Rise and Fall of the Labour Left* (Basingstoke: Macmillan).

―― and MINKIN, L. (1979), 'The Labour Party and its Members', *New Society*, 20 Sept. 1979, 613–15.

SHAW, E. (1988), *Discipline and Discord in the Labour Party* (Manchester: Manchester University Press).

SJOBLOM, G. (1978), 'The Swedish Party System in the Post-War Period', paper presented to the ECPR colloquium on 'Recent Changes in European Party Systems', Florence, 15–19 Dec., 1978.

TAYLOR, A. J. P. (1957), *The Trouble-Makers* (London: Hamish Hamilton).

TULLOCK, G. (1971), 'The Paradox of Revolution', *Public Choice*, 11: 89–99.

TURNER, J. (1978), *Labour's Doorstep Politics in London* (London: Macmillan).

VERBA, S. and NIE, N. (1972), *Participation in America: Political Democracy and Social Equality* (New York: Harper and Row).

VERBA, S., NIE, N., and KIM, J. (1978), *Participation and Political Equality: A Seven Nation Comparison* (Cambridge: Cambridge University Press).

VON BEYME, K. (1985), *Political Parties in Western Democracies* (Aldershot: Gower).

WARE, A. (1987), *Citizens, Parties and the State* (Oxford: Polity Press).

WATTENBERG, M. (1986), *The Decline of American Political Parties, 1952–1984* (Cambridge, Mass: Harvard University Press).

WHITELEY, P. (1978), 'The Structure of Democratic Socialist Ideology in Britain', *Political Studies*, 26: 209–31.

—— (1982), 'The Decline of Labour's Local Party Membership and Electoral Base, 1945–79', in D. Kavanagh, *The Politics of the Labour Party* (London: Allen & Unwin): 111–34.

—— (1983), *The Labour Party in Crisis* (London: Methuen).

—— and WINYARD, S. (1987), *Pressure for the Poor: The Poverty Lobby and Policy-Making* (London: Methuen).

WOLFINGER, R. (1963), 'The Influence of Precinct Work on Voting Behaviour', *Public Opinion Quarterly*, 27: 387–98.

INDEX

For reasons of space and ease of use the term 'party member' has generally been omitted from subheadings except where confusion might result. However, it should be assumed that all entries relate to Labour party members unless indicated otherwise. For example, subheadings concerning attitudes to various political issues refer to party members' attitudes.

Index compiled by Ann Barham